A CLINICAL APPLICATION OF BION'S CONCEPTS

Volume 3

A CLINICAL APPLICATION OF BION'S CONCEPTS

Volume 3

Verbal and Visual Approaches to Reality

P. C. Sandler

KARNAC

First published in 2013 by
Karnac Books Ltd
118 Finchley Road
London NW3 5HT

Copyright © 2013 by P. C. Sandler

The right of P. C. Sandler to be identified as the author of this work has been asserted in accordance with §§ 77 and 78 of the Copyright Design and Patents Act 1988.

All rights reserved. No part of this publication may be reproduced, stored in a retrieval system, or transmitted, in any form or by any means, electronic, mechanical, photocopying, recording, or otherwise, without the prior written permission of the publisher.

British Library Cataloguing in Publication Data

A C.I.P. for this book is available from the British Library

ISBN-13: 978-1-78049-068-7

Typeset by V Publishing Solutions (P) Ltd., Chennai, India

Printed in Great Britain

www.karnacbooks.com

To Ester, Daniela, Carolina, Clara, Luiz and Antoine

*To the memory of my parents, Dr Jayme Sandler
and Mrs Bertha Lerner Sandler*

Solomon saith, *There is no new thing upon the Earth*. So that as Plato had an imagination, that *all knowledge was but remembrance;* so Solomon giveth his sentence, that *all novelty is but oblivion*.

—Francis Bacon, 1625

One of their heirs who gave utility to their wisdom, Freud, made an observation out of this: *out of the creativity of a couple, claims to originality are but deluded omnipotence.*

CONTENTS

ACKNOWLEDGEMENTS xi

PREFACE xiii
Rocco Antonio Pisani and Mario Giampà

INTRODUCTION xix
Antonio Sapienza

PART I: THE MULTI-DIMENSION GRID

CHAPTER ONE
Scientific research in psychoanalysis 3

CHAPTER TWO
Verifying the truth value of verbal statements uttered in an analytic session with the help of the three-dimension grid 19

CHAPTER THREE
A hexa-dimension grid? 45

CHAPTER FOUR
A multi-dimension grid and a negative grid — 73

PART II: FREE ASSOCIATIONS AND FREE-FLOATING ATTENTION

CHAPTER FIVE
Freie Einfälle: the verbal irruption of the unknown — 89

CHAPTER SIX
Free-floating attention: the personal factor — 115

PART III: EPISTEMOLOGY AND TRUTH

CHAPTER SEVEN
Psychoanalysis and epistemology: relatives, friends or strangers? Paranoid-schizoid features in the paths of psychoanalytic practice — 135

CHAPTER EIGHT
Truth — 161

CHAPTER NINE
Two habits of mind: naïve idealism and naïve realism — 195

PART IV: GROUPS

CHAPTER TEN
A sixth basic assumption? — 229

REFERENCES — 267

INDEX — 279

ACKNOWLEDGEMENTS

This is the closing volume of the series *A Clinical Application of Bion's Concepts*. The completion of this whole series of books would not have been possible without the kind support of Drs Eduardo Berger, Waldemar Ortiz, Luiz Paulo Kowalski, Marcelo Ferraz Sampaio, Gisela Tinoni, Mauricio Ibrahim Scanavacca and José Eduardo de Souza, who have dedicated their own lives to help and care for other people's lives. A similar kind of gratitude is due to Drs Jayme Sandler and Ester Hadassa Sandler, and Mrs Francesca Bion. I was blessed by their constant inspiration and loving stimulus. The seemingly inexhaustible help from Mr Oliver Rathbone and Mrs Anna Nilsen followed on; the model of a midwife furnishes a pale idea of their joint work, which resulted in a readable contribution. Another kind of stimulus, remarkable for its timing, came from Drs Klaus von Röckerath and Thomas Hartung and the psychoanalytic group from Cologne; and from Dr. Abel Feinstein, from the International Psycho-Analytical Congress at Chicago, 2009, who granted me the possibility to do the first Official Course about Bion's work in the programme of the Congress—the critical contributions of its attendance allowed improvements in one of the chapters, The multi-dimension Grid. As was the case with the previous books,

I owe the making of this book to the patients who came to see me looking for help; for ethical reasons it is not possible to name them. In this sense, I hope that my personal need to share, which generated both this series of books and its "older brother" *The Language of Bion: A Dictionary of Concepts*, may prove to be rewarding and nourishing rather than a waste of time for the prospective reader. In contrast to love, time is the one and only unreturnable, unrenewable and irreplaceable good in human life.

PREFACE

Rocco Antonio Pisani and Mario Giampà

We have tried to combine the two currents, starting from the presupposition that there is no dichotomy in the scientific approach, but an integration of discoveries that have scientific value.

It is really extremely difficult to write a preface to this important book by Paulo Cesar Sandler. I have decided that the best preface to his book could be a synthesis of what we both share in a psychosomatic holistic outlook.

On the occasion of his Seminar held in Rome in 2004, Paulo participated as an observer at a Median Group conducted by me in the Department of Neurological Sciences in La Sapienza University. It was conducted in accordance with the theoretical, methodological and technical approach of S.H. Foulkes and Patrick de Maré, originator of the Median Group. Paulo was very impressed by the group's profound level of insight-outsight. He made some comments, which supplemented Bion's thoughts, on the group of basic assumptions and on the work group, in a context basically pertaining to Foulkes and de Maré. We commented that free floating dialogue, corresponding to the free association of the psychoanalytic session in a wider context, is the fundamental premise for transforming a group of basic assumptions in a work group. I was totally astounded by Paulo's vast knowledge that ranges from psychosomatic medicine to psychoanalysis, to group analysis, philosophy, anthropology, music, and generally speaking to every field of culture.

With Paulo I share *the psychosomatic approach to all medical problems*. In the Symposium on Psychosomatic Medicine entitled "Group analysis and Psychosomatic Illnesses" held in Rome at the Accademia Lancisiana in May 2004, we had an opportunity to compare our ideas on this subject. Citing Bion, Paulo declared that it is impossible to separate the body from the mind since it is an inseparable reality.

Foulkes also affirms that there is no contraposition between psychological illness and physical illness: everything that is psychological is at the same time biological and social, and vice versa: theory and the group analytic method do not have pseudo-problems such as biological versus cultural, somatogenic versus psychogenic, individual versus group, reality versus imagination (Foulkes & Anthony, 1965).

Psychosomatic disturbances express repressed unconscious meanings through somatisation. When the mind has lost its ability to symbolise it has also lost its verbal ability, and it is the body that speaks. The person has stopped speaking to himself, whereas it would be necessary to speak in order not to fall ill.

Paulo, with great perspicacity, points out that the purpose of analysis is not to interpret symbols but to understand that the absence of symbolisation and ways of expression are functions of nervous discharge, obstruction and acting out (Sandler, 2005b). I add that the translation of meaning rather than its interpretation, as group analytic practice teaches me, can encourage symbolisation when patients are ready and motivated to make the transition from the symptom to the meaning. It is a question of assessing the expediency of remodelling the psychosomatic defence mechanism. The question is this: is it expedient to demolish the defence mechanism or is it better to reinforce it?

I would like to return to some fundamental concepts expressed by Dennis Brown, which I feel are widely shared with Paulo. Brown is the group analyst who has studied psychosomatic disturbances most (Brown, 1985, 1989, 1997). Brown takes up Nemiah's and Sifneos' concept of alexithymia: the inability to find words to express sensations, emotions, feelings, fantasies and impulses.

For Freud (cited by Brown) the Ego is above all a corporeal Ego. Mental functions emerge gradually from bodily functions in the first and second years of life, from the original mother-child unity.

Development implies a process of desomatisation, a concept reiterated by Bion with the proto-mental state, beta elements and alpha function. Psychosomatic difficulties go back to preverbal, pre-symbolic experiences based more on psychotic parts.

An initial process can be the theory of alpha function where sensory impressions, including feelings, become elements that will form thinking, dreaming and memory (Sandler, 2005b). The child's physical experiences, from which his mental functions emerge, are basically influenced not only by the mother-child relationship, but also by the father, by the family and by the social culture in which the child is immersed.

Brown cites Joyce McDougall, according to whom the mind-body differentiation processes can be disturbed by the main attachment figures which may be very close and harmful or very distant at the moment when the Self emerges from the mother-child symbiosis and the mind emerges from the undifferentiated psychosoma. Real psychosomatic disturbances are more regressions to primitive preverbal states (Bion's proto-mental state). Genetic predisposition and environmental factors can be fostered by failures, on the level of mother-child interaction as well as on the level of familial communications and socio-cultural attitudes.

Physical symptoms represent a blocking of communication, and at the same time they are an indirect communication. Their treatment involves the creation of meaning and symbolisation on the part of individuals who remain chained to the somatisation of babyhood, in cases where this process is possible. Group analytic work consists of discovering the meaning of these symptoms at the most primitive (protomental) level so that they can be desomatised, translated into words and mentalised.

Sooner or later psychosomatic patients abandon their dependence on somatic forms of communication. The group proves to be a better container than one's own mother or family, frustration no longer inevitably activates the primitive (proto-mental) psychosoma. It is necessary to tolerate and control anxiety, pain, lack of help, dependence and rage (beta elements). The group facilitates communication and the conductor must facilitate communication on deeper primitive levels and eventually translate them into words (alpha function).

Psychosomatic disturbances, such as conversion hysteria, imply "the mysterious leap from the mind to the body". Their treatment, like dream analysis, can offer another "royal road to the unconscious" and to the "mysterious leap", revealing unrecognised and split affections within its matrix of relations from the beginning, before the mind-body differentiation.

Merendino (2003) studied cases of serious organic pathology: leukaemia, cancer, AIDS, etc. His opinion is that deadly disease in general and cancerous diseases in particular come from the subject's early loss, beyond a given threshold, of communicative ability with regard both to the outside world and to the internal world. For Merendino "there is no mental operation that does not have its correspondence in the soma, there is no somatic operation that does not have its mental correspondence". This means that in treating the mind we also treat the body, and in treating the body at the same time we treat the mind.

A similar concept to the one expressed by Paulo: "When Freud and Klein tolerated the paradox of the indivisibility of the life and death instincts, or Bion of the 'minus' ambit, which Green suggests calling 'negative', they gave us a way that sometimes allows psychosomatic medicine to be also somatopsychotic" (Sandler, 2005b).

Rocco Antonio Pisani, MD, is a psychiatrist and group analyst. He was formerly Professor of Psychiatry and Psychotherapy at La Sapienza University, Rome.

Even before reading the book, the chapters listed in the contents as well as the bibliography highlight "emotional disturbance" as W. R. Bion understands it: when two thinking minds meet. Here the reader's mind meets Wilfred Ruprecht Bion's mind and Paulo Cesar Sandler's mind. Mental becomes a word inadequate for describing psychic reality, which in my opinion is the purpose of the book. So we find we are reflecting between verbal thought and unconscious thought, when we put ourselves in the mental position of having little memory and little desire. Sandler encourages us to think again, together with him, about what Bion proposes in his "scientific psychoanalysis", namely, about experiences that cannot be learned through the senses, an attempt—not an easy one for us Westerners—to understand the autonomous life of the unconscious.

In 1977 Bion wrote that real life is a mystery, and real life is the concern of real analysis! We should think of the mystery! Psychic reality is Bion's field of study, and Paulo Cesar Sandler discusses this psychic reality in his book, examining it and reflecting on it from the dawn of the birth of thought, through philosophers and psychologists of the calibre of Julius Jaynes (1976), who postulated the existence of the bicameral mind and its collapse, up to and beyond Jacob Arlow (1996), who wrote about the concept of psychic reality. Sandler suggests that we should to go further in the knowledge we have of the functioning of the mind, recalling the Grid and the consequent structure of the apparatus to think the thoughts presented by Bion. The epistemologist Bion proposes the apparatus of the Grid, using the scientific deductive system in order to understand the individual and group unconscious both in psychoanalysis and in groups. To understand what there is in the myths of Babel, Eden and Oedipus and in the basic assumption of the messianic expectation that will free us from the nameless Terror. Undoubtedly he proposes a method for "scientific" thinking that unites Western thought and Asian thought. In a seminar in Rome, Parthenope Bion Talamo described her father as a Eurasian.

In this work Paulo Sandler is not alone, in that giving a "scientific" answer to the functioning of the mind is the theme of all modern thinkers. Roger Penrose, who investigates the fundamental laws of the universe, published *The Road to Reality* (2004), concluding that the answer to profound questions arouses even more profound questions. This is what Bion maintained and what Sandler re-proposes: the search for the formless, for the infinite, for the ineffable of non-existence.

Mario Giampà is a psychiatrist, psychoanalyst and group analyst. He is a Member of the Italian Society of Psychoanalysis.

INTRODUCTION

Antonio Sapienza

When I wrote the preface to *The Language of Bion: A Dictionary of Concepts*, published in 2005 by Karnac Books, I felt that it was a valuable contribution to practising analysts. In hindsight, provided by observation over a seven-year span, I see that I was not alone in such an evaluation. As a companion to the dictionary, the author has delivered another timely publication: *A Clinical Application of Bion's Concepts*, in three volumes. It presents many correlations which link remarkable theories from Bion with a detailed selection of personal clinical experiences spanning almost four decades of psychoanalytic practice.

In accepting the invitation to introduce the third volume, I was faced with the following eminently practical issues, often put as questions rather than affirmative answers by authorities: *A Multidimensional Grid, The Verbal Irruption of the Unknown, Free-Floating Attention: The Personal Factor; Psychoanalysis and Epistemology: Relatives, Friends or Strangers?* and *Truth*. The book ends with considerations on a theme which marked Bion's earliest incursions in the field: *Groups: A Sixth Basic Assumption?*

Sandler dwells on these issues, profiting from one among many of Bion's instigating questions, which pervades the whole text: "It seems absurd that a psychoanalyst should be unable to assess the quality of his work". The reader is invited to get in touch with theories of observation devised by Bion in the 1960s—which, alas, still are unknown to a sizeable number of members of the psychoanalytic movement. Starting from Bion, Sandler proposes models and modulating tools borrowed from Mathematics and Physics. He aims to get fundamental support to link to different clinical phenomena. For example: alpha function is related to capability to dream; levels of maturity obtained by the evolution from sensations and feelings towards the inception of thinking processes; preservation or destruction of the contact barrier, linked on the one hand to states of consciousness and on the other hand to intuition. Sandler also points out situations where emotional discharge and impulsiveness prevail; he assesses some characteristics that compose the psychoanalytic object through the use of formulations stemming from the philosophy of mathematics. Special care is given to describing clinical situations in which the presence of hyperbole and transformations in hallucinosis prevail. Sandler proposes some neologisms that may better describe the psychoanalytic posture, such as *desensifying* and *de-concretisation*, which may be gauged in the transition through the Grid categories such as A, B, C, D.

When I had the opportunity to write the preface to *The Language of Bion*, I focused on just one entry (Dream-Work-Alpha) in order to illustrate the general tone of the work. Now, what took my attention was the part of the work in which the author dealt with the multi-dimension Grid, an expansion from Bion's original two-dimension Grid. It was the result of theoretical and clinical research which took three cycles of about ten years. In the first one, Sandler proposes a tri-dimension Grid, composed of the psychogenesis of Thought Processes as its first dimension and Ego functions as its second dimension—corresponding to Bion's two-dimension Grid—to which is added a third axis, Intensity. They are represented graphically by three axes in a Euclidean-Cartesian plane. In the second cycle, Sandler introduces a fourth dimension: Time. In the third cycle, he resorts both to the research of Bion and to the research of modern physics, in a subtle way, proposing a six-dimension Grid: (1) Genetic development of thought processes, (2) Uses of the thought processes, (3) Instant intensity, (4) Dimension of the senses, (5) Dimension of Myth, and (6) Dimension of Passion. The author also explores the roots linked to the panel of mythical nature published by Bion in *The Grid*. Part I is a significant meta-psychological work and requests conditions of receptive minds, endowed with discipline and daring, to foster our adventure into exploring the Unknown in our clinical practice. Sandler's acknowledgement of what I would name the *phylogenetic consensual memory* unites Darwin, Freud and Bion with regard to the evolution which has as its starting point what Bion called, after Kant, the Pre-Conceptions. The evolution can be put as Bion did:

Pre-Conception → Conception → Concepts

Sandler chose the narrative of a dream with an atomic bomb related by a patient who makes moving incursions using Einstein's concepts as his free associations. It constitutes an exercise—to my mind, beautiful—of architectonic drama, which fairly expresses the reality of an analytic session, similar to fictional suspense in an environment made by the political and cosmological fields. The author emphasises Bion's claim that the psychoanalytical exercise provided by the Grid is to be cultivated and trained *outside the session* by each analyst. In this case, it was used to detect the continuous bombardment of beta elements, which Sandler had earlier (in Volume 2 of the same series, which expands the content of a paper published in the *International Journal of Psycho-Analysis*, 1997) classified under two types: the seemingly intelligible beta elements and the seemingly unintelligible beta elements, providing clinical descriptions of the seminal concept of the beta screen. They are among his expansions from Bion's concepts, in the proposals of an Anti-Alpha Function and the Minus Grid.

In Chapter Five, *The Verbal Irruption of the Unknown*, Sandler describes with precision the free associations, and the evasions represented by free dissociations, within the environment marked by the allowing tolerance of the analytic meeting. He demonstrates the real existence of conditions that allow dialogue and clinical investigation by the analytic pair.

Free-Floating Attention: The Personal Factor (Chapter Six) introduces a question: can free-floating attention be regarded as a personal factor or not? Some readers may feel the path travelled by Sandler as shocking: sometimes full of awe and frightful. As in most situations like that, it may promote sensible and energetic rewards. I dare to say that "A personal equation in two movements" demands a loving reader equipped with courage and strict confidence, and shielded by mature compassion!

Despite its eminently practical intention, the book presents to some readers agreeable surprises in the form of developing theoretical elaborations. Chapter Seven, for example, whose title is again formulated as an instigating question (*Psychoanalysis and Epistemology: Relatives, Friends or Strangers?*) leads to chapter Eight, synthetically and perhaps enigmatically entitled *Truth*. Both are part of Sandler's research in the transdisciplinary relationships and analogies between Psychoanalysis, Physics, and the origins of those fields from the theories of knowledge and scientific knowledge (epistemology). What could be the consequences for the reader's own personality raised by Sandler's proposition in "Epistemology is to knowledge as unconscious is to mind"? "An epistemological-psychoanalytic fable" provides another paradoxical irony that may cause one to lose sleep. The pitch is heightened with "A psychoanalytic vertex: two naïvetés". Sandler's forays into the theories of knowledge extend Kant's classical formulation of the existence of Naïve Realism (that is, the belief that the apprehension of reality is obtained exclusively with the use of the sensuous apparatus) with Naïve Idealism (the belief, equally wrong, that the world or reality is a mere product of an individual mind). A lower pitch, allowing for a breath of fresh air, is found in "Truth is Beauty, Beauty Truth" as well as in "at-one-ment".

Partial access to or apprehension of truth should be distinguished from lie; it must be distinguished from feelings of ownership of Absolute Truth. Equally, there is a need to elicit the search K → O, which unveils the theme related to destinies of mystics (genius or messiah). It is necessary to distinguish mystics from false prophets, liars and delirious personalities.

"'Passionate love' is the nearest I can get to a verbal transformation which 'represents' the thing-in-itself, the ultimate reality, the 'O', as I have called it, approximating to it" (Bion, 1975, pp. 197) is the quotation that heads the final chapter, which deals with groups—again, in a self-questioning tone: *A Sixth Basic Assumption?* If it is read with temperance, sobriety and serenity, mainly in the part "Some factors in the sixth basic assumption", the reader may see the emergence of the concern for life and consideration for truth that characterises "real psychoanalysis"—a formulation by Bion which is dear to Sandler.

Antonio Sapienza, MD, is a Training Analyst in the Sociedade Brasileira de Psicanalise de São Paulo.

PART I

THE MULTI-DIMENSION GRID

CHAPTER ONE

Scientific research in psychoanalysis

> It seems absurd that a psychoanalyst should be unable to assess the quality of his work.
>
> —Bion, 1970, p. 62

> I assume that the permanently therapeutic effect of a psychoanalysis, if any, depends on the extent to which the analysand has been able to use the experience to see one aspect of his life, namely himself as he is. It is the function of the psychoanalyst to use the experience of such facilities for contact as the patient is able to extend to him, to elucidate the truth about the patient's personality and mental characteristics, and to exhibit them to the patient in a way that makes it possible for him to entertain a reasonable conviction that the statements (propositions) made about himself represent facts. It follows that a psychoanalysis is a joint activity of analyst and analysand to determine the truth; that being so, the two are engaged—no matter how imperfectly—on what is in intention a scientific activity.
>
> —Bion, c. 1959, p. 114

> Indeed, I can say that an early casualty in trying to use the Grid is the Grid itself.
>
> —Bion, 1977a, p. 12

Proof and refutation of psychoanalytic research is best expressed by Freud's observation about free associations (Freud, 1937b). If the analyst utters something that propitiates an insight, the patient must react to it by uttering a free association. Conversely, if the patient issues a free association, the analyst must react through his or her own free-floating attention.

The cycle goes on, in a development which includes turbulence, setbacks, partial glimpses that can be regarded as good enough successes, trial and error, possible corrections, revision and expansion of something concluded earlier, and so on. The cycle can be expressed by Freud's formulations in "Analysis Terminable and Interminable" (1937a).

Bion expanded this scrutiny through a theory of observation drawn from mathematics, bringing the models and concepts of Saturation, Transformations and Invariants (1965), which were already intuited by Freud in "The Interpretations of Dreams" (1901). Bion's concepts of Saturations and Non-saturations have their origin in Freud's theory of bounded and unbounded instincts (for example, in "Instincts and their Vicissitudes", 1915a, and "Beyond the Pleasure Principle", 1920).

The medium of communication in psychoanalysis comprises semantic and non-semantic realms of talking. In other words: verbal, linguistic representations and non-verbal, ultra- and infra-linguistic expressive-impressive formulations. Both can easily be seen in artistic formulations; the former in poetry and prose, and the latter in the so-called expressionist and impressionist schools of painting or music, which rely on non-verbal modes of conveying emotional experiences. Starting from Klein's work with children, Bion and Winnicott were able, to an extent, to expand psychoanalytic apprehension of the non-verbal compounds which are always and constantly added to the verbal ones that were mainly studied by Freud. A disclaimer is due in order to avoid misunderstandings: this immediately previous statement does not imply that Freud did not notice the non-verbal compounds and their manifestations, which would be equivalent to denying his forays into the unconscious realm. But in many ways Freud was a harbinger and opened some broad avenues that were later expanded or explored by a few of his followers—a possibly apt designation due to the fact that they followed his path.

For some years (roughly from 1950 to 1964) Bion was influenced by part of the neo-positivist epistemology that attained high respect from the late 1920s to the early 1970s but had diminishing influence after that time. It looked for mathematical syntaxes in scientific statements in order to check their truth value. Interested readers who are not familiar with this may look at the work of Moritz Schlick, who had some indirect influence on psychoanalysis through one of its pupils, Roger Money-Kyrle; better yet, they might save some time with the work of Rudolf Carnap, who was born in Germany but moved to the United Kingdom. One of its last exponents was Imre Lakatos. It had almost nothing to do with the positivist school, even though the very name unavoidably recalls it, except that in both frameworks of knowledge there are attempts or pretensions to provide a basis for scientific thought and research.

With this inspiration, and armed with Freud's technique of the "talking cure", Bion devised a proposal to scientifically test the extent to which an analyst's intervention apprehended the patient's psychic reality. It was a psychoanalytic, non-positivistic view of proofs and refutations *to scrutinise both patient's and analyst's verbal formulations, according to as many vertices as one could possibly gather, in order to assess their truth value*. Bion hypothesised that this measure should increase the scientific value of psychoanalysis. The main difference between Bion's approach and that of others before or after him lies in a different underlying rationale. All approaches intend or pretend to have the same general goal. The latter usually believe in a more limited positivistic[1] outlook: limited for it is seen as the one and only science; limited in relying on conscious external appearances, thus risking putting itself outside of psychoanalysis. Leaving aside earlier attempts, nowadays there are emphases which include political backing[2] within the psychoanalytic movement on "empirical research" (as it is understood in the school of academic psychology devoted to consciousness) and on "neuro-psychoanalysis".[3] As such, they are not of concern to this study, which bears on psychoanalysis (Solms, 1995; Fonagy, 2001; Roth & Fonagy, 2005). Moreover, those approaches are the source of controversy. They are flawed by major epistemological and scientific drawbacks (Dornhoff, 2005), in my view due to their being based on positivistic tenets and their rival claims to have advanced beyond and/ or superseded psychoanalysis proper.

Material and methods

In psychoanalysis, both material and methods are one and the same: mind itself. This could not leave the analyst hapless, because other non-positivist sciences, like modern physics (post-Einstein and post-quanta) share the same feature. Research into the unknown in physics is based on probabilistic calculus of a measured interference of energies between a given known particle and a given unknown particle. Interference, in mathematical, musical and psychological nomenclature, is a synonym of relationships.

Our twofold method consists of excerpts of analytic sessions and a Grid expanded from two dimensions to n dimensions. Bion's original Grid proposed a two-dimensional representation that constantly conjoined two individual axes. One axis was numbered from 1 to infinity and represented a genetic development of thinking. Understood after Georg Cantor's set theory of ordinal and cardinal numbers, the unconscious as a kind of infinite set was a model explored by Matte Blanco. Cantor gave preference to the term transfinite, which means not absolutely infinite but, paradoxically, infinite as far as it is submitted to research. This use of his theory does not mean approval of the theory as a whole, which is beyond a psychoanalyst's task, or even as the one and only mathematical theory as a contribution to psychoanalysis. It is quoted just to use this definition, which is useful to analysts who accept dealing with the infinite. Adding Brouwer's intuitionist theory and other criticisms to Cantor (for example, Russell's paradox) may furnish a more workable contribution to psychoanalysis. The other axis, lettered from A to G (with an infinite inner classification still waiting to be named), represented the functions of thinking (or ego-functions, after Freud in "Formulations on the Two Principles of Mental Functioning", 1911a). Each cell plotted in relation to the two axes can be used to characterise each verbal statement coming from both components of the analytic pair. Therefore, according to the vertex under which it is uttered, *any verbal statement may fall into one or many different grid categories*. Even one category may fall into another one.

This allows us to formulate statements that avoid descriptions of particular clinical entities being made to fit some quite different clinical entities: "Correct interpretation therefore will depend on the analyst's being able, by virtue of the grid, to observe that two statements verbally identical are psychoanalytically different" (Bion, 1963, p. 103; 1965, p. 116).

This observation has a seminal importance to the practising analyst. Each assigned category changes kaleidoscopically according to each moment of the sessions and according to each vertex assumed by the patient and/or the analyst.

Why assign one particular category to a statement instead of any other? The decision depends on an "analytically trained intuition" (Bion, 1965, pp. 34, 50). The Grid was intended to improve it, together with other means. Chief among them, the analyst's personal analysis: "the best possible one analyst may get" as Bion emphasised many times (1977, 1979). The Grid attempts to convey the human apparatus of thought as an observational theory in psychoanalysis and this nature and intent have as an intrinsic factor the truth-seeking function.

When Bion states that the Grid has some functions, it is obvious to state that the Grid must have a *functioning*; this endows with value the idea of a mental apparatus and a mental apparatus of thinking—which are truthful formulations that come from Freud and were followed by Bion.[4] The functioning of the original two-dimension Grid elicited, at least to me, two additional dimensions implicit in it: the axes of intensity and time (Sandler, 1987, 1999).

Bion had doubts about the success of the bi-dimension Grid to effect the improvements mentioned above, for he noticed its built-in representational flaws (1963, 1977, 1979). In principle, the Grid has in common the limitations of any human representations that strive, but cannot present reality as it is—in any given realm (artistic or scientific), which has any given discipline and media it may adopt, according to its nature, artistic or scientific. But it was soon discovered that the Grid (again, in common with some of the psychoanalytic tools that preceded it and also with those which followed it in time) had more than its share of limitations. For example, at least in my experience, it was comparatively rare to find people who realised that the Grid is endowed with a functioning.[5] Also, the implicit dimensions of intensity and time have been difficult for many people to realise. It became noticeable (even in Bion's time, a fact detected by him) how a great many students of his work seemed to be imprisoned by the representational formulation of the Grid—which seemed to them, thanks to its form, something like a prison. The clinical utility of the Grid was put into doubt, with no reference to the availability of capacity or possibility in the onlooker or student to have grasped it, halting the studies in its very medium. Was the medium a problem? If it was, it may be useful to consider that any medium must be within the spectrum of human catchment and apprehension. This apprehension may be extended beyond the human sensuous apparatus through our technical ability to augment it. In order to address this issue of improving the "analytic intuition utility" of the Grid in diminishing the flaws imposed by the chosen media, it was suggested that two additional representations should be added that focus on the dimension in which realisation was hitherto lacking. The present expansion tried to follow some steps in the history of science as exemplified by its earliest manifestation, mathematics. As occurred in the mathematical realm, the suggestion of a three-dimension Grid, with an axis of magnitude or intensity, expanded the two-dimensional Euclidean space of the original Grid into a three-dimensional space.[6] A decade of further clinical experience indicated that the three-dimension Grid still had some limitations; a fourth axis, to represent time, was added. Again, the three-dimension Grid was encompassed by a four-dimension Grid; in both cases there was no replacement, just expansion. Therefore, the four-dimension grid had two axes added to the earlier two-dimensional representation in order to represent intensity and time of phenomena (Sandler, 1987, 1997). Ten years later, a representational formula for a six-dimension Grid was proposed, using other observations from Bion conjoined with data obtained in further clinical experience: the added dimensions encompassed the realms of the Sensuous, Myth and Passion, representing a more detailed scrutiny of both intensity and time axes. As in the earlier proposals, the six-dimension Grid tried to integrate scattered observations found in other parts of Bion's work.

It seemed that the six-dimension Grid, based on the achievements of the two other powerful methods of apprehension of reality, mathematics and physics, could not represent the multi-dimensional reality of psychic reality. The same situation also occurred before with mathematics, whose researchers had to, and now are able to think along n dimensions. Therefore, both three- and six-dimension Grids are provisional steps towards a more precise model to appreciate the truth value of analytic statements in the analytic session. The original Grid and its three- and four-dimensional expansions may help the reader to realise the instrument step by step. I do not claim to make more than provisional, albeit developed, expansions.

Clinical validation of psychoanalytic constructions[7]

Freud's empirical-clinical criterion: There is nothing to be gained by telling the patient that which he already knows; the obverse is valid when he tells us what he knows. A correct construction (or interpretation) in the context it is given allows the emergence of renewed free associations. These access psychic reality to the extent that they display love of truth and regard for reality, and dispense with fraud and evasion: "The unconscious is the true psychical reality; in its innermost nature it is as much unknown to us as the reality of the external world, and it is as incompletely presented by the data of consciousness as is the external world by the communications of our sense organs" (Freud, 1900, p. 613; 1937a, pp. 237, 238, 248).

Extensions from Freud by Bion: "Correct analysis ... formulates what the patient's behaviour reveals"; verbal interpretation dispenses with "an emotional discharge (e.g. countertransference or acting-out) ... If analysis has been successful in restoring the personality of the patient he will approximate to being the person he was when his development became compromised". A successful outcome of analysis depends on "resolution of the Oedipus complex". "Considering any psychoanalytic session as an emotional experience, what elements in it must be selected to make it clear that the experience had been a psychoanalysis" and not "an *imitation* of psychoanalysis rather that what is genuine"? "The work of the analyst is to restore dynamic to a static situation and so make development possible ... the patient manoeuvres so that the analyst's interpretations are agreed; they thus become the outward sign of a static situation". "In reversible perspective acceptance by the analyst of the possibility of an impairment of a capacity for pain can help avoidance of errors that might lead to disaster. If the problem is not dealt with the patient's capacity to maintain a static situation may give way to an experience of pain so intense that a psychotic breakdown is the result". And vice-versa: "The interpretation given the patient is a formulation intended to display an underlying pattern". The underlying pattern is unconscious: "The psychoanalyst tries to help the patient to transform that part of an emotional experience of which he is unconscious into an emotional experience of which he is conscious" (Bion, 1965, pp. 35, 143; 1963, pp. 94, 14, 62; 1967a, p. 131; 1965, p. 32).

Bion's term "real psychoanalysis", in its original formulation, is free from moral judgments. It allows discrimination between true and false. The moral vertex turns "true *and* false" into "right *or* wrong". "And" present a paradox which calls not to be resolved; "or" turns it into an idea of attaining an absolute truth. Bion quotes Darwin: *"judgment obstructs observation"* (1962, p. 86).

> The "real psychoanalysis" to which we aspire is at best only a reaching out towards that "real psychoanalysis". But it is real enough to make people aware that there is "something" beyond the feeble efforts of psychoanalyst and analysand. I think it optimistic to suppose that we do more than scratch the surface in our struggles to achieve it. [Bion, 1979a, pp. 509–10]

It focuses some states of the analyst's mind:

> I suggest that for a correct interpretation it is necessary for the analyst to go through the phase of "persecution" even if, as we hope, it is in a modified form, without giving an interpretation ... Again, he should not give an interpretation while experiencing depression; the change from paranoid–schizoid to depressive position must be complete before he gives his interpretation ... The interpretation should be such that the transition from *knowing about* reality to *becoming real* is furthered. [Bion, 1967b, p. 291 and 1965, p. 155]

The Grid

This epistemological tool (or a tool to gain knowledge), developed from 1963 to 1977, performs a critical scrutiny, outside the analytic session, of the analyst's recall of verbal statements issued by patient and analyst (Bion, 1965, p. 128). This method respects the basic psychoanalytic tenet: free association. It is implicit that the analyst's recall must provide a correspondence whose nature is the same as free associations, having the *nous* of sincerity. The Grid allows discrimination: "The elements of psychoanalysis are ideas and feelings as represented by their setting in a single grid category" (Bion, 1963, p. 103).

This indicates how Bion was influenced by the neo-positivism of Schlick, Neurath, Carnap and the young Wittgenstein, brought to England by Braithwaite and Bradley.[8] I have observed that many confuse German and Austrian neo-positivism with the French positivism of Auguste Comte, which constitutes a mistake. That which became the "Viennese school" of epistemology had sought a mathematical syntax seen as powerful enough to verify the truth value of scientific propositions. In neo-positivism, this mathematical syntax would be "theory-free", so to say, "above" (or "below") the individual discipline or field, whatever it may be. From this project, epistemologists used to affirm that a criterion for some discipline to attain a scientific level or qualification is that it must be made mathematical; an early and still continuing offshoot of this is the application of probability mathematics to many aspects of scientific research as well as the evaluation of results, therapeutic or not. The neo-positivist posture contrasts with positivist beliefs, namely: (i) predictive cause-effect relationships; (ii) neutrality of the observer; (iii) favouring material reality at the expense of any other form, trapping thought in intra-sensuous apprehension; (iv) consequences such as the location of phenomena in Euclidean space; (v) disparagement of intuition.

Construing *cell categories* dynamically linked through the intersection of two axes, Bion offer a dynamic Grid to integrate Freud's formulations of the two principles of mental functioning with Klein's discovery of the paranoid-schizoid and depressive positions (Freud, 1911a, 1920; Klein, 1940, 1946, 1957). To differentiate the two axes, Bion resorts a visual form: a bi-dimensional geometrical representation of a vertical and a horizontal line divided by categories. The former is numbered and the latter is lettered. Bion emphasises that the Grid represents in a bi-dimensional field, though crudely, both evolution and involution of thinking processes. The Grid does not "serve to real contact with the patient", but rather as a prelude to this contact, as training for the psychoanalytic intuition. Nevertheless, the Grid can be put into a kind of "introjection" service when it is used to enhance the analytic intuitive contact with emotional experiences. It does not serve as an aid to self-analysis, but can be seen as a portable supervisor:

> Although home work is not done in an atmosphere of emotional tension, grid and transformation theory is applied to the recollection of such situations. The analyst's intuition, which it is the object of these reviews to exercise and develop, is operating in contact with the tense situation. It is important to distinguish between the grid (as it appears in my scheme) operating in tranquillity on recollections, and the grid as part of the analyst's intuitive contact with the emotional situation itself. [Bion, 1963, p. 75–6]

Moreover, it furnishes truth-verification for this contact, perusing the verbal statements uttered by both sides of the analytic pair (Bion, 1958–1979, p. 195; 1963; 1965, p. 39–47, 50, 74–75, 96–100, 126, 167–169). For those readers who are unfamiliar with Bion's grid, the reading of the quoted texts from *Transformations* (1965) seems necessary; also, Bion, 1967; 1971; 1977b; 1977c, pp. 57 and 92.

Bion's representational construction in two axes seems to be inspired by the bi-dimensional mathematical notation from Euclidean representations often learned in school mathematics and physics, such as the study of linear or parabolic functions. Their representation uses two coordinate axes (usually called x and y, abscissa and ordinate).

The horizontal axis consists of numbered columns representing the uses and functions of thinking processes. Columns 1 and 2 may be called the "Platonic-Kantian categories" to represent a primitive functioning of mind. The first column is innate pre-conceptions, or definitory hypotheses, things-in-themselves felt as absolute truths. The second is ψ, which relates to facts and other elements known to be false by the patient; moreover, these facts enthrone statements against the obtrusion of any development in the patient's personality involving catastrophic change (Bion, 1977b, p. 11). That which is false has a function when one is bound to learn from experience with reality. It constitutes the "test of reality" (Descartes, 1637; Freud, 1910a). It includes the epistemological function of error; in psychoanalysis, it is contained in "unconscious phantasies" (Freud, 1900, 1905, 1910a, Isaacs, 1948). Its function is analogous to the blind man's stick when the issue is not walking, but the unconscious mental maturation; metaphorically, a "walk" in one's life. The unconscious phantasy has a link with natural instincts, or needs; at the same time, it contains wrong pre-conceptions to the extent that they seek avid, complete satisfaction of desire. There are some leanings to one side or another—frustration or satisfaction. The outcome and aftermath depend on each person's abilities to hate truth and disregard life, linked to primary narcissism and envy as described by Freud and Klein (Bion, 1958–1979, pp. 125, 133, 262; Klein, 1957). The blind man's stick, the natural tendency of the unconscious phantasy towards developed apprehensions of reality, transmutes itself into a herald of ignorance, manifested in delusions, illusions and fetishism. These nourish paranoia or psychopathic behaviour if the phantasy leans towards its error rather than to reality. Anyway, the perception and existence of lie is a necessary situation to attain glimpses of truth.

> Epistemologically a statement may be regarded as evolved when any dimension can have a grid category assigned to it. For purposes of interpretation the statement is insufficiently evolved

until its Column 2 dimension is apparent. When the Column 2 dimension has evolved, the statement can be said to be ripe for interpretation; its development as material for interpretation has reached maturity. [Bion, 1965, p. 167]

The "Original lie" in its earliest, primitive manifestation seems to be that the desired breast exists at all; the pre-conception of breast would be wholly, greedily satisfied. Nevertheless, the reality is that any offered breast, which will serve as a realisation, never is—and cannot be—the desired breast, as if it were custom-made. Frustration is the begetter of thought: no-breast, therefore a thought. Columns 3, 4, 5 and 6 are the "Freudian" categories of the grid to represent ego functions: notation, attention, enquiry and action (Freud, 1910b).

The vertical axis consists of lettered rows, a psychogenesis of thinking processes. Those categories historicise thought processes within a continuum: from less developed to developed classes (science and algebraic calculus). Rows A, B and C "shelter" or indicate, respectively: β elements; α elements; myths, dreams and dream thoughts. They evolve from a "de-sensifying" to a "de-concretisation". Human beings are able to catch a limited (but good enough for some tasks) range of stimuli, external or internal. Our human sensuous apparatus mediates this catchment. After being sensuously apprehended, the process of apprehension continues in a series of transmutations (analogous to physical transducers) that are at their most hypothetical, whose elucidation is just beginning, but they occur and may be intuited by analytic research. Psychoanalytic research is based on intuition, in the same vein as any research around the world in all scientific disciplines known to humanity since the inception of science. Pascal, Kekulé, Poincaré, Fleming, Planck, Einstein, Sabin and Schechtman (winner of the 2011 Nobel Prize in Chemistry) furnish telling examples. Chemical and neurological (now also called "neuro-scientific") research still suffers from its positivistic shackles—here understood as a belief in cause-and-effect reasoning—as well as from exclusively conscious reasoning, which may be submitted to twisted and hasty conclusions. For example, the causal links hastily hypothesised and even more hastily elevated to the status of proven thesis around the discovery of neuro-mediators and enzymatic processes associated with them: adrenalin, dopamine, serotonin and the inhibitors to their uptake. Computerised neuro-images based on anatomical macro-findings, like any images obtained by computerised techniques, are much more the work of the computer engineers' minds and their ideas of what reality should be than counterparts of what functional reality is. It seems that avid audiences often forget that the "neuron" is still a hypothesis: the reticular theory cannot easily be dismissed, making its possible counterparts in reality the object of controversy.

The transduced form of the received stimuli is expressed by what analysts call thinking, dreaming and memories. The reader may recognise here Bion's theory of alpha function. This theory has an intermediary stage that Bion regards as the formation of α-elements. The first stage is represented by the data that demands to be apprehended: the raw external and internal sensuous stimuli. The last stage is expressed by memories, dreams and thinking, a mixing of α-elements. Bion calls the external and internal stimuli β-elements, which occupy a specific category in the horizontal axis, as I have just mentioned (Column 1). They also occupy the same place in the vertical axis: the definitory hypothesis. The sensuously apprehensible stimuli are the origin of everything and anything. Sense organs, albeit incomplete in their range of amplitude of apprehension, are our port of entry for everything and anything. Some misapprehensions of Bion's writings disparage the sensuous apprehensions (see Sandler, 2005, p. 832). Perhaps their simplification overlooks Bion's remarks that the problem is not with them, but with some individuals who keep themselves frozen in the initial reaction, refusing to de-sensify the stimuli or to de-concretise them. To keep one in the sensuous perceptions is equivalent to degrading *Homo sapiens* into *Homo sensorialis*. Conversely, β-elements transform (transduce) themselves into α-elements; so α function can be regarded as the mind's de-sensifying function, even though the hypothetical α- elements, formulated just as a model, used for memorisation, dreams and so on, have as their raw material real experiences. It is easier—and psychoanalysis was keen to furnish this method—to examine events from the most elementary, primitive and earliest forms it is possible to describe. Among the advantages is that they are simpler to describe and usually serve as prototypical models, in terms of transference patterns. Thus there are sensuous impressions that are involved in a baby's annihilation terrors, such as the cold air that pierces through its pharyngeal space, larynx membranes, and alveolar spaces in the lung. It goes on with the first contact with the breast, which can result in breasts felt as good or otherwise. The hitherto available hypotheses are based on very limited observations *in utero*, and pre-natal life cannot start from the same experience. For life itself, in its "complete" material and psychic existence, is not at stake before the time of the baby's first contact with air to provide oxygenation. Respiration and nourishment come in a readied form from the mother throughout the baby's pre-natal life. Both are freely given to the unborn child as final products rather than initial stimuli (both external and internal), as happens in post-natal life. Lack of a good enough, real hypothesis leaves some researchers free to imagine. In this case, one should ask how an α-element could be used to form memories, dreams and thoughts before birth. After all, it would only be after birth that the baby will acquire knowledge for the first time. The template which will—and must—be used to acquire knowledge is a built-in preconception, a part of what Freud described as *Trieb*. Phylogenetic inherited instinctive drives push the baby; he or she has to look for a breast in order to survive. From this time on, how does the baby acquire knowledge? The sensuously apprehensible experience is linked to hunger. How could hunger, survival, annihilation (in other words, how the life and death instincts are manifested) be "re-acknowledged" and in this sense already form part of a primitive "ur-memory of pre-concepts"? My hypothesis is that it is an inborn part of the common-sense phylogenetic memory acquired by Darwinian selection.[9] Thus the innate pre-conception of the breast is the "Kantian" amendment (Column 1) to Freud's ego functions. Coordinated with Row A, this "Kantian" amendment results in a category named A1. The same is valid for the second innate pre-conception suggested by Bion, Oedipus.

When β is transmuted into α and then, from α to dreams, myths, etc., the primitive thoughts and thinking processes are located in A1, B1, A2, and B2. Bion's quasi-mathematical notation with the relationships of letters and numbers reflecting the intersection of the two axes proved, to many readers, to be a maze. This seems to be the reason for the abandonment of attempts to use and improve the Grid as a tool (Sandler, 2005, p. 306). So a scan of the symbols, "translating" them to their original meaning in colloquial language, may help; it will suffice to use the two axes. Therefore: A1 means definitory hypothesis made of β-elements; B1 means definitory hypothesis made of α-elements; A2 means lies made of β-elements; B2 means lies made of α-elements. All of them may function as Row D, which corresponds to Pre-conceptions. The reader may ask: does the term "pre-conception" apply to A1, A2 and D (1–6)? The answer is both "Yes" and "No". The thoughts which function as pre-conceptions in D differ from those which function as such in A1 because the former are not necessarily innate, but they may be products of learning. Bion found it useful to coin another term, a non-hyphenated "preconception" to denote theoretical starting points or vertices from the analyst. To quote an example, if one focuses on Oedipus as used by a baby, it has the hyphenated form; if used by the analyst, it has to be written with no hyphen. Those pre-conceptions may match with realisations, albeit incompletely. Why incompletely? Because this incompleteness warrants its evolution: the offered or available breast *never* can match in an exquisite way, such as the coupling of precisely machined pieces, the "breast pre-concept" which, in the actual movement, will have no way out of being a preconceived breast rather than a pre-concept. From the other side, the unavoidable, real incompleteness provides the no-breast, or a good enough mother as depicted by Winnicott. The no-breast is a frustrating as well as a good enough experience, which allows to the baby to think about the breast when it is absent. This is Bion's theory of thinking; it appears in the successive "saturations" and "non-saturations" that cast the evolution of Row D (pre-conceptions) to Rows E, F, G and H: respectively, conceptions, concepts, deductive systems, and algebraic calculus—more developed thinking modes.

The two axes, vertical lettered and horizontal numbered, can be constantly conjoined, and from this conjunction they construe a common sense: "The two axes should thus together indicate a category implying a comprehensive range of information about the statement" (Bion, 1963). Using the bi-dimensional graphic way idealised by Bion, the conjunction which forms the categories is made simultaneously from above to below, A to H (or its obverse sense, from below to above, H to A) *and* simultaneously in the diagonal vector.[10]

One may state that from an epistemological vertex, Bion's original Grid forms an authentic *tour de force* to the extent that it is a concentrated

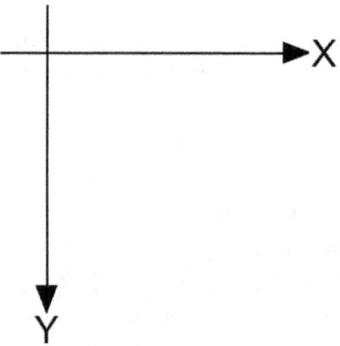

Fig. 1: Euclidean coordinates

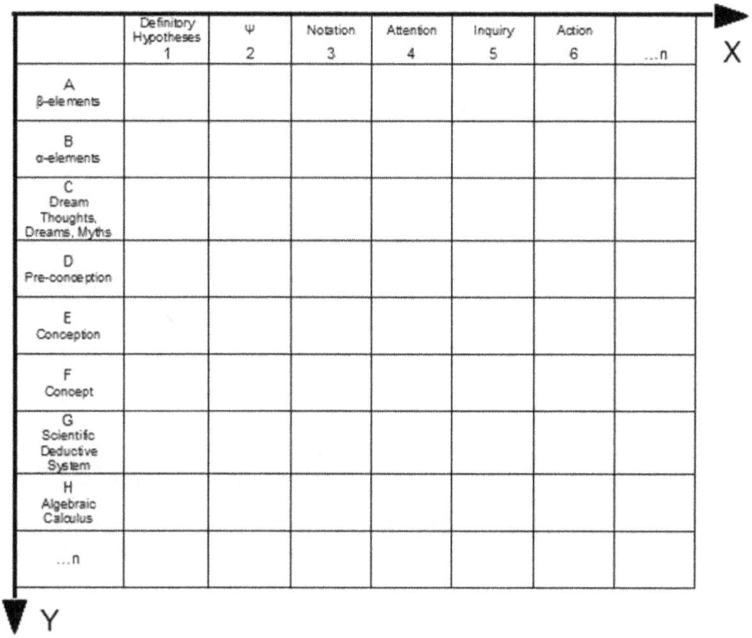

	Definitory Hypotheses 1	Ψ 2	Notation 3	Attention 4	Inquiry 5	Action 6	...n
A β-elements							
B α-elements							
C Dream Thoughts, Dreams, Myths							
D Pre-conception							
E Conception							
F Concept							
G Scientific Deductive System							
H Algebraic Calculus							
...n							

→ X
↓ Y

Fig. 2: The Grid (Bion, 1963)

integration of fundamentals from Locke, Hume, Kant, Freud, Klein and neo-positivism. As mentioned before, the concepts are, respectively, common sense, constant conjunction, pre-conceptions, ego functions, and emotional theories of thinking.

Bion's representational construction in two axes (see Figs. 1 and 2) seems to be inspired by mathematical notation from Euclidean representations. Usually people learn these when introduced to the study of mathematics and physics in school, through learning functions such as the linear or parabolic functions. In Fig. 2, the horizontal axis corresponds to Functions of the Ego; the vertical axis corresponds to the genetic development of thoughts.

Notes

1. "Positivism" is regarded here as an attempt to find consciously discovered uni- or multi-causality, dismissing intuition of underlying immaterial facts, beliefs about special localisation, and the erection of absolute truth.
2. Which adds to the extra-psychoanalytic realm.

3. This approach postulates that no psychoanalysis is neurological and no neurology is psychoanalytic. Under this basic assumption—which is unquestioned—there is an invitation (seen by its authors, and popularised by some audiences, as novel) to reunite the two fields. Freud's work offers questioning alternatives, more often than not forgotten, to this assumption.
4. Albeit much criticised in the fashion for relativism so typical of our present days.
5. The International Psychoanalytical Association promoted a course about Bion's work as an official event in its Congress in 2009—forty-six years after the introduction of the Grid. Or, the establishment may feel less vulnerable learning about this tool half a century later. The living experience of this course, if its attendance can be seen as a representative sample, echoed the findings already hinted before—surprise and shock at realising that the tool had a function and worked.
6. I do not use Euclidean and Cartesian in the popular sense of the terms, which attribute to Descartes the representation of space in three dimensions. According to the history of mathematics, both two- and three-dimensional systems of representation came from Euclid. Descartes was one of those who enabled us to expand Euclid's view by freeing it from the range encompassed by our sensory apparatus through algebraic calculus. The exclusive use of the former limited our mental apprehension of reality. Persian mathematicians provided a development of this algebraic expansion. Nevertheless their acquisitions remained unknown for centuries due to the Roman Catholic prohibition of knowledge. Most of their achievements were kept in Damascus and secretly in monasteries. This prohibition of knowledge in Western countries can be seen in the myths about it, reviewed by Thorner (1981) for psychoanalysts.
7. Or Interpretations (Freud, 1937b).
8. Bion seemingly did not know of Imre Lakatos's attempts. It seems that neo-positivism died with him; perhaps both died too early. We cannot know if this "dying" will be eternal or if there will be a phoenix-like event; the "resurrection" of truth is a well-known fact in the history of ideas in Western civilisation. Truth is durable (transcendent) even if perception of it may be fragile (immanent).
9. Freud's and Bion's acknowledged allegiance to Darwin's discoveries allows for this hypothesis.
10. I have observed that the few people who publicise a kind of work with the Grid usually use just the vertical sense, with no regard to the diagonal movement.

CHAPTER TWO

Verifying the truth value of verbal statements uttered in an analytic session with the help of the three-dimension grid

> Anyone who examines the Grid both on psychoanalytic grounds and for scientific methodological rigour will be dissatisfied ... In time someone may evolve a more generally acceptable system and proceed from that to the formation of grids suitable for particular types of difficulty, different disciplines.
>
> —Bion, 1977b, pp. 12, 20

In 1977, Bion proposed a more detailed view, and even a complete Grid devoted to Row C, Dreams and Myths. Another particular Grid was to be devoted uniquely to Column 2 (lies). And a Negative Grid was included in the same suggestion, forming part of what I propose to call the Realm of Minus (see Volume 2, Part I). Fourteen years after his proposal of the two-dimension Grid, in his talks in New York, Bion expanded it into a "grating", a suggestion of a three-dimension Grid, albeit with another name (Bion, 1979).

One of those evolutions may be a fresh view of its visual display. Even presented as a two-dimensional picture, Bion's Grid has an implicit *third* dimension. This constitutes the *variation in magnitude* of each category, which is made visible in the clinic. By adding a third axis

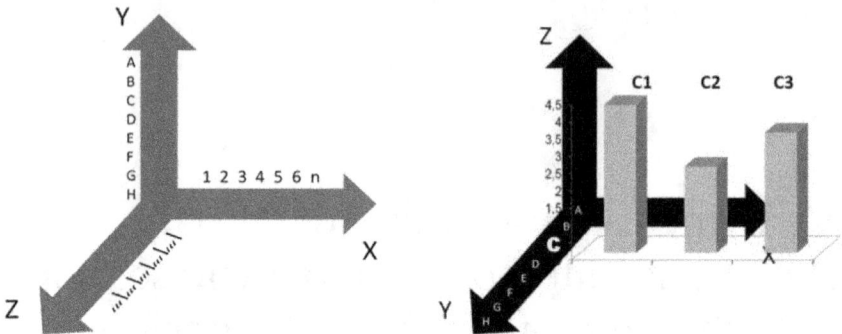

Fig. 3: The Tri-Dimension Grid   Fig. 4: The Grid in time

over the existing two, one may represent the intensity, or magnitude, of the constant conjunction of the genetic and function axes. There is no attempt to suggest the replacement of the original two-dimension Grid with the three-dimension one. The third dimension expands and helps comprehension of the existing two, though at the same time perhaps making the Grid more cumbersome.

The following example tries to illustrate, through an earlier proposed Tri-Dimension Grid (Sandler, 1987; 1999), a clinical situation where the tool was used to make a clinical hypothesis after one session and as a prelude to another one. The theoretical models are drawn from *Elements of Psychoanalysis* (1963), *Transformations* (1965), *The Grid* (1977a), and *Cogitations* (1958–1979).[1] The model, again, stems from Euclidean spatial representations through the adding of a third axis over the previous two. This third axis represents the intensity or magnitude of the constant conjunction of the genetic and function axes: in Fig. 3, the x axis represents the ego functions, the y axis the ontogenesis of thought, and the z axis the intensity of phenomena.

The Tri-Dimension Grid may represent different mental states over time: Fig. 4 shows the evolution of Category C, as an example.

Attempt to verify the truth value of verbal statements uttered in analytic sessions: second thoughts with the aid of the three-dimension grid

A way to demonstrate this expansion on Bion's original Grid can be seen through its use as an extra-session activity.

The task confronting the analyst is to bring intuition and reason to bear on an emotional experience between two people (of whom he is one) in such a way that not only he but also the analysand gains an understanding of the analysand's response to that emotional situation, and does so through an appreciation of the evidence to which the analyst is drawing attention in the course of his interpretations. It is not enough for the analyst to be convinced that there is evidence for the truth of his interpretations; he must have enough evidence available to afford the analysand the opportunity of being persuaded, by his reason, of the cogency of the interpretation. [Bion, 1958–1979, p. 91]

The work of the analyst is to restore dynamic to a static situation and so make development possible ... the patient manoeuvres so that the analyst's interpretations are agreed; they thus become the outward sign of a static situation ... In reversible perspective acceptance by the analyst of the possibility of a capacity for pain can help avoidance of errors that might lead to disaster. If the problem is not dealt with the patient's capacity to maintain a static situation may give way to an experience of pain so intense that a psychotic breakdown is the result. [Bion, 1963, pp. 60, 62]

I suggest that for a correct interpretation it is necessary for the analyst to go through the phase of "persecution" even if, as we hope, it is in a modified form, without giving an interpretation ... Again, he should not give an interpretation while experiencing depression; the change from paranoid–schizoid to depressive position must be complete before he gives his interpretation. [Bion, 1967b, p. 291]

Verbal statement: A patient overtly displaying a mildly frightened demeanour, and wanting to give this kind of impression in the onlooker (the analyst), lay down on the couch and immediately said: "I dreamt about an atomic bomb."

I, the "analyst",[2] thought in connection with this and suddenly that the patient was expressing his aggression and destructiveness. Some few agreeing comments were made by both, agreements made in a rational way. In rational connection with those comments, the patient stated many "confirmations" of the idea. In other words, the patient willingly swallowed the interpretation I gave him, agreeing with it.

"Yesterday, I was ready to smash my neighbour's crying cat, which only seemed to be able to make irritating meows ... are you surprised, to smash the smooth skin of a cat? Smashing, this must be my title ... I was very hard on my employee; it was not his fault, but I would willingly have stabbed him if I had a knife ..." The analyst's emotional experience shows him the dichotomy between what is related verbally and what is actually going on; an advertised guilty but lifeless account. Anyway, echoing the patient's attitude, the analyst soon dismisses the underlying lack of "colour" and resorts to verbal agreement. That seemed to elicit, explicitly and consciously, the patient's approval of the analyst's interpretation about the same patient's aggression.

Nevertheless, I remained dissatisfied with work that seemed to me, on second thoughts, drab. The dissatisfaction was tinged with persecuting guilt. After the patient left, I thought that the session had no roughness. On the other hand, it had plenty of plausible teleological conclusions that gave me final "answers", with no furthering free associations. This disquieted me—how can a session where aggression furnishes that kind of tone and pitch evolve with no aggression at all? Moreover, it seemed to me that both I and the patient were talking about a third party, a "patient" who was not there. At this moment I was reminded of some of the phrases uttered: "... ready to smash ... smooth skin ... was very hard on my employee ..." What seemed to me like free associations lacked the quality of free associations; they were "propaganda" (Bion, 1965, chapter IV) that refers to outside-the-session unobservable facts.

I was now in the status of a "would be-analyst that wasn't", becoming increasingly aware of a disturbing sense, that of entertaining doubts about the session and about my intra-session posture. I was not comfortable with the fact that the session was tidy and plausible. Mutually held agreements flowed easily, devoid of any sensation of the anxiety which was experienced after the session.

At first, there was a comforting feeling given by the appearances which indicated that everything was smoothly right. Now, that very same reason that was felt as comforting displayed itself as a source of discomfort. An analyst never ceases to see that rationalistic explanations have no place in analysis, except when the patient resorts to them; but even in this case they demand to be discarded after careful questioning and analysis.

After experiencing what can be seen as a tandem movement, being rescued from a false feeling of calmness and flowing into a persecutory state, some spontaneous reminders emerged in my thinking. I suppose that I was entering into a depressive emotional experience. This emotional experience seemed to correspond to Bion's recommendation about the timing of a good-enough intra-session interpretation (Bion, 1963, 1965, 1967). The inception of a lie and awareness of it—I felt I issued a false interpretation—may also be the opportunity, like an entry door, to reach a true statement. Unfortunately, they happened *after* the session. Paradoxically, I supposed that they also happened to be *before* a planned new session. The spontaneous flow of reminders was:

1. I, the would-be analyst, was in a favourable position to make use of Bion's grid: an extra-session musing about a specific analysis.
2. In the form of a visual image (akin to both a pictographic record and a hallucination, but at the time I could not tell which) the figure of my second supervisor's face emerged, in a grandfatherly deportment. This man was a fairly well known and respected psychiatrist who had greatly helped the founders of the local psychoanalytic society. In a non-admonishing, but also worried tone, he said to younger psychiatrists working at his mental hospital who gathered around him: "You are enthusiastic about psychoanalysis. You must avoid situations such as one where, after five or six years, you and your patient should discover that both of you have wasted your time" (Yahn, 1971). What worried me was that I could be held responsible—before myself—for wasting my patient's time.
3. I was reminded of Freud's warnings about patients who agree with the analyst's comments, as well as his statement that nothing is gained when the analyst tells the patient that which the patient already knows (Freud, 1937).
4. Perhaps my free-floating attention was functioning—alas, outside the session. Better late than never, I thought. My next memory was Bion's paper "Evidence" (1976): he hypothesises and questions whether the whole of psychoanalysis might well be a vast paramnesia to fill the void of one's ignorance. Bion's report was about a verbal interchange with interpretations and agreements marked by softness, with no resistance at all, as if everything was "going well"—until evidence emerged that something had not

gone so well. His patient returned home, went to the kitchen and gassed himself.
5. Another recommendation, this time from my first supervisor: "If you notice that you are too hasty to deliver what seems to you a wonderful interpretation, then it's high time to refrain from talking" (Sandler, 1970).
6. After this wave of guilt pervaded me, I felt—again—a reassuring remembrance in the form of a paper written by a rather famous or fashionable analyst that dealt with a similar utterance in a similar way. His patient mentioned something similar to a bomb and the two agreed that it was exclusively linked to the patient's aggression. Suddenly I felt saved and resorted to an "authority", instituted by myself. Short-lived reassurance, anyway; I noticed that a tandem movement between persecutory feelings and alleviation was occurring in my mind. I shall spare the reader from quoting this specific author, for my intention is not to carry out a professorially disguised witch-hunt based on a self-attributed moral role. Conversely, I suppose this is a fairly common situation shared by many analysts. Therefore the following exercise may prove useful to some readers.

Those recollections, which included fatherly supervisions (both literally and symbolically) whose emotional effect on me was *Take care, do entertain second thoughts,* enabled me to tell myself: "I regarded the statement *I dreamt about an atomic bomb* as a report about a factual dream."

Increasingly, realisations about obstacles to the analytic evolution of the session became clear. I noticed that something Freud recommended to interpret dreams was remarkably absent: free associations (Freud, 1900; Sharpe, 1937). I noticed that I had willingly been kidnapped by the manifest content, something acoustically apprehensible. My patient and I attributed the same meaning to the words "dreamt" and "atomic bomb". There was no working through, no transformations at all that could elicit some latent contents. Under this light, I concluded that my feelings of failure were not exactly feelings, but an emotional experience of misunderstanding and misapprehending what would be happening in reality. It became crystal clear that the whole intra-session situation served the function of resistance to pain. Again and again, I saw that second thoughts extricated me from the reassuring rational and logical reasoning—as soon as I became well enough aware of it. This was a clue to the reassuring smoothness and rational plausibility of that session and to the patient's reaction to my colluded "'interpretation"—in inverted commas because this is a kind of pseudo-interpretation. The session now displayed another face: something was lacking. What was it? Some analysts usually experience persecutory feelings followed by sensations of depressive emotional experiences *before* giving an interpretation, but in this case this was occurring outside the session. All that remained was the persecution about some unknown failure. Was it a mere sensation? Was it a personal problem to be dealt with in my own analysis? Or was it a real perception of a fact?

As it occurred in the session, I could not go on. No wonder, because I colluded with the patient and in our shared hallucination we agreed that both of us "owned" an absolute truth. There was nothing to be confronted with.

Trying to improve my work, I supposed that time was ripe to use both the original and the expanded three-dimension Grid in order to appreciate the truth value of both the patient's and my statements (verbal formulations). We will see that this use produced at least one possible alternative, which could be compared with the events in the session.

How to display the actual session in the Grid

Even though it was not explicitly verbalised by Bion, it is implicit in the design and function of the Grid that it presents *possibilities of analysis*, under given vertices, which function as postulates or starting points. The three-dimension Grid seems to *represent* in a different, hopefully better, visual shape the possibilities *presented* by Bion's original two-dimension Grid.

Let us display the Grid at specific points in time as well as representing the three axes: ego-functions, development of thinking and magnitude of events. The variegated points in time may correspond to a fourth dimension, whose function could be didactic to follow the course of the analytic training or development. Ideally, these representations can be displayed as animated images through computer aided design (CAD), like a kind of cinematic film.[3]

Let us examine the three-dimension Grid in detail. One of the dissatisfactions centred on the soft effect of a hitherto undoubted absolute truth (thing-in-itself, β-element). Trying to make the best of this idea, I made a hypothesis: the patient's statement and my statement could serve as a "definitory hypothesis in β-element". This cannot do as a psychoanalytic interpretation. Now I think that our work was restricted to category A1. I try to get a naïve regard, disciplining and eventually trying to divest myself of theories and previous approved codes. Those codes include linguistic codes—patients and analysts usually use the same language with grammatical rules which are mostly even. The already known codes shackle and chain the observer into manifest contents. For analytic experience shows that patient's and analyst's vocabularies and the semantic field attributed to them are similar only when just outward appearances are taken into account. The analyst thinks: "I kept myself grounded in the social meanings of the phrases, restricting the patient's verbal statements and formulations to their superficial meaning. Why does one need an analyst who apes that which conscious, academic psychology already states?" I suspect that at that moment I made a dictionarised pseudo-interpretation clothed in psychoanalytic parlance which resulted in another imitation: a lifeless session. I had a glimpse of this in the actual session, but I denied the hunch.

Therefore a *folie-à-deux* session occurred; both felt entitled to have ownership of an "absolute truth":

$$\text{Atomic Bomb} = \text{Aggression}$$

in a kind of symbolic equation first described by Freud (1924) and expanded by Klein and later by Segal.

An alternative hypothesis sprouted from this postulate, which did not last as such, giving way to the consideration of its opposite. Now I had a scientific doubt due to the presence of two alternative hypotheses making for a dual-track (Grotstein, 1981), paradoxical state, rather than an absolute, monocular truth:[4]

$$\text{Atomic Bomb} = \text{Aggression}$$
$$\text{and/or}$$
$$\text{Atomic Bomb} = ? \text{ (meaning: unknown)}$$

Troubling questions about my practice; but at the same time, when I faced up to them, the questions enabled me to conclude that my precocious and hasty answer to the patient, focusing a particular linguistic meaning, did not allow for mutual analytic development. Rather, it continuously enabled the patient-professional pair to replace the would-be analytic couple. The pair remained glued to a shared lie, or agreement.

In the session, it installed a "Thus far and no further" posture (Bion, 1975). In this case, I used the stalemate as my leverage to think further. "There is nothing either good or bad in analysis, but mind makes it so" could be a fairly respectful paraphrase of Hamlet.

My doubt allowed me to locate the statement in Column 2: lies. As soon as I made this hypothesis, it became clear that both were working at a high intensity as well as in a restricted area of the tri-dimension expanded Grid. If we represent the mental state of the session, it depicts a definitory hypothesis of a beta-element which turned into a lying definitory hypothesis. But the lying hypothesis jumps to a conclusion, because it is either an *a priori* or an *ad hoc* pseudo-hypothesis, or a non-scientific already-proven idea, as soon as it is stated. Liars made plausible and rationally convincing theses rather than hypotheses. Shared plausibility does not imply that a truthful statement was made.

It takes into account the magnitude (or degree, or intensity) of the focused manifestation, amended to its genetic development conjoined with functions of the Ego. If the Grid has—as I have some evidence that it has—the power to represent facets of psychic reality, the magnitude has to do with an instinctive urgent pressure (*Drang*: Freud, 1915a; Sandler, 2000b). The Euclidean bi-dimension space system of representation that marks an area of restricted space submitted to high intensity can be likened to the physical concept of pressure (force applied to area). To the reader who does not loathe symbols or is accustomed to its corresponding worded notation, Bion's quasi-mathematical parlance may serve: A1 (beta-element as a definitory hypothesis). The "interpretation" and its collusive reassurance are symbolically noted by A2 (lies as a definitory hypothesis, with no transformation from beta-element).

Another category reached by what happened in the session is assigned to A6, acting out a definitory hypothesis. Both patient-analyst relationship and the analyst's interpretation can be seen as an acting out, as defined by Freud and reviewed by Fenichel.

Like the two-dimension Grid, the three-dimension Grid encompasses Melanie Klein's contributions: the analyst becomes aware, after using the tool, that he had hitherto unconsciously succumbed to an emotional climate full of projective identification. This climate was created by the patient. The analyst could now furnish a less incomplete version of what had happened in the session: the patient was issuing projective identifications of his love and life instincts. It was as if he was getting rid of his true self (in Winnicott's sense), and this was felt as painful. The patient feels that his capacity to love could be denied and split. Lost in the darkness of the unconscious, it would materialise itself in the external environment, as a projection into the analyst. It is clothed in a hallucinated collusion of a pseudo-loving agreement, manifested by "the same idea": aggression. It constitutes a resistance, in its classical sense discovered by Freud, accompanied by projective identification, which results, in the here and now of the session, in a "reversion of perspective": it turns a dynamic situation into a static one (Bion, 1963, pp. 54, 55, 61).

Thanks to depressive feelings, I became free to move on when I considered that I was going along the *same lines* as the patient, imprisoned by the patient's manifest wording. Now it was clear to me that I attributed to this wording the same concepts and meaning that the patient was attributing: "dreamed", "atomic bomb". All seemed to be the same to both of us; "all colours will agree in the dark", as Francis Bacon said in his essay "Of Unity in Religion" (1625). Therefore I decided to see what would happen if the patient's statement could be considered anew. Experience in analysis shows that it is always possible for the analyst to divest himself of his own previously known social and individual codes, vocabulary and meanings; from the social meanings of any statements taken at their face value. This corresponds to Bion's discipline of memory. I also tried to maintain a discipline over my desire, when I gave up the reassurances of being freed from the pain of having failed. A hitherto unrecognised face, fearful, appeared: a different kind of bomb ... the statement now "sounds", in my recollection in the calm outside the session, like a closed, saturated statement allowing no creative developments; which means that there is a death of thought. It came to me as something that has the features of a postulate. My idea seems to be confirmed by my own spontaneous recollection of my interpretation, which now appears to be unequivocally linked and colluded to the manifest content: "he is expressing his aggression and destructiveness".

Outside the session, I was at least free enough to exercise myself with the aid of the Grid. My experience of persecution and perception of it happened again, but not so briefly, because it was not under attack. The realisation of "being overwhelmed" in Column 2 allows me an alternative to that situation, which includes renewed thinking processes.

Questions which are felt as troubling have a beneficial consequence, often overlooked when fear of pain and the unknown prevail. There was now a possible opportunity, that of a different attempt. Lies and envy, like cancer, create uncreative growth rather than development; they demand the continuous idealisation of more lies as an attempt at constant repair. The analyst and the patient have growing layers of lies—immense stocks of nothing.

Therefore I ascribe to them the categories "a thing-in-itself as a definitory hypothesis" for the verbal statements about "atomic bomb" and "dreamt" (A1) and "a lie occupying the place where a dream should be" (A2) to depict what was going on in the session. The "atomic bomb" and "dreamt" were taken as ultimate truths, beta-elements. This kind of representation can be made using both Bion's two-dimension Grid and the expanded three-dimension Grid, if one sets out to see the intensity of the phenomena. The Z axis of the proposed three-dimension Grid displays a high intensity (Fig. 5).

Through the use of the Grid I had confirmation of the unpleasant feeling of an acting out in the session (A6). The patient's collusive reassurance also acquires the same taste. The analyst's Grid and the patient's Grid are identical and superimposed. I realised once more that I was dazzled by the acoustic—therefore sensuously apprehensible—stimulus. I also realise that, being *static and ecstatic,* blocked in a definitory hypothesis of a beta-element, A1, I simply had not resorted to my own previous experience with the patient and had not waited for more associations. This is the same as saying: *I did not deal with the patient's statement as an unknown*. The graphical depiction of the three-dimension Grid displays an impoverished figure as corresponding to an impoverished analysis. Adopting a three-dimension grid, the intensity of the

Fig. 5: Three-dimensional representation of the first session

phenomena increases towards A1 and A2 and jumps into A6. What is the advantage of doing this graphical exercise? It is the advantage of having a pair instead of a single; this creates an alternative choice. From a pair a couple may evolve, meaning real creation. Now I had my memory of the session and the use of the Grid. Both pointed in the same direction. If two wholly *different* vertices point in the same direction, furnishing a "hetero" instead of a "homo" vision, there is an enhanced probability that the orientation is nearer to the truth. One may compare this situation with the "confirmation" *a priori* displayed in the session.

Let us focus another problem of this situation, quoted briefly earlier. Those facts, at least in the analyst's mind, cropped up outside the session, for the analyst did not permit himself to experience the full cycle from paranoid-schizoid position to depressive position and back (Bion, 1967a, p. 291). He was halted with the pseudo-agreement; therefore, a realistic interpretation could not come into being. The use of the Grid seemed to serve as a warning of this state, analogous to an interlude.

The Grid categories display acting out phantasies of owning absolute truth, A6 (acting out of a lie). It is pseudo-scientific, because it was an intuition-less, rational deduction acted out on false premises. G6 (acting out in pseudo-scientific deductive systems) and H6 (acting out in algebraic calculus) construe a false theory. There prevailed direct, non-complex ideas on the "patient's destructiveness" borne in the statement. The patient understood his dream, but no insight had ensued. I concluded that the patient therefore set out to produce many reassuring pseudo-associations to keep the shared lie in constant repair, convincing both of us that we were living in a Panglossian state, the best of all worlds. To the extent that our activity in the session had no counterpart in real life, we were not making real analysis (Bion, 1977b, p. 307).

Now what was reported as a dream appears to me as a beta-element, the extent to which I had dealt with it as if it were a thing-in-itself becomes clear. I think, lamenting not having thought this during the session: "If only I had disciplined myself in my desire to interpret and to understand, if only I had been able to discipline myself with my memory on the social meaning of terms such as 'dream' and 'bomb' …" My doubts assumed a manageable form: "Was it a dream? Was only that the dream? Does 'atomic bomb' *really* mean something aggressive and destructive?" In more normal terms hitherto used by analysts, there was collusion. In reaching functions, the same initial phrase ("I dreamt about an atomic bomb") now constitutes an open work, after being kidnapped by the manifest content. The return to the analytic vertex, through the use of the Grid, propitiates a realm in which the analytic couple can be enabled to move with freedom, unbounded by the concreteness of one's own speech. Freedom from constraints imposed by other people is an unrivalled experience obtainable through the liberal, amiable and mutually fruitful activity that Freud called "psychoanalysis" and Bion emphasised as "real analysis". Some people experience it as fearful.

I cannot answer my questions, but now I have questions instead of absolute truths that impede progress in the research. The answers of the patient now seem definitely collusive, falsely compliant and feigning depression where there was none. The lifeless, smooth, "insightless" climate of the session now appears coherent to the whole. All of this was a defence against the emergence of painful feelings, as we shall see. The "smooth skin of a cat" acquired an alternative hypothesis of interpretation; it could be a hitherto unnoticed, but straightforward unconscious comment about the here and now of the session. The act of "smashing" could also be an inchoate insight about smashing an analytic session; the "neighbour" and "employee" appear as a transference situation linked to what he felt was me. In that moment of recollection in tranquillity (devoid of the in-session fire) I remembered that this man usually deals with me in a condescending way. It seemed to me a condensed image such as we see in dreams (corresponding both to a dream work hitherto unnoticed and to an ego mechanism of defence).

I allowed that "my Grid" would develop from the β-element definitory hypothesis (A1) status of the statement "I dreamt about …" into an unknown which allowed me renewed considerations, in the guise of new hypotheses: Is the patient's statement a hint that he, the patient, is dreaming that he is in a session of analysis? Is the patient setting up an exploration to see my (the analyst's) reaction?

Almost a century after the inception of the psychoanalytic movement a ritualistic canon obtruded; it is a banalisation of an otherwise powerful analytic tool. The patient is expected to recall dreams, and it is now quite common to find the prejudice that one ought to report dreams to an analyst. The same applies to the obligatory rule of talk; but we analyse despite the speech, not due to it, in a paradox one must cope with. I now hypothesise that the statement qualifies as a definitory hypothesis of a dream, C1, or a definitory hypothesis appearing as a dream, having passed through a de-sensifying process, alpha function—but in a very different sense compared to Possibility 1: the patient has a kind of day-dream that he is in a session of analysis.

Interlude between sessions

Possibility 2 is represented graphically by Figs. 6 and 7. The previous tri-dimension Grid (Fig. 5) depicted a high intensity in A1, A2 and A6. It was this extra-session examination which enabled the analyst to complete the tandem cycle of the Positions (PS⇔D). Thus armed, he considered a second hypothesis. It could be stated as a question: is it the "I dreamt about ..." which evokes the agreement about "aggression"?

In subduing the second part, the communication would be a hint: the patient dreams that he is undergoing an analytic session; a wish-fulfilling dream intended to ignite a pleasant reaction in the analyst. One century of psychoanalysis seems to have created a banality of an earlier powerful analytic tool, a ritualistic canon common to patients and analysts: the former are expected to recall dreams.

The analyst checks his idea through the tri-dimension Grid (see Fig. 6). The picture obtained displays an enriched pattern *vis-à-vis* the first Possibility. It is endowed with intensities spread over added categories, especially in those columns representing ego functions. Now it has elements belonging to notation and attention (Columns 3 and 4), as well as a new element from Row B, that is, an α-element. This element denotes the transformation of raw sensuous data into an element of thought: firstly, the raw sensuous data, taken as a β-element, is manifested as a phenomenal fact: "I dreamt about an atomic bomb"; and

Fig. 6: The analyst's second thoughts

Fig. 7: The analyst rescues the analytic view

then the element of thought, formed through α-elements, can be seen as the analyst's working through of the experience: "We (the quasi-analytic pair, pretending to be an analytic couple) had a hallucinosis, enslaved by pleasure, enthroned on the altar of a superior, colluded idea, that we were enjoying a psychoanalytic session". The intensity in categories A1 and A2 lessens; A3, B2, B3, C1, 2 and 3 obtrude. To those unfamiliar with the quasi-mathematical notation: beta-elements are replaced by lies as alpha-elements and notation of alpha-elements, which in their turn are transformed into dreams construed with beta-elements, which are transformed into dreams with alpha-elements and notation of dreams (which allows for its reporting as manifest contents). In Fig. 6 a richer picture emerges, diminishing the overloading of categories A and B and spraying the intensity over other categories from Row C.

The functioning of the three-dimension Grid, like the mental apparatus, can be seen in an entropic equilibrium between the many categories, under Fechner's principle of homeostasis, quoted by Freud in his model of the mental apparatus. This pre-psychoanalytic work, or would-be-psychoanalytic work, or pretending-to-be-analytic work, which could not yet be called psychoanalytic work, now had a chance to become that. In colloquial terms, an immateriality—expressed by the statement about a shared hallucinosis—springs from materiality. The patient's words, which were taken at their face value initially, are not any more. In Freud's terms, at first (Possibility 1) the pair was restricted to the examination of material reality; psychic reality was not reachable. After the session, the analyst makes a hypothesis (Possibility 2), through psychic un-reality (hallucinosis) functioning as a port-of-entry or dischargeable capsule. In Winnicott's and Bion's criteria, the analyst's work with the Grid allowed him to make a second cycle of transformations (Possibility 2), which differs from the first cycle (Possibility 1). The movement can be regarded as going from the first to the second cycle of transformations. The first belonged to the patient (in Bion's notation, Tp); the second belonged to the analyst (Ta), and *now* differs from Tp. All of this, having occurred outside the session, makes for mere hypothesis; further contact may or may not confirm it. But at that moment there was no certainty that the patient would come back.

If the analyst can "dream the session"[5] as recommended by Bion, the Grid seems to have helped me to confirm that my "interpretation" in this case was hastily linked to the manifest content, the spoken version of the patient without further elaboration and transformation. In Bion's later quasi-mathematical notation: Tpβ. Resorting to verbal notation: the final product of the transformations that the patient makes out of his initial inner stimulus, "Op". Literally: the patient's truthful experience is "O", Bion's notation for the numinous realm. I took the patient's statement at its face value, and even though it is reported as if it were a dream, I suppose now that it was not in fact a real dream; this idea—that both of us shared—was a conscious, assigned value. It does not qualify to be placed in Category C. Both I (the analyst) and the analysand relied on Column 2 beliefs, not knowing their Column 2 nature, and until that moment I did not know they were false. Consciously built, deductive rational explanations followed, as usual.

The final emotional experience and the analyst's mental state can be subsumed by Fig. 7. It may be compared with the patient's grid (Fig. 5).

A6 is a result of the spraying of all A categories, and as it has a C6 counterpart, cannot be seen as acting out; it is a short way to say: "The patient dreamt he had a session of analysis", a wish-fulfilling dream.

Still using the quasi-mathematical notation from Bion, which seemed to him more compact and synthetic, we may see that in Possibility 1 the final products stemming from the analyst's transformations (Ta) and from the patient (Tp) were the same, while in Possibility 2 they were not.

$$\text{Possibility 1: } Ta\beta = Tp\beta$$
$$\text{Possibility 2: } Ta\beta \neq Tp\beta$$

In this case, the second possibility is restricted to a hypothesis to be confirmed or not if, and when, the patient comes again. Hopefully, both cycles of transformations have to do with the same invariant, or "O". The reader who is familiar with Bion's work knows this author's notation to represent the numinous realm. This is intuitable, but remains ineffable. It was described by Plato, and later by Kant (Bion, 1965).

Furthering analysis: a further session

Possibility 3 is represented by Figs. 8–11. In this case, hope was casually replaced by fact; a question of contingency, ruled by unruly chance. Due to his innate disposition, the patient came back. Perhaps it is an effect of compulsion to repetition (Freud, 1920), not regarded as a pathology but as a last resort of health. It was not possible to know in what part of the spectrum he was: whether he returned, at one extreme, looking for analysis like one who longs for something he has not had (prototypically, having had the experience of a no-breast); or, at the other extreme, because he did not want analysis and had good confirmation from what had happened in our environment until that time that he would be sure not to get it. Probably it was a mixture of both, for he furnishes a renewed opportunity for analysis and for the analyst, added to his coming, which can be seen, albeit partially, in the monochord tone of his tune: "I dreamt—again—about an atomic bomb"'.

I decide to wait, aided by my extra-session musings propitiated by two factors: dissatisfaction and my own association with the use of the Grid. Instead of issuing the habitual hasty "interpretation" I tell myself: "It seems to be the same thing as yesterday, but there is a chance that it is not the same; I do not know what he is talking about; this seems to be an indication that we did not do our work properly yesterday." I was not caught unaware by the invitation offered through the use of the word "again". Regarding the communication under a different vertex (what was seen as rational was not rational), coupled with the silence of the analyst (coherent with the fact that he was kept in the dark), seemed to help the analytic couple. Would a pattern obtrude, as in Charcot's recommendation that so impressed Freud?

After having his own free-floating associations, the analyst is able to reconsider the whole case. There is a diminishing feeling of ownership of "absolute truths"; therefore, nothing in Category 6 emerges initially.

The analyst observes a subtle piercing stare and a sudden movement of the patient's hand; now a concrete piercing, through his own ear.

Fig. 8: Possibility 3, initial image

Fig. 9: The area that appertains to statements known to be false diminishes in intensity

Fig. 10: The highlighted area reflects the enriched approach

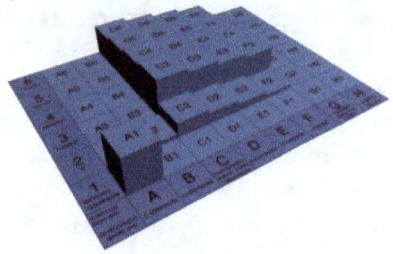

Fig. 11: The patient reacts to the analyst's free associations

It is not a cleaning action, as is most usual in some uneducated persons; the patient is polite and the movement may have some seemingly unconscious intent. The analyst makes an intervention formed from a compound of suggestion and affirmation: "I observe that you are thinking of things other than what you choose to report, which is the same as what you told me yesterday. It seemed to me that you were piercing …"

This action proved to be propitiatory to analysis. The patient interrupts the analyst and says, straight away: "Something strange happened. As you pointed this out to me, I was reminded of a recurrent dream I have. For the hundredth time I was helping to build an atomic bomb … I was in the laboratory occupied by Professor Oppenheimer, the physicist, I was his subordinate … my job was to finish the bomb's carcass, so to say, I had to pierce a hole in its shell".

This displayed an already existent idea thus far covered by hasty conclusions and false pleasurable agreements. This recurrent dream, despite being dreamt before the uttering of the association, is itself a free association to the later one and displays the latent content of it. It did not present an atomic bomb (the later dream's manifest content); quite the contrary: it was a creative, sexual act.

This new-old dream reminded the analyst of earlier sessions, months ago, when the patient dwelt on the history of the Second World War. I say "new" when the vertex is the manifest content in the analytic session, and "old" when the vertex is the patient's mental state, which includes what is latent and hitherto unknown. There seemed to be no immediate connections other than a preferred, pleasurable reading of the patient.

In those sessions, he related a history interspersed with his political and historical comments on World War 2: "Sir Winston Churchill was someone who could put an atomic bomb to good use. It was almost impossible that he would attack Hiroshima. He was not a political scoundrel like that Mr Truman. Poor Dr Einstein, Professor Oppenheimer's friend … he had given advice to Mr Roosevelt to push the bomb project but how could he know that he would die so early? Fools … From Los Alamos to Hiroshima, the Atomic Mushroom!" Silence; the analyst waits. The patient resumes: "Just as happened with the other fool, Santos-Dumont. As soon as he learned that they were using his invention to bomb defenceless civilian people, he killed himself."

The uncovered material conjoined with my spontaneous dreamy recall: a kind of rescue of what the patient had said before but did not make sense at the time. I decided to furnish my associations to the patient because they were not restricted to my mind's creations, but rather statements coming from what the patient said, as offshoots or siblings. All of this seemed to be propitiated by the previous use of the Grid; both patient's and analyst's utterances share the features of *freie Einfälle*. In Bion's expansion from Freud, there is a difference between acting under the aegis of unconscious memory and intuitively following "dream-memories". The former corresponds to Freud's "repeating"; the latter to a mix of "working though" and "remembering" (Freud, 1914a). Possibility 1 (represented by Fig. 5) displays "repeating", through the use of preconceived linguistic patterns stored in memory.

In Possibility 2, freedom promotes a playful talk with the patient's psychotic part, or taking part in hallucinosis in order to depart from it later (represented by Figs. 6 and 7). After Klein, the analyst may inspire himself in the play technique and furnish the adult's toys, his own free associations, from his free-floating attention (Klein, 1932; Bion, 1957a, 1970).

As soon as I recalled the patient's comment on Churchill, Einstein and Roosevelt, the patient seems to be able to issue his own free association ignited by the analyst's recall: "I am a mushroom eater … in fact, lover. Where there is life, you can see, there are mushrooms. Grandpa used to call new-born babies mushrooms; they are the essence of life. He marvelled to see Japanese babies; he said the Japanese procreate like mushrooms … Grandpa loved babies and babies loved him."

These statements, made in a non-racially prejudiced mode—"Japanese people", "grandfather", people killed and not killed by bombs, with the sense of life going on—radically modify Possibility 1 and confirm the error that hallmarked it. I suppose I apprehended that the patient was struggling with, and is now working through, his instincts of life and death: he was dealing, through toleration, with the paradox first described by Freud.

Possibility 1 had dismantled the paradox and concluded that there was a split between the two, favouring the opposite of life, emphasising destruction and death, instead of coping with the paradox. Freud's discovery of the fusion and de-fusion of instincts demands a tolerance of paradox with no attempt to solve it. The pre-analytic pair which was formed by this patient and myself made a double error, focusing on the manifest content of aggression and the corresponding acted out theatrical display (aloofness, etc), and splitting the instincts of death and life. This hampered or perhaps successfully precluded the possible evolution of the session, as seen later. No free-floating attention from the analyst could ensue because no attention was being paid; no new associations from the patient could emerge because the matter was resolved once and for all. But unconscious thoughts were going on, waiting for their thinkers: the manifest content "atomic bomb" sheltered an "atomic mushroom", "from Los Alamos to Hiroshima", that is from something linked to life, vectoring to death—no real difference from the natural history of humankind. The reference to Grandpa included the fact, remarkable for the patient, that he had survived the war. All of this has the value of "babies" in his mind and heart, also expressed by the reference to the "essence of life", told *en-passant*.

After this session, I renewed my use of the three-dimension Grid to make an assessment of the truth value of my interpretation. My earlier exercise with the tool seemed to allow me to realise that which the patient could understand (theoretically) but could not apprehend (the involved intra-psychic and relational psychic reality). The patient could talk about analysis, rather than making analysis—an exclusive fact, uniquely feasible in the analytic section. The pseudo-understanding was based on raw sensuously apprehensible data coming from the patient. In Possibility 1, the sensuously apprehensible raw data remained processed just in the sensuous system and were viewed as if they were an absolute truth. It came from the patient—in a Grid devoted uniquely to the patient: A1—and was restricted both to the patient and to A1.

The analyst's Grid in this case is symbolically equated to the patient's Grid. Possibility 2 began as a Grid devoted to the relationship between patient and analyst; this is an A1 (beta-element as a definitory hypothesis) that differs from A1 in the patient's Grid. The difference undoes the saturation of the patient's statement because an unknown (like a mathematical unknown) obtruded. The road to research is paved.

To take a part for the whole typifies schizophrenic thought as well as thinking more typical of those people who inhabit the paranoid-schizoid position. The "atomic bomb dream" proves to be a part rather than a whole. In the exercise of free-floating attention, a paradoxical whole emerged, which is made of both pacifists and warlords ("Oppenheimer", "Einstein", "Truman", "Roosevelt", and "Churchill"). Perhaps functioning as the analyst, I evolved towards a category of Notation (Column 3); and now I was enabled to pay attention to it (Column 4).

As soon as I reached a state that can be seen as dreamy, I became at-one with the patient's report but kept myself apart from it: the analyst "dreams the session" when he allows himself to spontaneously (that is, not through rational or intellectual thought) remember something said by the patient. The patient's associative reaction to this analyst's dream proves its utility. Its Grid correspondences are assigned to Row C: the dreamy recall (C3), attention to it (C4), and enquiry, when I offer it to the patient (C5). In this case, the patient inseminates himself with this and reacts according Freud's criteria, that is to say: the patient produces a new free association emerging from the unknown.

To have an idea about a genuine new free association, one may use its "negative rationality factor". The more plausible it is, the less the chance of it being a free association. To the extent that it conserves its "unknown" factor, it will be illogical under the laws of formal logic. The memory of the patient about "Sir Winston Churchill", who waged war in order to obtain peace, and "Santos-Dumont", whose split loving impulse (a conscious will to do good things for humanity) led to odious inhumanity (suicide), contributes to eliciting the loving, life-preserving aspect inhabiting an apparently odious impact. The "atomic bomb dream" proved to be a fragment; a pacifist appears as well as a sexual—life producing—activity within it, the "holes". I did not know what it meant, and this allowed me to transform it into an α-element. So I could not only to progress up to the point of making a notation but could also be attentive to it, in order to reach a dreamy attention and notation: C4 and C5. In other words, a free association of mine ensued—my remembering the "Churchill" remark that displays the loving, life-preserving aspect of an apparent hate. Thus the statement and the associations qualify for Rows D, E and F (pre-conception, conception and realisation), encompassing all functions of the Ego (Columns 1–6) at an extremely high intensity (magnitude). Antonino Ferro would call it, after Bion, a "narrative element" (Ferro, 2001). The patient is inseminated by it and reacts not with reassuring confirmations or disclaimers but with a fresh new association on "the stuff of life". Fig. 11 attempts to represent the patient's state at this time. The patient's hidden associations offer a different view of "aggression"; the ensuing representation is much richer than the former.

Reassuring agreements as seen in the earlier session are replaced by an association which presents (rather than represents!) "an essence of life". The Grid diagram displays a richer picture, as rich as the session was *vis-à-vis* the earlier ones.

A few weeks later, the patient referred in a subdued voice, almost in passing, to having inseminated his wife. He had a kind of married experience. Nevertheless, he had until then refused to perform his manly function and help her to procreate, always giving arguments and silly rationalised explanations. His wife persisted, and his usual reaction was to mistake her persistence for insistence—which formed part of his accusations against her.

The Grid seems to have helped the analyst to win over the analytic vertex, by leaving a more superficial approach. The analytic couple could enter into constructions of underlying senses. They had gone from hermeneutics to function, meaning to sense. Sense is used in the same way one might use the word vector, to borrow a term from physics. Its vector value reflects a tropism, as in biology. Sense should be used in psychoanalysis to display a step equal to sensations and feelings, as a sensuous precursor that comes before affects and emotions.

Psychiatric and psychoanalytic diagnoses seen through the three-dimension Grid

A most basic fundamental tool in practice, psychiatric and psychoanalytic assessment through nosology may be seen with the use of the Grid. Each reader may discover his or her own uses; the following are briefly quoted as illustrative examples. If the previous plates display a

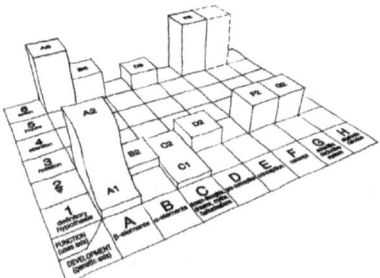

Fig. 12: A psychotic moment

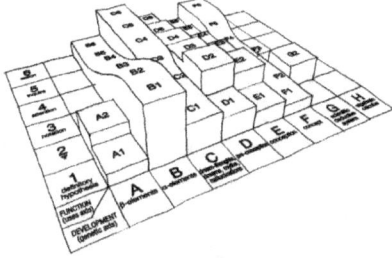

Fig. 13: A practising psychoanalyst at work

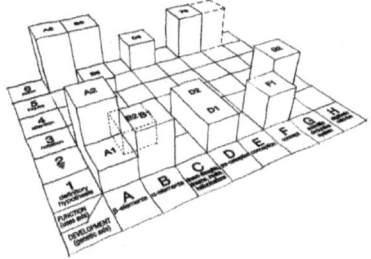

Fig. 14: An initiating psychoanalyst

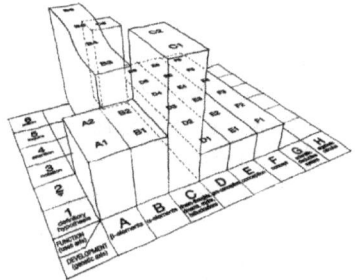

Fig. 15: A good enough psychoanalyst at work

film, the three-dimension Grid may give a psychodynamic diagnosis as if it were a photograph.

No-thinking, as a special form of thought (belonging to the negative or minus realm; see Volume 2), appears at full bore. In this kind of mental functioning, which tends to become a static situation, there prevails a clinging to the paranoid-schizoid position, in an exclusive dedication to it, a full-time job. There is a high intensity of Categories A1 and A2, corresponding to a large quantity of beta-elements. The person phantasises the ownership of ultimate truth. Beta-elements are the stuff of which definitory hypotheses (attributable to Category A1) are made; but extremely few of them attain the status of alpha-elements. They jump to conclusions, accepting no doubt, speeding into the categories of Column 6, which construes acting out. Beta-elements also compose Row C as hallucinations, indistinguishable from wish-dreams and wishful thinking. There is some alpha function, restricted to Column 2 and also nourishing acting out (Column 6). Categories F and G appertain to misunderstandings (-K); usually they are endowed with an internal rational and logical coherence, but they have no counterparts in reality. They qualify to erect deductive systems, which are pseudo-scientific but usually pass for scientific, thanks to rationalised acting out. They dispense with ego functions (horizontal axis). Psychiatric practice with people labelled as schizophrenic provides examples of these kinds of F and G productions. Therefore, Category G6 is represented by a dotted line to emphasise its virtual, rather than real, nature. The matching of pre-conceptions with realisations is extremely rare, and the three-dimension Grid represents it through a lack. It may exist at the service of physical survival, rather than emotional and thinking life. The area of notation is exclusively at the service of Column 2 (lies). The realms described by Freud as attention, as well as investigation, are useless in this kind of mental functioning which denies what is mental (in other words: non-mental functioning). If they emerge from repression, they give rise to an unbearable anxiety, due to immensely high levels of pain introduced by doubt. They are usually "resolved" through rationalisation belonging to Categories F6 and G6.

One may compare this figure, obtained unknowingly, with Possibility 1 described above.

Transient and fugacious, an analyst may occupy what Melanie Klein called the depressive position when he or she is enabled through attention, personal analysis and a good enough knowledge and control of his or her personal factors (see chapter 9, part II). With this capacity, the analyst may issue an interpretation, a construction and a model (see Volume 2, Analytic Function), maintaining good enough contact and preservation corresponding with a given patient's invariants (see Volume 1, Transformations and Invariants). In this case, there remains a low intensity of A1 (definitory hypothesis about a beta-element), rescued by personal analysis from reaching A6 (action of beta-elements and beta-elements acted out). This corresponds to the analytic discretion, or keeping analysis in the realm of discipline over desire. Freud called it "abstinence". The reader may notice the presence of all Column 2 categories (lies), access to which can be made through the analyst's personal analysis. The analyst's alpha function, quite independent from the way it is performed, is also a constant (similar to Column 2), but it suffers a softening in intensity when the analyst issues his interpretation or construction. The "provoking filter" of the decrease is the inception of alpha function, as far as its containment function is concerned.

One may regard the analyst's discourse or talk, or even simple remarks intended to be parameters, or facilitating comments, or exploratory comments, as belonging to Column 6, when action is distinguished from acting out. In any case, at the exact moment they are uttered, they cannot carry any thought processes. They convey their final transformations instead—and only. Row C must be free from memory and constitute the analyst's armoury of experience, including his analytic and life experience. In Row D, or Pre-conceptions, it is useful to recognise a heightening of Column 2. It can be counterbalanced, despite or because of the pain it may inflict, by a partially conscious heightening of Columns 3, 4 and 5 (Notation, Attention and Inquiry). Row E (Conception) keeps the same profile. Many of them cannot match conceptions, but hopefully some of them do, through the exercise of attention and discipline on analytic method. Therefore a few of them arrive at F (Concepts). It is safe to put G as alien to psychoanalysis, in that it is inimical to what is new (deductive propositions can only arrive in a circular way to their own premises) and intuition. The representation can be put into G2 and G6, that is, scientific deductive systems that are lies or acting out. H categories (algebraic calculus) cannot be reached at the present time in the psychoanalytic realm. Therefore the three-dimension Grid is empty in H.

Notes

1. Even though the tri-dimension Grid proves to be cumbersome to construe, at least from its graphical representation, one may think, as an analogy, of the representational leap that occurred when humankind progressed from Egyptian painting (bi-dimensional) to Greek painting (tri-dimensional).
2. Truthfully, at the specific moment focused by this report, the correct term is the "so-called analyst". It refers to the author of this book; therefore, the existence of criticism in this text must be regarded as self-criticism.
3. The author can send any interested reader a CD copy of a CAD movie of this example; requests may be made through the publisher.
4. See analytic function, binocular vision (Volume 2).
5. For example, *Cogitations*, pp. 38, 39, 43, among other contributions.

CHAPTER THREE

A hexa-dimension grid?

Analysts who try to maintain a scientific posture are used to self-criticism, a seminal factor in scientists. No experienced analyst would ever think that it would be impossible to describe mental functioning in a still more precise way. So complex a system challenges any attempt at description. We already have more profound (because basic) descriptions, and in this sense they furnish more precision. Freud provided the psychoanalytic endeavour with initial discoveries endowed with this precise value, due to their (his) clinical intuition. He was able to immerse his clinical observations into earlier descriptions from art and philosophy, the first attempts to apprehend psychic reality in Western civilisation—which were, by themselves, hallmarks of the inception of this civilisation. Freud formulated—and in this sense, discovered—the two principles of mental functioning. Until then, only the first principle was known; the principle of pleasure and displeasure. It had already been depicted by Homer, described by Hobbes, Shakespeare and Locke, among a legion of thinkers and poets. Freud brought out the principle of reality, for the first time in Western thinking. It was implicit in Shakespeare's and Goethe's prose and verse, but a fuller individual awareness that is possible in the scientific endeavour, in order to be practically applied to human individual beings, had to wait until the advent of medicine, and within it Freud's achievements.[1]

The detection of a fact, namely, unconscious mental processes and their relationships with the hitherto almighty consciousness (as Freud had put it), was constantly coupled with some of his stroke of genius and scientific outlook, which led him to hypothesise theoretically that the latter instance could be regarded as a sensuous organ to apprehend the psychic qualities of the unconscious. Its ways of performing this exacting function included dream work, in order to maintain the principle of homeostasis. Freud then formulated mechanisms of defence, such as reaction formation, transformations into the contrary, regression, transposition of affects, and so on, which were later expanded into the realm of the ego, more than night dreaming activity.[2] All of this made for another way to describe mental life, in addition to Freud's developed theory of instincts.

In attempting to produce more accurate depictions, Klein, Winnicott and Bion continued under Freud's own psychoanalytic pattern, with no borrowings and transplants of extra-analytic models (such as philosophical, sociological and so on). The non-split (or non-Kantian, but Hegelian: Sandler, 2001a, 2003) notion of space and time is included in Klein's "Positions" theory,[3] as well as in Klein's observations of the many forms assumed by unconscious phantasies. The list is fairly long and, most of all, useful with patients: Klein's and Winnicott's precise observations about the formation of internal objects and imagos; Bion's expansions (still in Freud's own terms, but integrating them with Klein's achievements) of the simultaneity of the two principles of mental functioning as well as of the conscious and unconscious mental processes (Bion, 1962; Sandler, 2005).

It is this scientific evolution of the concepts of which this work seeks to form part. It is scientific due to its attempt at precise definitions of terms, their empirical origin and background, as a step towards a partial and transient glimpse of reality as it is. We will try to integrate, as a constantly conjoining relationship, the three sensuous, visual dimensions of the Grid which represent the axes of thinking in its measuring ways, genetic functions, and intensity, as they occur through the "arrow of time"—which already depicts, albeit crudely, the space-time unit (Eddington, 1933; Coveney & Highfield, 1990)—with Bion's other realms of interpretation as described in the same book in which he introduced the bi-dimension Grid, *Elements of Psychoanalysis* (1963).

Bion regarded that which is seen here as "realms" as "dimensions": the dimensions of sense, of myth and of passion (Bion, 1963). We will return to some consequences of this hypothesis later. For our present purposes, we can see that they admit a measuring parameter as far as depth or profundity are concerned, and therefore qualify as "dimensions". When one examines Bion's evolution, in terms of the history of his ideas, one concludes that he increasingly moved from a more sensuously based apprehension of mental functioning—for example, when he adhered firmly to the psychiatric and sociological vertex of pathology—one feels authorised, in the interests of precision, to call his "dimensions" "realms", to mean something beyond "dimensions", with more "some" than "thing" in the "something". The name "realm" may help to divest that which it purports to designate from the sensuous and concrete penumbra of meanings that the definition of "dimension" seems to entail. Psychic facts are not "dimensionable"; rather, they are dimensionless and infinite (or, better, transfinite, if one uses Cantor's suggestion).

Would science, and within the scientific discipline, Mathematics and Biology, be the most developed scientific methods (using the term after Kant) humankind has at its disposal? Freud and Bion thought so; and seeing Melanie Klein's observations and profiting from psychiatry, she seemed to follow the same lead. Is there some confusion in the use those great authors made of earlier attempts to apprehend reality? Many adherents of the psychoanalytic movement seem to be too fascinated by the earlier attempts: they try to throw psychoanalysis back to pre-psychoanalytic times, which have the advantage of apparently being less complex. In other cases, there is an undervaluing of psychoanalytic achievements through the transplantation of earlier methods that were typical of those attempts. Freud, Klein and Bion explicitly and heavily used earlier artistic, philosophical, neurological and psychiatric contributions. I suppose that if one considers that art, philosophy, neurology and psychiatry are earlier methods to apprehend reality, and therefore could regard psychoanalysis as the next in the sequence, there would be no undervaluing of psychoanalytic patterns.

One may use the concept drawn from mathematics: the circle of confusion; or in a Venn diagram, an area of overlap between a common object made by human mind and its imbalances and sufferings as well as concern for truth. In other parts of this work we emphasised the existence of earlier, pre-scientific methods that may be more scientific than epochal approved science (such as positivism). In this proposed classification—that ordains the obtrusion of the earlier attempts in time—non-verbal methods (expressed by music and plastic arts) as well as a growing access to verbal methods (such as myths, which evolved into theatre) were all always encompassed (even in variable grades) in an enriched way in the philosophical methods derived from them. The forms came as philosophy-in-itself, poetry, prose, opera and operetta. Their conjoined modern guise is represented by movie-making.

I consider psychoanalysis to be a scientific activity, as Freud and Bion did. It can use earlier activities as tools rather than finalities; as organons rather than canons. Psychoanalysis can be seen through what it is not; for example, it is not a *Weltanschauung* (other than scientific), as Freud remarked. Analogies, as a transdisciplinary aid, provide mutual collaborations between psychoanalysis and related fields such as philosophy, mathematics, and whatever it may be that is of interest to mental functioning and truth. Interest here is not a matter of the opinion of any researcher (including, and foremost for our purposes here, the analyst). To reduce research to the realm of reality, to the opinion of the researcher, mistakes the precise description of the researcher's vertex for opinionated ideas: a common degeneration of the psychoanalytic movement, which is so devoted to idolisation. But the vertices, which can and must be described, are externally bounded by reality; they can be seen under each discipline as "objects" (after Aristotle), as well as how the specific discipline treats them.

Both psychoanalysis and physics discovered that it is impossible for the observer to be axiologically neutral, with no disparaging of "observation-in-itself". Both disciplines improved not only the concept but also the precision of observation, when they knew more about its pitfalls. The observer interferes in the observed phenomenon; the observation obtrudes as a functional part of the observed phenomenon's ethos as well of as its "ecosystem".

The efforts of psychoanalysis to minimise this fact are subsumed by that which Freud called "the personal factor" or "personal equation"—through the analyst's personal analysis (see Chapter Nine). Physics, correspondingly, minimises it through the widest possible knowledge of the behaviour and features of a given energy/matter's bombardment of (that is, interference with) another unknown energy/matter. Both deal with probabilities, and this has replaced the illusion of predictions: the aftermath of linear, formal, logically determined cause-effect relationships. Both deal with the paradoxical coexistence of immateriality with materiality, beyond illusions of sensuous-concrete perceptions which have bent into the concept of physical locations (valid in conditions within the human range of sensuous perception), good enough for some of the large (or Newtonian) particles, but not in quantum conditions, which are both micro (sub-atomic) and macro (of the great universe). Both deal with the limitations of Euclidean geometry, and in doing so they reach that which belongs to infinite sets and timeless realms.

The following proposal is *not* a "mathematisation of psychoanalysis"—something that does not exist at all except in the realm of hallucinosis and envious attacks. Rather, it tries to see to what extent both mathematics and psychoanalysis, in mutual collaboration, enable an improved view of reality itself.

Bion regarded psychoanalysis as a thought waiting for its thinker, until Freud came to think it. It is a realm[4] that through the history of Western ideas may be likened—as a model—to migrating birds: constantly looking for a safer heaven to survive. Art and philosophy could not provide it; psychoanalysis still seems to be an improvement, through the Enlightenment-medical view, which translated into an individual care.

But the psychoanalytic movement, a mere century later, shows signs of not being up to this task (Sandler, 2001a). This is due not to the exhaustion of the movement, but rather to the perhaps early formation of yet another (as if there were any scarcity of them) Establishment, leading to the obtrusion and final prevalence of political factors.[5] The former enforces the enshrining of dead exoskeletons or single-celled earlier knowledge, which is turned into established knowledge and ownership of absolute truth. The latter enforces networks of elitist, personal (narcissistic) influences alien to, and contrary to, processes of knowing and becoming. In the light of evidence reflected by the growing claims that "Freud is dead",[6] there has been a decrease in the quality of people who look for analysis. This can be measured by the loss of interest from young people when they conclude their graduate training in universities; also by disappointment over unfulfilled promises taken under the umbrella of psychoanalysis, which amounts to the misunderstanding of psychoanalysis, and attempts to co-opt it into the encircling establishment, be it political or pseudo-scientifically political. It will be no wonder that our object of study—mind and mental functioning, as well as consciousness and unconsciousness—is increasingly becoming the object of study by mathematicians, biologists and philosophers of mathematics and physics (see Penrose, 1994; Einstein,

1916; Schrödinger, 1944; Heisenberg, 1958; Sandler, 1997b) who were precociously labelled "mystics".

Taking into account those forays, our model tries to use the philosophy of mathematics that contains correspondences and analogies with psychoanalysis, contributing to a mutual collaboration, with no preponderance of one over the other (Sandler, 1997b). Freud, Planck and Einstein emerged in the same epochal moment—a difference of something in the environs of five years is negligible in historical terms. This brings to the fore immateriality, uncertainty and probability, vector-driven movement and infinity. Both disciplines are deterministic; but the determinism is of functions, beyond the positivist determinism of causes.[7]

Presentation, representation, model and reality

Freud's and Klein's work *presented* psychic reality[8] and also *represented* it with verbal symbols. From this work, derived concepts and theories were developed, which came to be subsumed by Bion's contribution through quasi-mathematical or mathematical notation systems. Some of the concepts were expanded, making for derived concepts: for example, projection and identification as first observed by Freud flowed to projective identification; mother functions flowed to good enough mothering, and so on. The expansions and derivations embodied the former concepts and their evolution; except in the work of Winnicott and in just one area (death instincts), the evolution was neither made through replacement of nor through dismissing the original concepts. In short, Klein's and Bion's work was not done under the aegis of rivalry—which in itself constituted a sizeable part of their study!

Bion's work contributed to an evolution which includes a great deal of making explicit—and then reviving—Freud's sources in Western thinking, the Enlightenment and Romantic movements, the nest of psychoanalysis. His contribution includes:

1. *Quasi-mathematical symbols*, in order to facilitate communication among researchers: the double arrow ⇔ for the living movement PS⇔D; Tα and Tβ, respectively, for the processes and results of mental transformations following sensuous experiences; M ψ ξ as a representation of the psychoanalytic object; hyperbole[9]
2. *Biological terms*: ♀ ♂ to represent container and contained; tropisms

3. *Philosophical, poetic, medical and "mystic" terms*: "O", at-one-ment, language of achievement, catastrophic change, hallucinosis, psychotic and non-psychotic personalities.

The Grid constitutes a representation which concentrates many contributions and embodies a long history. In this "epistemological *tour de force*", the Grid unites the items listed above in a visual representation in order to communicate some factors in thinking processes. In other words, *it is a model to represent a function and two activities (or factors) of psychic reality*.

Since a tri-dimension Grid was first proposed (1997), attention has been given to its continuing flaws, both as a representation and in its application in analytic work. The two Grids, the original and its derivation, are heavily rooted in space, which is, in itself, an inadequate representation of the mental realm.[10] Consequently, it depicts a non-existent space; any description of nothingness is equal to hallucination, hallucinosis and delusion, according to psychoanalytic knowledge (please see Volume 2 Part I for details, including the difference between nothing and nothingness). This flawed concept of space, which applies to a very limited range of physical facts but leaves unobserved the vast majority of physical and non-physical (immaterial) facts, is usually called the three-dimensional Euclidean space. Obviously, this measure dating from Ancient Greece widened the field of research: for example, if one started from circles, one could reach spheres and so achieve an enriched depiction of reality. At the risk of repetition, perhaps it would be useful to remind ourselves once more that this kind of flawed (but in some cases useful) representation is still erroneously known, outside mathematical circles, as the "Cartesian space".[11] The French thinker René Descartes made use of the Euclidean space: he expanded it in a remarkable way through algebraic calculus, removing its dependency on visual concreteness. Much later, a Russian and a German—Lobachevski and Riemann—were able to discover the possibility of a non-Euclidean geometry, expanding mathematical research not as all-destroying revolutionaries or conquerors but as contributors (Whitehead, 1911; Penrose, 1989, 1994).

Scientific models may represent and convey, by their scientific design, their counterparts in reality. Sometimes (though rarely) they do more than represent, and present reality to the observer. In this latter case they are realistic, or scientifically valid. The mutual counterparts between science and reality (truth) were called "correspondence" in Spinoza's and Kant's parlance.

Many good enough scientific formulations fall into a somewhat limited range: on the one side, a shorthand; on the other side, a caricature which exaggerates some partial aspects in order to present the ineffable whole which is intuitable, visible to and graspable by the good enough expert in that field. Winnicott's good enough mothering has its counterparts in scientific formulations and within the scientific mind.

The first instance of apprehension is perceptual, through our human sensuous apparatus, whose range is extremely limited. We are able to "see" a point on a railway where the tracks meet, even though this unitary event does not exist. We cannot see the stars when the sun is bright; and cannot see the waves emitted by mobile phones, radio and television transmitters or radioactive elements—a fortunate fact, after all, even if coincidental, or a collateral effect of what is known as the wisdom of nature in not endowing us with an eye able to see this kind of radiation. Our sight is unable to distinguish the individual frames in a movie, giving a false "cinematographic" impression (illusion) of movement to that which is still, not-kinematic in reality as it is. Under the same shadow of illusion, we *feel* that bi- and tri-dimensional spaces do exist in reality.

Plato and Kant were two people (among others) who dealt with this illusion in a more detailed way. "Reality as it is" is larger than any human attempt to encompass, convey and represent it. But despite the problems of perception and representation, presenting it depends on the capacity to tolerate existing reality's "infra" and "ultra" immateriality in the moment it occurs. Like a flame, it exists as long as it lasts.[12]

This tolerance was furnished by Einsteinian (and post-Einsteinian) physics and Freudian (and post-Freudian) psychoanalysis. The infra- and ultra-sensuous unconscious shares the features of timelessness and quasi-spacelessness, as well as the one-sided boundaries, of the infinite, expanding greater universe as described by Einstein.

In the mental realm, the one-sided boundary can be expressed by each one's personality (who the person is). Both different "systems" and "levels" also partake of the same gravity force that flows deterministically (or when probabilistic indeterminism turns into a functional determinism) into free associations in the psychic realm and stellar formations in the realm of the expanding universe. The unconscious is immaterial like the quantum realm.

The features of the unconscious realm of the Id (*das Es*) allow one to warn that the model of a six-dimension Grid which we will suggest below belongs to the fields of caricature and shorthand. One must not take it concretely. It has, for the benevolent reader, the status of a provisional model on the way to something better.

The temptation of giving it a material form, thus preventing analysts having to exclaim in perplexity like Isidor Rabi when he found a microparticle in 1936 which had no weight (Penrose, 1994; Sandler, 1997b), made us briefly toy with the cumbersome attempt to seek inspiration in M. C. Escher's drawings to represent the six-dimension grid.[13] Even if it could serve as a diversion for the lazy or challenge the artist's proneness to draw, the attempt never came to fruition for two main reasons. The three- and four-dimension Grids had already proven their impracticability for daily use, and the sensuous concrete stimuli that this kind of drawing could give, inviting or provoking (rather than evoking) a concrete interpretation from the onlooker, could be too much to stand. A perversion of the original intent would be produced, or would have a high probability of being produced.

Even though mathematicians and physicists have at their disposal mathematical equations as a most precise way to represent and communicate reality as it is, perhaps the most precise form hitherto devised, some of them resort to verbal representations, as in Dirac's classical textbook of quantum mechanics (1930).[14] Psychoanalysis usually (perhaps always) resorts to verbal formulations, even though it purports to encompass the infra- and ultra-verbal goal, the realm of insight.

Movement, matter, energy, space and time

In order to construe the model of a six-dimension Grid into a verbal formulation, we need some firmer idea of concepts and models derived from the philosophy and history of mathematics and physics that—at least in our own experience—seem not to be well known in the psychoanalytic movement.[15] A firmer notion of movement, matter, energy, space and time may help the psychoanalyst's daily work. As such, those concepts and realisations are seminal to the use of the six-dimension Grid, which relies on them.

Bion suggested that mathematics is an early (perhaps the earliest) human attempt belonging to the realm of thought to deal with psychosis (Bion, 1965, p. 56; Sandler, 2005, p. 417). It remains to be observed, and thus a matter of conjecture, whether there are realms other than thinking processes involved in this attempt. Anyway, it is safe to put them, if they exist, outside the job of a psychoanalyst. With the inception of mathematics, we human beings became able to deal with real objects without their concrete presence. As mathematics developed, algebraic geometry freed mathematicians from the need for visual figures that were the hallmark of Euclidean geometry. Later developments included matrix calculus and probability. Nevertheless, robust minds such as Pascal, who improved once and for all the theory of probability, declared himself terrified by "infinite spaces". Newton's enlightened view framed a broad alternative to authoritarian dogmatism—then embodied by the Roman Catholic Church—which talked about a universe whose order was immutable, eternal and static. Scientists suppose, through observation of facts; authoritarian rulers affirm, through abhorrence of observation of facts.

Newton provided the investigation of the realm of "mechanics", the science of both movement and its lack, under the headings of static, kinematic and dynamic. The study of movement finally resulted in a less incomplete and thus more precise comprehension (as distinct from from understanding) of the outer or external world.

This step, today taken for granted, cannot be overstressed. If and when one knows the exact point in space in which an object is, as well as the time that it needs to reach another known point in the Euclidean space, Newton could calculate its velocity. The unknown value can be used to make previews of each other variable, so a quite accurate study of movement and restricted ideal previews could be made. The real preview soon found its obstacles, like the attrition forces against movement, but it could be managed as a theoretically ideal preview that gave a good enough account to a restricted practical area, such as ballistics. A paradox awaited this step forward, namely, it also contributed to a backward movement later named "positivism". The myth of prohibition of knowledge enlightens those paradoxical steps in the history of human ideas; it corresponds, in the realm of thought, to movements "to-from" which are typical of PS⇔D (see Volume 2, Chapter Ten).

Sir Isaac Newton's progressive discoveries linked to the study of "movement" also allowed the possibility to perform differential and integral calculus. "The importance of differential calculus emerges from the very nature of the issue: mathematical consideration towards the increment of functions...the fundamental idea of movement is the basis of all perception we have from phenomena, and soon suggests the investigation about rates of change" (Whitehead, 1911, p. 179).

Differential calculus implied an uncertainty. Newton may be regarded as having the same reaction as Pascal to what was infinite, but with no comparable consciousness of terror at the appearance of uncertainty in Physics—due to his own contributions to it. Newton was not afraid of uncertainty; he embraced it in his use of infinitesimals (described by critics as "ghosts of departed quantities") in "fluxions"— his term for differential calculus. Pascal was a religious man, but Newton saw himself as different. Nevertheless, the development of self-awareness had to wait for the advent of psychoanalysis. The gifted Englishman resorted (perhaps appealed) to religious explanations for this discovery. He involved himself in a bitter diatribe with Bishop Berkeley, who accused him of irreligiosity. At the same time, Newton felt that Leibniz was guilty of plagiarism. Mysteriously, a fire broke out in his laboratory when he was asleep, and he was rescued from a dreadful death with moments to spare. Newton survived physically but his life—that may be considered a unity of material and immaterial facts, like any human life—continued on a path of decay. As an acknowledgement of his contributions the authorities of his time gave him the job of master of the Mint. Newton could never return to his main job, that of mathematics and physics.

In any case, "Movement" constitutes an insight about a central feature of life as it is, and an analytic session as it is. Freud's object and instinctual cathexis describe immaterial movements, as well as affects and emotions. In brief, the unconscious as a dynamic system in Newton's sense expanded psychoanalysis into the infinite realm, as it had also expanded physics itself, even though Newton could not profit in a personal way from all of his later discoveries.

If the models and analogies drawn from a tiny part of the history of philosophical ideas of mathematics and physics are valid, they tell us that babies, psychoanalysts, scientists and any people need to have a "mathematical nucleus of the mind" in order to cope with a breast when it is absent. The "nucleus" may be called—as Freud called it—an instinct, and this instinct may be more specifically described as "scientific", or "psychoanalytic", or, in a more general sense, "epistemophilic", being responsible for the human "urge to know" described by Aristotle.

One must cope with that which was implied in Newton's loss of his judgment, with no need to restrict our life to the "Mint", meaning concrete, rationalised[16] establishments with their attendant bureaucracies that impose the fitting of the patient's material into a previously learned jargon as well as into *a priori* theories. Or, conversely, one may try to reach the patient's material in order to justify them through the rationalised use of an *ad hoc* theory:

> P.A. Mystery is real life; real life is the concern of real analysis. Jargon passes for psychoanalysis, as sound is substituted for music, verbal facility for literature and poetry, *trompe l'œil* representations for painting. [Bion, 1977b, p. 307]

> P.A. You heard that fellow Bion? Nobody has ever heard of him or of Psychoanalysis. He thinks it is real, but that his colleagues are engaged in an activity which is only a more or less ingenious manipulation of symbols. There is something in what he says. There is a failure to understand that any definition must deny a previous truth as well as carry an unsaturated component. [Bion, 1975, p. 92]

Our clinical exercise with the Grid attempted to mirror some features of a clinical analyst's everyday work. Namely, movement and its attendant, transient and fleeting experience, despite its fundamental function[17] (Freud, 1916).

> His Satanic Jargonieur took offence; on some pretence that psychoanalytic jargon was being eroded by eruptions of clarity. I was compelled to seek asylum in fiction. Disguised as fiction the truth occasionally slipped through. [Bion, 1977b, p. 309]

In the hope that the following definitions will not dishearten the prospective reader to the point of not carrying on reading due to unfamiliarity, at least to the psychoanalytic endeavour, it might be useful to learn that in the microsphere of sub-atomic particles there is a concept called *spin*, which defines the particle's angular speed. The realisation of this concept is dependent on previous realisation of another concept, called "momentum". What is this "momentum"? It is defined as the product of a given particle's speed (defined in Newton's terms as the distance gained by a moving particle divided by the time taken to gain it) and its mass. I will spare the reader the symbols used to represent those concepts. Perhaps the verbal formulation suffices; let us return to historical details.

Phase space

William Hamilton was a researcher well known in his field but not so outside it. He was a harbinger and provided a decisive milestone in the development of modern physics, allowing the possibility of the appearance of Einstein, Planck, Minkowski and Poincaré, among many others. He had shown the relative importance of a particle's spin *vis-à-vis* its (Newtonian) speed, which is defined, as we have just said, as the relationship between the distance a particle moves and the time it takes to do so.

Hamilton's discovery changed the way physics could research real phenomena. He opened avenues that can be described, under a psychoanalytic vertex, as "de-concretising"[18] the realm of Physics. After him, the illumination of the chemical basis of physics obtruded. This realm began to be regarded as "energetic", probabilistic, and "wave-istic" too; he allowed the perception and tolerance of yet another paradox.

In observing the particle's momentum, physicists began to work with something they define as "phase space". Phase space is not amenable to being grasped through human visual abilities, even though some of its consequences have visible counterparts in reality. For example, it can be approached by mathematics and it can be adequately measured by calculus.

From the realisation and use of phase space, Albert Einstein could precisely calculate the paradoxical material and immaterial nature of Light,[19] first in the form of a hypothesis and then in the guise of calculation of the relationship between matter and energy—which opened yet more avenues in Physics that are still being researched.

From that epoch on, time should be regarded not according to Kant's ideas—in other words, his error that time would constitute innate preconceptions, split from space. If Immanuel Kant was nearer to the truth in observing preconceptions, especially after observing the categorical imperative, later called superego by Freud, he was mistaken in his detection of time and space as being the other two. It seemed to me that time must be regarded after the observation of the second law of thermodynamics, which describes the irreversibility of some phenomena—first and foremost, the path of time, which Sir Arthur Eddington called the "arrow of time", after Einstein (Eddington, 1933). Like the irreversibility of the path followed by heat, which flows from a hot body to a cold body but cannot flow from a cold one to a hot one, time flows in just one direction, from "new" to "old". A very robust mind like Newton's had serious difficulties with this, which also marked his mental decay; in fact, fabulous fables, or phantasy flights in a "time-machine" and "travels to the past and the future", as well as pseudo-reliance on memory (past) and desire (future), have always occupied popular fantasy and imagination, indistinguishable from popular delusion. Again, a firm grasp of these realisations seems to be useful to a practising analyst, even though "popular fantasy" (beautifully illustrated by Mackay, 1841) had displayed a strong resilience in accepting the more precise idea stemming neither from fantasy nor from imagination (for it cannot be turned into images) but from scientific progress. Under the religious vertex, useful to demagoguery, *vox populi, vox dei* (the voice of the people is the voice of God), a belief which under the scientific vertex would be stated as "*vox populi* may be *vox dei* or not", depending on the case. In other words, sayings of "popular wisdom" may reflect either popular wisdom or popular error; sometimes both, but in any case they are always popular. Freud observed that the psychoanalyst should discipline himself not to adopt the commonplace as a guide. Confusion between commonplace and common sense lingers on.

The usefulness of the mathematical-physical analogy to the psychoanalytically trained reader does not need to be demonstrated mathematically; some concrete analogies allow one to better introduce the concept of phase space. The concreteness of an analogy can serve either to display or not the ethos of the reality that a given analogy purports to elicit. The reader who is able to make the tandem PS⇔D movement may construe a dream through an inner de-sensifying of the concrete analogy, while another reader unable to de-sensify the concrete analogy might find that it clouds his/her perception of the reality the analogy represents. The insight on reality is thus paved; reality itself has a chance to obtrude. Conversely, the same concreteness of the analogy may serve to a different reader to cloud its corresponding reality or its counterpart in reality.

In the end, the model obstructs the realisation of the analogy. The truth content of the model is of relative importance. If it is there, fine, but if it is not there, the work may be done by the reader in order to apprehend at least part of reality as it is. Models and their concrete forms are far from reality as it is, even though they may seem to be equated to it. In the exact proportion that their concreteness is far from reality, models seem to us to be closer to reality—a paradox one may cope with in order to digest and discharge it as soon as it has achieved its function.

This is valid both for scientific models and in a session of analysis: the decisive, here-and-now instant of the nourishing interpretation and its "swallowing" by the "nourishable" patient.[20] The concrete models may act, as usually occurs, as a provisional and dischargeable aid to the apprehension of reality.

There are many examples of flawed and false models that perform this function for humankind, as may be seen in a rather humdrum example such as "the sun rises".[21] Given its vertex and usages, this statement was useful for some purposes. In the times when watches had not been invented—or even today, if time measuring devices are perhaps not available for whatever reason—one may conjecture that a group of people who want to gather in order to, say, go fishing, their assembling in the same space-time may be feasible through the use of this imaginary, albeit sensuously visible device. The form it assumes functions merely as scaffolding.

Keeping these warnings in mind, let us now imagine (using the human capacity to put real events into visual images, outside flights of fantasy) a pendulum, suspended from above and then set in motion (Figs. 16–18).

Figs. 16–18: A pendulum set in motion back and forth, like any pendulum …

The movement of the pendulum can be visually likened to the shape of a cone—again, one should put one's waking dream work into action (Figs. 19–21).

This movement creates a phase space with two axes. One axis is given by the pendulum's spin or moment acquired in more easily measurable figures when a given speed is obtained. The other axis is given by the same pendulum's position in the Euclidean space. Their equivalents in drawing appear in Figs. 17, 18 and 19. One may also imagine each point in this "'phase space" and, in doing so, construe, even if in imagination,[22] a geometrical figure "drawn" by the translation of the pendulum.

The variegated "to-and-fro" movements determined by that coming and going of the pendulum "construe" the base of the figure, which can be represented by a circle. The "sides" unite in an imaginary point, its apex. The whole figure is first a conic section and then a cone (Figs. 20 and 21).

Now we may represent a particular state of this system, when the pendulum has a given position and moment (a unit that was defined earlier). If the system's state changes, the point which represents it changes too, as well as its concrete values. Taking into consideration that the state of the system is an ever-changing one, it still has to keep its "pendulum-function", the underlying reality—"O"-pendulum, using Bion's nomenclature—which does not vary.

Even if one "sees" the cone, as one sees its three-dimensional representation put onto a piece of a two-dimensional paper, with marks and shading that can give the viewer the impression (illusion) of a three-dimensional shape, this cone is a figment of the imagination.

To paraphrase Shelley on Shakespeare, and Bion on Conan Doyle (in *A Memoir of the Future*), in certain cases which call for accurate

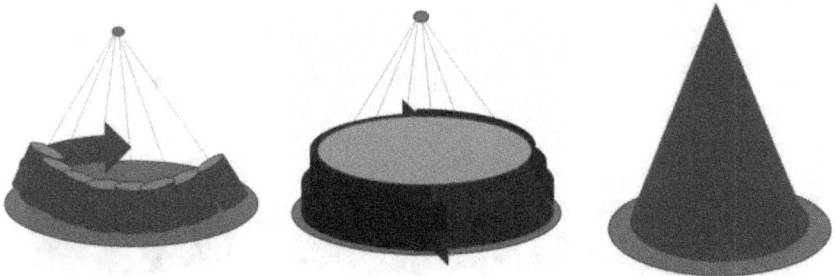

Figs. 19–21: ... until it takes the shape of a conic section, and finally a cone

description of conditions and vertices of observation, some figments of imagination can give a better realisation of reality than a great many real things—including human beings. Or, sometimes, depending on the audience or onlookers, truth seeps into fictional characters and makes them more real than real people.

Provided that one may immerse oneself in and emerge from the present scaffolding-imagination, the six-dimension Grid, we suggest that the psychoanalyst, when he or she construes an interpretation or construction in analysis, operates at least in a six-dimension level, or a space-time that can be likened to phase space as defined by Hamilton.

The "figure" it displays tries to reflect the unfolding reality as it is; such a reality may be intuitable by the members of the analytic couple. The "figure" usually constitutes provisional caricatures, like metaphors and models of persons, things and events in the patient's life, as unconsciously "seen" by him. All of this goes beyond, for example, the concreteness as it was seen in the previous chapter as a conscious report about an "atomic bomb". It would be analogous to the manifest content described by Freud in dreams, with the expansion previewed by Freud but more fully realised by Klein in the play technique and later by Bion in the everyday waking dream-work (please see more details in volume 1 of this series).

Each associative production can (or must) be put in terms of free associations, corresponding, in our gross analogy, to the "visualised, imagined cone". What is of interest to the analyst and the patient is the "pendulum-ness", the feature that allows something to be a pendulum, which is different from being anything else. This is paradoxically betrayed by the imaginary figure of a cone. These associations represent the pendulum as soon as they are regarded as "movements", or an ever-moving reality—drawn by the pendulum translation—the living whirling here and now moment (or micro-moment) of each session.[23]

The analyst must abstain from concreteness, as mathematics and physics do, or as any scientist does—the abstinence emphasised by Freud, and Bion's expansion of it: discipline of memory, desire and understanding. I would add: abstention from concreteness, in order to perform the quantum leap needed for the analytic posture.

Phase space descriptions developed through the observations of Joseph Liouville, another prominent researcher in physics. He demonstrated that the *quantity* of particles in a given phase space volume keeps itself constant regardless of the variegated forms it may assume. As we could see in the model of the pendulum, something moves but paradoxically does not move. In order to realise what this finding means, one may resort once more to a visual analogy: a device made of soluble ink, a dropper and a suitable solvent for the ink. One drop of the ink will spread over the volume of the solvent. In a given period of time, the *volume* of the drop and that of the solvent are constant, but the *form* of the ink, which starts as a tiny drop and develops into a sprayed colour, will vary. The way to realising what an invariant is was paved. As we have seen elsewhere (Sandler, 2005, 2006), two British mathematicians working together, Sylvester and Cayley (who lived at the same time as Liouville), demonstrated the existence of other invariants in algebraic terms. From this, other mathematicians and physicists (and at least a psychoanalyst and a philosopher) discovered that there are no facts in the universe that do not happen through invariance and transformations (Dirac, 1932; Bion, 1965; Nozick, 2001).

In the hope that the reader has grasped the rudiments of the concept of phase space, one may keep in mind that phase space has at least six dimensions, here visualised by the three Euclidean coordinates, together with its moment, made by three more coordinates (depicted by the models of the pendulum and the ink). Phase space furnishes an improved presentation of reality *as it is* in relation to the former and still popular representations restricted to Euclidean space.

From this hexa-dimensional space, mathematicians developed methods to deal with infinite-dimensional spaces, including non-dimensional phase spaces, which, having no dimension, cannot be measured. If Einstein started from Hamilton-Liouville insights, he proceeded to an ever-expanding universe—thus unbounded, infinite—born from infinite emptiness (black holes) where nothing existed due to infinite existence (immeasurably huge and compacted mass), generating gravitational forces that can be measured. The paradoxes lingered on; as already seen in that which exists in matter and energy, or the wave and particle nature of photons—two different forms from an ultimately unknown same existence—which we call "light". In analysis, the same insight about the need to tolerate a paradox—even if the form and content of paradoxes can be said to be different because the object studied is different—was reached through the eliciting of two different forms of the same existence, psychic and material reality (Freud, 1900). The psychoanalytic realm—like the mathematical realm—has infinite dimensions. Could a few of them be intuited, used and transiently caught?

The six-dimension Grid

The purpose of this six-dimension Grid remains the same as that of the original two-dimension Grid: to verify the truth value of the analyst's and the patient's statements under a given vertex. Let us re-summarise, with slight modification, the "first" three dimensions that characterise our proposed expansion of the Grid: [24]

1. *Genetic development of thought processes* as seen in the vertically bounded positive (downwards) and negative (upwards) movement from one category to another, A to H. One may consider that the interval between the categories and therefore the categories themselves may be described by Cantor's set theory: transfinite would-be categories, depending on the empirically founded future observations of each reader, eventually placed after H; this set theory allows for a more precise location of phenomena between categories and within each category (between O and 1 there are infinite numbers);
2. *Uses of the thought processes,* ego functions according Freud, 1 to 6, horizontally bounded positive (right) and negative (left) movements, amended by the two Kantian categories (Columns 1 and 2) as well as by Cantor's set theory: infinite categories between the categories and within each category (depending on the empirically founded future observations of each reader);
3. *Instant intensity,* as seen in each bi-dimensionally conjoined category of the Grid.

What was stated above as categories "between" and "within" categories helps to describe a movement and interpenetration of categories which was already prefigured by Bion's concept of saturation (inseparable from de-saturation) as well as by his own revision, which comprised a whole Grid devoted to Rows B and C (Bion, 1977b). The pre-conception categories have shortcomings in conveying the reality they purport to convey, as can be seen in some writing tribulations in the naming of their functions in Chapter Sixteen of *Elements of Psychoanalysis* (1963). In my view, the source of the problems is the Grid's bi-dimensional "demeanour". Some of them can be solved by either three- or four-dimensional proposals. Whether this "some" means "extremely few" or "not enough" depends on the experience of the user.

Geometrical representations may display Space through a Euclidean representation but cannot do the same with Moment. Space-time and Moment may be represented by algebraic notation and calculus, but this method cannot be applied to mental states under the present conditions of knowledge—both in psychoanalysis and in mathematics. There is no present indication that this will be done in the foreseeable future. Conversely, there are also no indications that it will not be done—the same state of affairs as was displayed much earlier by Gödel's theorem (Sandler, 1997b).

Having dispensed with symbolic and drawn figures to represent the six-dimension Grid and thus returning to the typically psychoanalytic verbal formulations, I finally noticed—and I suppose that anyone can notice too—that Bion *had already suggested three further categories in the same book in which he had proposed the Grid* (Elements of Psychoanalysis). These remaining three categories enable the observer to see perspectives in the clinical material which were not encompassed by his original two-dimension Grid; a six-dimension Grid can integrate the three further categories with the dimensions defined earlier. Let us be reminded of them: they are the dimensions of the Senses, of Myth, and of Passion.

The same problem found with representations of what Physics named "Moment" appears when one tries to represent Bion's remaining three dimensions: Euclidean representations are still available for the first three dimensions of the Grid, but we have no algebraic notations and even less calculus to represent senses, myths and passion, Bion's remaining three dimensions, in order to attain an analytic interpretation. Nevertheless, each dimension allows for verbal expansion.

The *Dimension of the Senses* is a realm that can be measured; it functions through the earliest (or most primitive, under the phylogenetic vertex) human device and mechanism designed by nature (or reality, or biology) to apprehend outer stimuli. The neurological catchment "power" that makes for what is known as an Autonomic Nervous System has another neurological attribute whose function is conduction: that leads to sophisticated functions typical of mammals' verbal and non-verbal experiences belonging to the Central Nervous System; what began as a sound stimulus ends in a chemical process, probably belonging to the realm of quanta, still to be discovered.

Freud illuminated some psychic functions of the central nervous system; today, neurologists and self-styled neuroscientists are not against the conception that the unconscious system is part of the central nervous system, and increasingly accept it. Bion furnished a theory to account for those still unknown processes: alpha function, described in the original Grid though the categories most concentrated in the far left (Rows A, B, and C, Columns 1 to 6).

If one resorts to the still very primitive and general knowledge provided by neurology, the same processes described by Bion can be seen as the conduction of stimuli from the autonomic nervous system to the central nervous system. It was discovered that this conduction generates electrical and, as a consequence, magnetic fields that may be measured—the field of electroencephalography. Unfortunately, the measurements have been proved to be excessively rough to allow for the precise study needed to know emotional experiences and affects, the non-verbal output and expressions of the central nervous system. Novel computerised techniques, which create illusions of localisation through colours planned by computer information engineers who still cannot count with clinical principles outside positivism, cannot attain much more. The inner quantum phenomenon is still impossible to describe and observe; non-existent theories and no key concepts (due to the lack of intuition that would demand the appearance of people with Freud's and Einstein's abilities and gifts) condemn present day tomography and magnetic resonance to serious limitations. In other words, the researcher is put into the position of measuring phenomena that demand a device graduated in nano-microns armed with a "ruler" graduated in miles. The sparse and split data are collected with no previous generalising key concepts or theories (usually given by philosophy, which points to the ways of science: Kant, 1781; Sandler, 2001a), and are doomed to form an incoherent collection of data swiftly described as "causality theories", such as the link between "depression" and enzymes involved in the metabolism of specific catecholamines. Psychoanalysis has no tools to attain quantum phenomena either, but it has clinical observations made coherent by Freud's intuition amended by a few other authors who followed him. Therefore analysts are better prepared to deal with the verbal and non-verbal experiences issued by the central nervous system. A prodigious output, by the way; so a fair analogy is to state that a hunter with a bow and arrow is better prepared than a more primitive one armed just with his fists. One may resort to the verbal statements of our clinical example as presented in the three-dimension Grid earlier to illustrate the task: "The analyst's emotional experience shows him the dichotomy between what is related verbally and what is actually going on; an advertised guilty but lifeless account. Anyway, echoing the patient's attitude, the analyst soon dismisses the underlying lack of 'colour' and resorts to verbal agreement." In other words, I, the analyst, erred in having, up to a point, jettisoned the sensuous experience as it occurred in the session. "Up to a point" because the same analyst was able to describe his dismissal of the lack of colour—albeit almost unwitting and partially unconscious, hidden, made *en passant*, diluted among other parts of the report of the session—that could be rescued when reviewing it "posthumously" (after the session) with the help of the Grid.[25]

Both positivistically oriented researchers and psychoanalysts put their epistemophilic instinct to work. The former have a strong tendency to privilege a most treacherous activity of the epistemophilic instinct, sensuous apprehension, at the expense of other perception activities such as sensible intuition. Many psychoanalysts have the same tendency, expressed in taking the patient's parlance as things-in-themselves—a fact already examined in previous parts of this work. Thus this kind of researcher undoes the whole work that the autonomic nervous system and the central nervous system had previously done. The practitioner's irremediable fate is to be unable to look for that which underlies it—the invariant (see Volume 1 of this work).

Sensuous impressions are the home we start from; they may ignite an equally primitive reaction, that of the instincts (*Trieb*; Freud, 1915a). A disclaimer is necessary now in order to avoid oversimplifications that made for fashionable trends in the analytic movement: to emphasise the deleterious effects (when the purpose is to apprehend reality) of privileging sensuous impressions does not mean that the dimension of the senses is something to be held in contempt. Any partisan tendency whose outcome is to overturn things leaning towards a single path disturbs the mind's and the body's homeostatic principle. As a consequence, there is no dismissal of what is related by the patient. The port of entry of anything in life is made by sensuously apprehended data. No analyst with a good enough awareness and experience of his or her task would denigrate anything that comes from the patient, and much less the manifest content, expressed by what he says.

A Portuguese-Brazilian motto is that "half a word is enough for an understanding person". From "being told" to "saying" (or "doing") may (or may not) entail a long (or short, respectively; and infinite time measures in between) journey, but in any case, a journey. The same applies from "hearing" to "listening", "looking" to "seeing", "sensations" to "affects", "feelings" to "emotional experiences" . This was studied in Volumes 1 and 2 of this work. The question is to discriminate and order the communication made. To be halted in the manifest content is like going to a party but stopping at the front door of the host's home, without ever moving into the party room.

The *Dimension of Myth* was represented in the original Grid as Row C, comprising dreams, myths and dream thoughts. One of the expressions of these in the activity of writing and reading is metaphor, which acts as an igniting device. Bion provided us with verbal expansions based on his knowledge that the original Grid missed some points, suggesting that this specific category of the Grid should be noticeably expanded to the point of meriting a Grid of its own; hence the metaphorical fables "death of Palinurus" and "tomb-robbers" (Bion, 1977a). Row C (Dreams, Myths) corresponds simultaneously to Plato's Ideal forms *and* to Aristotle's "nous": the mind thinking about itself and simultaneously presenting the universe, human nature and, above all, itself to itself.

This is a remarkable category of the Grid to which Bion gave most of his attention, for myths are powerful enough to convey macro, universal truths which are also valid at the micro, individual level, as part of the "primitive apparatus of the individual's armoury of learning". Bion states explicitly that myths were the earliest scientific approach made by humankind, developing observations from von Herder, Schopenhauer and Nietzsche, as we will see in a more detailed way in Part III. Bion considers the myth a "fact-finding tool" and states explicitly: "I wish to restore its place in our methods so that it can play the vitalising part there that it has played in history (and in Freud's discovery of psychoanalysis)" (1963, p. 66), rescuing Freud's way for analysts. Bion's practical applications or lessons scrutinise the Oedipus myth (1963) and the myth of Babel (1958–1979, p. 226); he confers on "liars" (1970, p. 101) and "tomb-robbers" (1977a) the mythical roles of Protectors—of human physical survival and of science, respectively.

A verbal statement made in a session was examined using the Grid, and this process is illustrated graphically in Figs. 5 to 12. The proposal of an integrated verbal formulation of a six-dimension Grid may prove to be less time-consuming than the physical construction of a three- or four-dimension Grid. It demands neither drawing talent nor previous training in CAD computer software. Both the intra-session statement and the graphics attain the dimension of a myth. This can be emphasised with the use of the six-dimension Grid. I suppose that, like the construction of the three-dimension Grid, a renewed effort towards another Grid to further scrutinise the issue may not only prove to be equally cumbersome, but—due to the complexity of mental phenomena—it may also have an increased chance of being an excessively complicated model. Through the three-dimension (and four-dimension) Grid we were able to observe and describe the obtrusion of a life-producing, sexual activity—in the clinical illustration, it was manifested by the holes in the bomb's shell. Analytically trained intuition[26] authorised a hypothesis: the visual production is an individual presentation of Oedipus, which may be regarded as the basic invariant of the whole material.

The analyst acquired a kind of serenity which enabled him to single out his earlier failure to enter into a "truth realm". His initial statement, strictly based in the manifest content, or appearances of words uttered, failed to see that it did not express just hate, but also a split love. This could deepen the work done to the point of turning it into a real analysis. What is the patient's psychic reality? He was researching the nature of life. The very research is enlivened by the actual session—a fundamental *raison d'être* of psychoanalysis.

The *Dimension of Passion* illuminates an expression of instincts: in other words, affects, emotions and the emotional experiences which are presented through three links (Love, Hate and Knowledge), corresponding to the three named groups of instincts hitherto known (epistemophilic, life and death). The links, indissoluble from their emotional experiences (Bion, 1962, p. 42; the detailed description is in Sandler, 2005) that at the same time present the instincts, mould passions through trying to affect second and third parties (and so on; therefore we may speak about affects). The outcome of affects depends on the "affectability" of the second, third or more parties. Passion, as a manifestation of instincts, depends on biological traits, chiefly on primary narcissism and primary envy, as they were called by Freud and Klein respectively.

To return to the clinical example, the "atomic bomb", the eventually passionate analyst allows himself to be driven by a kind of humane surrender. It means a good enough abandonment (or discipline) of self-pleasure and desire. One of its manifestations is a "caring" attitude: in other words, not being enslaved by an ideology that could be described as "it is better to receive than to give". This particular analyst, who can be seen as belonging to this classification due to his self-critical posture about his work (still not well) done, met a collaborative and insemination-prone patient, whose return for another session, both despite and due to the relative failure of the previous one, may be evidence of this personal feature. The analytic couple thus endowed toiled for development. A mutual insemination appears when both return to the session, in the wake of the "germs of life" of which Mephistopheles complained (Goethe, *Faust*: Part I, Scene 3). The aftermath, like a baby, was a free association producing entity, analysis itself (see more detailed study in Volume 1, container and contained).

The original Grid by Bion and its extension with the added four dimensions seemed to help the analyst to gradually improve his approximation of each patient's psychic reality at a given moment, under a given vertex, as well as the analyst's psychic reality and the ensuing momentary relationship experienced by them. Through a scrutiny of verbal statements stemming from the analytic couple and their development, the ensuing saturations and non-saturations, or processes of transformation, could be scrutinised too.

The six-dimension Grid, using a transdisciplinary approach, may offer an integrated view of some observations which were scattered throughout Bion's work. It suggests a model, albeit still provisional and utterly incomplete, that may increase the analyst's possibilities to deal—outside the session—with aspects of timelessness and infinity of unconscious, as it unfolds and presents itself in an analytic session.

It was not possible for me, other than a mere toying inspired by Escher's drawings, to draw a visual depiction of a Grid whose dimensions are ≥ 5 without incurring more problems than solutions. Mathematicians may do this with algebra and non-Euclidean geometry; but they do not resort to visual means.

Notes

1. Many suppose that they earn insight and real development through reading prose and poetry, apprehending philosophy and being exposed to other artistic stimuli. In individual beings, those claims may be verified and appreciated, especially before the inception of psychoanalysis.

If those attempts could be really useful and durable, there would be no need for the obtrusion of psychoanalysis.
2. Please see Volume 1, Part I.
3. The Positions theory can be seen as expanding Freud's view of the unconscious, which can be likened to Einstein's insights about the greater universe with space-time, a monistic unitary entity, phasing out illusions about absolute units of space and time as they were hitherto seen. In the Positions, the space-time unit is more clearly seen in the intra-psychic mental universe (see Sandler, 2001a, 2003, 2005).
4. We also avoid the term "entity" because of its anthropomorphic connotation.
5. Is the psychoanalytic movement—as distinct from psychoanalysis proper—an aping of the fashionable gatherings around ideas and movements and counter-movements which gave birth to totalitarian social movements such as Communism and Nazism?
6. Widely-read and popular weekly magazines as well as—alas—voices within the analytic movement make this claim. In other words: psychoanalysis could deal with external enemies, but will it be equally successful in dealing with its internal enemies?
7. The distinction between determinism of functions and determinism of causes was made in Sandler, 1997b.
8. *Anschauung*, in the German term used by Freud.
9. The reader unfamiliar with Bion's notation and his definition of the concepts to which it corresponds may refer to his works (Bion, 1962, 1963 and 1965). For the reader who prefers not to run after them, as they are scattered through his books, they are collected in a dictionary (Sandler, 2005).
10. I prefer not to dwell on a criticism of the concept of "mental space" as introduced by many authors. I hope that the criticism, which deals with the restrictive outlook of this view, will be made clear in the advancing of another model, which bases itself on the space-time unit.
11. Please see Chapter One, Note 6.
12. This verbal formulation paraphrases the observations of the poet Vinicius de Morais on love.
13. The first association between Escher's drawings and Bion's ethos of work came from a graphic designer, Mrs Mari Pini, when I asked her to produce a cover for my second book in the Portuguese language (*Fatos, a tragédia do conhecimento em psicanalise*, Imago, 1990; an English version of its title could be "Facts: the tragedy of knowledge in psychoanalysis"). Mari Pini, a professional who was determined to create a cover only after reading the book for which the cover was intended, instantaneously choose Escher's drawings, without any previous

knowledge of Bion or acquaintance with the Grid. This use as an illustration differs from any other attempt to use Escher's drawings as a model for psychoanalytic theories and clinical work. As regards the revamping of this theory from four to six dimensions it would be just an ad hoc activity, taking a purely artistic work by a gifted Dutch illustrator based on exclusive use of illusion, akin to *trompe l'œil* which is normal for artists but would be anti-analytic for psychoanalysts.

14. Due to the relative complexity of the mathematics of quantum mechanics.
15. This study includes a brief summary of them; a more detailed view can be seen elsewhere—albeit written in a less widely used language (Sandler, 1997b).
16. "Rationalised" after Freud in the case of Schreber (Freud, 1911b).
17. To attempt does not imply success; in writing, the outcome depends on the reader.
18. To avoid semantic confusion, the neologism "de-concretising" has nothing to do with the term coined by post-modernism, "deconstruction". The former tries to focus on an act that makes events less dependent on their sensuous basis, belonging more to an immaterial world, inseparable from the material but not confused with it. In analysis, the term "de-concretising" displays the range of the spectrum {psychic reality ⇔ material reality}.
19. Light, the thing-in-itself under study, or absolute truth, in itself, remains an unknown. The relationships between things-in-themselves, which remain unknown, can be known, even if partially and transiently, in their given, and thus describable, usable states according to equally describable vertices.
20. Please see Volume 1, Part III.
21. The example is given by Bion in *Cogitations* and other works, expanded in its explanation here.
22. Imagination is the capacity to make mental images to be discarded as soon as they have fulfilled their purpose, as stated just before, with regard to the concrete form of models and analogies.
23. Among many confusions and misunderstandings there is an excess of "little learning", intended or unintended plagiarism. They subsume denial of Bacon's observation that there are no new things upon the Earth, just oblivion. In the analytic movement there are specific factors that belong to a spectrum which comes from a tendency to be lax on definitions, resulting from the immateriality of the object of study (psychic reality), which seem to justify to many professionals the lack of a habit of scholarship. Therefore, the "here and now" observational concept in psychoanalysis is popularly attributed to people other than

Freud. This is scientifically unjustifiable and, being so, unfair to truth and truthfulness. Other instances of the same fact (the invariant is untruthfulness in the psychoanalytic movement, usually driven by narcissistic drives disguised by "political" importance) are the concepts of unconscious phantasy, symbolic equation and object relations. All of them come from Freud, but they are attributed to other authors. Some of these authors—I am referring to Klein, to whom some attributed the creative act—never claimed personal authorship of those concepts. Apostolic fanaticism is the act of second and later generations.

24. "First" does not imply importance, just an ordinal classification based on time of appearance or elucidation of the dimension, for didactic purposes.
25. The model can be of the clinical-anatomical meetings in surgery and general practice.
26. Bion, 1965.

CHAPTER FOUR

A multi-dimension grid and a negative grid

Another step allowing one to realise the n-dimensional psychic reality could be the naming of other elements of psychoanalysis. The Euclidean representational system still furnishes a helping hand towards its realisation, through polyhedral construction. Again, the human sensuous apparatus can cope with representations of polyhedra with six, eight, ten, twelve and even twenty faces. The mind could be represented, albeit imperfectly, by its sensuous bases which also confer a kind of comprehension, by an n-dimension polyhedron whose faces are not equal to each other (Fig. 22).

This representation allows for the visualisation of "external" and "internal" realms, separated by a semi-permeable "contact barrier" as theorised by Freud (1905) with amendments by Bion (1962).

Our next step in describing an n-dimension Grid beyond the six-dimension Grid is to focus on Biological-Instincual Function—in short,

Fig. 22: A polyhedron with unequal faces (model by the designer Miss Adriana Miotto)

Trieb-Function. It was already present in Bion's original two-dimension representation, akin to a linear function constantly conjoining two dimensions of the function that can be named "Thought processes": the genetics of thought processes and uses of it by the ego. Any function allows for a double or ambivalent (in the sense that it has two valences at the same time) description, forming paradoxical pairs. They can be seen as functioning basic invariants. In philosophy they were described as thesis and antithesis. In psychoanalysis neither one can prevail over the other, which could be described as thesis *or* antithesis. It is rather a question of balance, as in the homeostatic principle first observed by Fechner and later used by Freud.

Clinical practice allows us to specify expressions of the *Trieb*-Functions, expressed by elements of psychoanalysis (Bion, 1963).

Concern for life ⇔ Death

A more precise focus on the dimension of passion can be put into the humanitarian (enlightened) medical ideology about the discipline of desire—above all, sadistic desire—which dictates that analysis is an exercise of availability within the boundaries of elected tropisms or affinities, to paraphrase Goethe.

Focusing still more, it can be likened to a conjoint consideration, paradoxically oriented to living life and concern for death. "Living life" is an expression of the real interests of the patient and the analytic couple as a tool to observe and living it in the here and now of the analytic session. It is a collaboration between a couple that "should be healing and rewarding … It is doubtful whether the transformation of the analysis into something wounding is expected from a real analyst" (Bion, 1965, p. 25). "An analyst is not doing his job if he investigates something because it is pleasurable or profitable … anyone who is not afraid when he is engaged on psychoanalysis is either not doing his job or is unfitted for it" (Bion, 1979, p. 516). Analytic function is nourished and kept through a capacity and availability expressed by "a capacity for compassion" (Bion, 1965, p. 143), in other words, regard for an individual's life as it is.

Pain ⇔ Growth

Bion suggested the two elements that may be seen as a coupled conjunction, as an expansion of what he observed, and the development is implicit in his later works. Here it is made explicit, to be used in a session.

Growth is intrinsically related to pain—common sense and medical wisdom observes "growing pains" (Bion, 1963, p. 63). In discussing the reversible perspective, that is, the attempt to turn a dynamic situation into a static one (Bion, 1963, p. 60), Bion states that the reversal of perspective, through the excessive use of projective identification, is "evidence of pain".[1]

Any development has painful aspects; it can lead to catastrophic changes and abandonment of cherished habits. But to study growth, one refers to events separated in space and time in unbridgeable ways. When one refers to "growth", one may start from the very dubious assumption that there are no particular difficulties in its perception either by the growing object or the object that stimulates growth. In fact, their relationship with precedent phenomena is obscure and separated in time, and one should consider this in any reference to growth and development, in order not to jump to pseudo-theories constructed with undue, hasty over-simplifications, avoiding research into what is complex. In doing this, one would have learned from Freud's, Klein's and Bion's contributions.

Freud, embedded in the rescue made by the Renaissance and the Enlightenment of ancient forms of transmission of experience—myths—furnished a helping hand to scientists concerned with growth and pain. Like Herder, Schopenhauer and Nietzsche, Freud saw myths as providers of succinct statements of "psychoanalytic theories which are relevant in aiding the analyst both to perceive growth and to achieve interpretations that illuminate aspects of the patient's problems that belong to growth" (Bion, 1963, p. 63).

Some myths developed ways to show that growth and pain are constantly conjoined in tolerable ways, and may have been an attempt to work through both. Bion suggests at least three myths as primitive models for mental growth: those of the Tree of Knowledge, the Tower of Babel, and the Sphinx. Growth is also linked to the imbalance or even conflict between narcissism and socialism as components of the Oedipal situation.

Pain was regarded by Bion as one of the elements of psychoanalysis (Bion, 1963; Sandler, 2005). This means that pain qualifies as something basic and fundamental, endowed with a structuring function in the human mind. As a matter of consequence, pain is a function in any analytic session.

> The case for acceptance of pain as an element of psychoanalysis is reinforced by the position it occupies in Freud's theories of the pleasure–pain principle. It is evident that the dominance of the reality principle, and indeed its establishment, is imperilled if the patient swings over to the evasion of pain rather than to its modification; yet modification is jeopardised if the patient's capacity for pain is impaired. [Bion, 1963, p. 62]

This is in stark contrast to the popular view, endorsed by the vast majority of professionals in the field of so-called mental health, that one must unquestionably extinguish any pain, with attention neither to its quality nor to its quantity; much less to each individual's way of dealing with it.

Freud introduced a different view, but he was not heard; Klein and Bion tried to rescue it, in popular terms, to no avail; the psychoanalytic establishment is tainted with religious hallucinations of cure and attainable whole happiness. Human willingness to entertain wishful feelings has inhumane consequences: with the help of judgmental values, it downgrades suffering either to a non-useful status or to sadistic profit. It can be said that the most fervent wish of children is to have qualities they see in adults—especially the power and strength to fulfil their desires. The project is flawed and may be corrected or not by experience. Adults who displayed this hallucinated belief and cannot learn from experience display the same idea, in its obverse or specular vertex: they ardently want to be children, driven by the imagination that they can have a life free of pain and sorrow. Experience is always seen, under this vertex, as "awful", hence the popular idea of "awful reality". Shakespeare observed a different situation: "there is nothing either good or bad, but thinking makes it so" (*Hamlet*, II ii).

Outside wishful thinking many thinkers deal with pain, avoiding being prey to attempts either to extinguish it or to co-opt it through sadism. Bion quotes one of them:

> John Donne said that "affliction is a treasure and scarce any man hath enough of it. No man hath affliction enough that is not matured and ripened by it." No one today is likely to complain that there is any shortage in this commodity, but is it possible that our elaborate machinery, social as well as individual, for the denial

of the existence of everyday troubles and difficulties has led to a
revolt that has taken the form of an artificial production of calamity
on a vast scale? [Bion, 1958–1979, p. 346]

Bion was seemingly referring to his life experience; but this had not changed in social terms, despite the negative growth of greed which gave way to consumerism, communism and wild capitalist casinos (Grünwald, 1992).

Psychoanalysis, with its recommendation of discipline of desire and pleasure, was already hinted by Freud's advice on the need for abstinence, which tries to help humankind to find alternatives and ways under the aegis of the principle of reality, both within and outside the session. This recommendation is usually mistaken for the hallucination of an axiological neutrality of the observer, typical of positivism.[2]

One phantasises that the world (originally the breast) must be that which one desires it to be, and further phantasises that it cannot be that which it is in reality. Intolerance of frustration indicates a prevalence of the principle of pleasure/displeasure. There is an imbalance which implies a prevalence of aspects of the paranoid-schizoid position. It implies intolerance of pain. One feels the pain but it cannot be said that one suffers it (Bion, 1970); one is always trying to evade it. This action further worsens one's predicament. The issue is not limited by the imposition of desire, for it may well be that a necessity is at stake. Due to the prevalence of innate paranoid and narcissistic traits, one phantasises that all one's needs must be satisfied. This can be enhanced or counterbalanced by the environment.

Pain cannot be absent from the personality. An analysis must be painful, not because there is necessarily any value in pain, but because an analysis in which pain in not observed and discussed cannot be regarded as dealing with one of the central reasons for the patient's presence. The importance of pain can be dismissed as a secondary quality, something that is to disappear when conflicts are resolved; indeed, most patients would take this view. Pain, like Death, has no alternative, no opposite counterpart. Analgesia is just a question of sensuous perception.

> Furthermore it can be supported by the fact that successful analysis
> does lead to diminution of suffering: nevertheless it obscures the
> need, more obvious in some cases than in others, for the analytic

> experience to increase the patient's *capacity* for suffering even though patient and analyst may hope to decrease pain itself. The analogy with physical medicine is exact; to destroy a capacity for physical pain would be a disaster in any situation other than one in which an even greater disaster—namely death itself—is certain. [Bion, 1963, pp. 61–62]

The presence of unfathomable and non-sensuous pain can be measured by the presence of reversal of perspective and the projective identification which accompanies it.[3] Bion proposes that the analyst who is doing his or her job must try to "restore dynamic to a static situation and so make development possible". He furnishes a scientific observation easily reproduced[4] by any practising analyst:

> The patient manoeuvres so that the analyst's interpretations are agreed; they thus become the outward sign of a static situation … In reversible perspective acceptance by the analyst of the possibility of a capacity for pain can help avoidance of errors that might lead to disaster. If the problem is not dealt with the patient's capacity to maintain the static situation may give way to an experience of pain so intense that a psychotic breakdown is the result. [1963, pp. 60, 62]

The word "static" can be seen as a verbal formulation of a manifestation of the death instincts; conversely, "dynamic" is the hallmark of life itself. There is an added complication, linked to the "economic problem of masochism": sadism is a way of establishing and inflicting pain in order to achieve pleasurable sensations.

The psychotic creation of pseudo-pain is akin to sadistic relationships; together with incapacity to suffer pain it runs parallel to, and disguises, the capacity to feel pain. This is highlighted in Bion's work in many ways. Most useful is dependence on one's capacity to keep in touch with one's mind:

> There are patients whose contact with reality presents most difficulty when that reality is their own mental state. For example, a baby discovers its members; for example, its own hand; it might as well have discovered its stomach-ache, or its feeling of dread or anxiety, or mental pain. In most ordinary personalities this is true, but people exist who are so intolerant of pain or

> frustration (or in whom pain or frustration is so intolerable) that they feel the pain but will not suffer it and so cannot be said to discover it. [Bion, 1970, p. 9]

Growth is related to an increased capacity to face the unknown, to abandon cravings for explanations and understanding of perception of one's destructiveness, in Klein's sense, of a transition between the paranoid–schizoid and depressive positions. Growth would include, from the time that Bion wrote *Transformations*, a respectful awe of the existence of truth, "O"; he introduces the term "at-onement" to the relationship between the human being and "O". The psychoanalyst accepts the reality of reverence and awe, and the possibility of a disturbance in the individual which makes at-onement, and therefore an expression of reverence and awe, impossible.

> Growth, + or -, remains inaccessible to thought, if unmistakable to feeling. Conceptual thought and passionate feeling are impossible to relate within the confines of existent universes of discourse. [Bion, 1975, p. 138]

Thinking can be viewed according to its degree of sophistication. The scanning of Bion's original, two-dimension Grid (1963, p. 86) represents growth of thought processes: categories run from A to H and from 1 to 6, as well as from a constantly conjoined scrutiny of both axes, from A1 to H6. Growth, like Pain and Death, has no alternative. Decay is not its obverse, because it is another state.

A specific kind of growth expresses itself, in analysis and in the outside world, as Work. Both are related to pain. The capacity to work and the capacity to tolerate pain develop in parallel and are proportional to each other. Analytically, the measuring device can be marked by an imaginary scale whose unit could be pain due to the unknown and pain due to frustration of pleasure. Both may be augmented by analytic work.

Tolerance of paradoxes

One of the n dimensions of a multi-dimension grid may be called that which is also an analytic function in the session: the tolerance of paradoxes with no attempt to resolve them.

The basic and prototypical paradox is integration and splitting: the person needs to discover and integrate the fact that the object that is loved and the object that is hated are one and the same object. Marriage, parenthood, and any intimate contact propose paradoxes with which we human beings display some difficulties in coping. The human relationship with truth is another paradox: truth, which is the food of the mind, is also subject to hate from the same mind it nourishes, as Bion observed. Again, the prototypical situation is our relationship with anything that smells of or marks dependence, such as the nourishing breast. "The systematic separation into two objects, good and bad, conscious and unconscious, pain and pleasure, ugly and beautiful, had provided a framework which seems to have facilitated the development of knowledge, but the element of growth appears to have escaped formulation especially since it resembles maturation" (Bion, 1975, p. 77).

Is growth an increased capacity to tolerate paradoxes, the prototype of those paradoxes being the internal object that demands to be perceived in its loved and hated aspects as the one and only object? All of Bion's texts seem to indicate this, to the extent that he usually displays at least two faces of the situation; in some cases, more. Growth is also seen as a growth of meaning, accretions of meaning in thinking processes and in the relationship of container and contained, resulting in growth of container and of contained. This is extremely important in a single session of analysis, to the extent that an authoritarian, supportive, idealised professional can work as an analyst. He or she and the patient will evolve and grow into the unknown through "tolerated doubt" (Bion, 1962, p. 92) to the extent they allow each other to hear, to associate freely and to "inseminate" each other.

The emotion to which attention is drawn should be obvious to the analyst, but unobserved by the patient. An emotion that is obvious to the patient is usually *painfully* obvious, and avoidance of unnecessary pain must be one aim in the exercise of analytic intuition. Since the analyst's capacity for intuition should enable him or her to demonstrate an emotion before it has become *painfully* obvious, it would help if our search for the elements of emotions was directed to making intuitive deductions easier (Bion, 1963, p. 74).

The negative grid

Another dimension which was present in the original two-dimension Grid which challenged representations in any sensuously apprehensible way is the realm of the negative, which also can be seen as a psychoanalytic function in the here and now moment of interpretation and insight. It gives to both their "truth value" through a counterpoint—the extent to which they carry lie. Bion's first attempt was to represent it by a numbered column (2). It was just this category that seemed to merit more attention, together with Row C. He thought that they needed a Grid of their own.

Later researchers saw the hypothesis of a negative Grid in a different way adumbrated here. The absence of a list of their names and papers here does not imply dismissal. Nevertheless, the psychoanalytic environment still has an abhorrence of scientific criticism, which just adds pseudo-controversy,[5] much tainted with narcissism:

> Much psychoanalytic "controversy" is not controversy at all. If listened to for any prolonged period, say a year, but preferably two or three, a pattern begins to emerge, so much so that I can write a chairman's address suitable, with the alteration of a phrase or two, for practically any paper by anyone at any time. Thus: "Ladies and Gentlemen, we have been listening to a very interesting and stimulating paper. I have had the great advantage of being able to read it in advance, and though I cannot say I agree with everything Dr X says," (chiefly because I haven't the faintest idea what he thinks he is talking about, and I am damned sure he hasn't either). "I found his presentation extremely—er—stimulating. There are many points that I would like to discuss with him if we had time," (thank God we haven't) "but I know there are many here who are anxious to speak" (in particular our resident ex-officio permanent bores whom no one has succeeded in silencing yet) "so I must not take up too much of our time. There is, however, just one point on which I would like to hear Dr X's views if he can spare the time." (At this point I prepare to give one of the favourite bees which reside in my own bonnet its periodical airing. It does not matter in the least how irrelevant it may be, or how unlikely Dr X is to have any views whatever on the subject, or how improbable that I would want to hear them if he had—the time has come and out it goes.) "It has often occurred to me" (and only the poor devils in my Society know how often that is) "that ... etc ... etc." [Bion, 1958–1979, p. 303]

No questioning would be maturely valid if not accompanied by an alternative, which Bion provides later:

> Controversy is the growing point from which development springs, but it must be a genuine confrontation and not impotent beatings of the air by opponents whose differences of view never meet. What follows is a contribution to bringing different psychoanalytic views together in agreement or disagreement.
>
> Hearing psychoanalytic controversy I have felt that the same configuration was being described and that the apparent differences were more often accidental than intrinsic; different points of view are believed to be significant of membership of a group, not of a scientific experience. Yet everyone knows that what is important is not the supposed use of a particular theory but whether the theory has been understood properly and whether the application has been sound. It may be objected that to establish this would involve consideration of every individual analyst and of the circumstances of every individual interpretation .... Even so, many difficulties could be obviated by more precise definition of the point of view (vertex). [Bion, 1970, p. 55]

Taking into account that one of those authors, Donald Meltzer, granted me some personal contact and made himself available in an amiable conversation as well as through an exchange of letters, I will quote his opinion as emblematic of those of others. He took the possibility of a negative Grid under a moral vertex. This is a popular view: judgment replaces comprehension; taking sides replaces apprehension. Donald Meltzer felt that a negative Grid mirrored "philistinism" and "envy" (Meltzer, 1986, 1998). Bion observed some conditions that make the obtrusion of value judgments inevitable:

> Intolerance of frustration is not so great as to activate the mechanisms of evasion and yet is too great to bear dominance of the reality principle, the personality develops omnipotence as a substitute for the mating of the pre-conception, or conception, with the negative realisation. This involves the assumption of omniscience as a substitute for learning from experience by aid of thoughts and thinking. There is therefore no psychic activity to discriminate between true and false. Omniscience substitutes

> for the discrimination between true and false a dictatorial affirmation that one thing is morally right and the other wrong. The assumption of omniscience that denies reality ensures that the morality thus engendered is a function of psychosis ... There is thus potentially a conflict between assertion of truth and assertion of moral ascendancy. The extremism of the one infects the other. [Bion, 1961 p. 114]

In other words, when one loses sight of what true and false are all about, the lack of this kind of discrimination creates an unbearable vacuum. The vacuum itself is abhorred by the personality that puts fulfilment of desire above all else. This posture fuels a vicious circle. More hate of reality ensues. Truth seems to be exceedingly unattainable. Therefore one tries to resort to judgmental values in order to fill the vacuum.

The achievement of *correlation*, which would enable the psyche to tolerate the fact that paradoxes admit no resolution but require forbearance, is hampered or precluded. The forbearance is of the very paradox, which excludes omniscience and demands tolerance of the unknown that would remain as such, or the unconscious, id, "O".

> Patients show* that the resolution of a problem appears to present less difficulty if it can be regarded as belonging to a moral domain; causation, responsibility and therefore a controlling force (as opposed to helplessness) provide a framework within which omnipotence reigns. In certain circumstances, to be considered later, the scene is thus set for conflict (reflected in controversies such as those on Science and Religion). This situation is portrayed in the Eden and Babel myths. The significance for the individual lies in its part in obstructing the PS⇔D interaction.
>
> *And not only patients. The group is dominated by morality—I include of course the negative sense that shows as rebellion against morality—and this contributed to the atmosphere of hostility to individual thought on which Freud remarked. [Bion, 1965, p. 64–65]

Alternatively, that which I regard as the negative Grid should avoid (this is the ethos of the term negative) some stances. Generally, this corresponds to discipline of desire, memory and comprehension (Bion, 1967c). Negative discipline equips some other dimensions already stated. The prominent avoidance expressed by absence or negative demeanour has to do with judgmental values. Therefore, the n-dimension Negative Grid must have an *absence of judgmental values*: apart from the work of Kant, which attributes to the activity of judging a pathognomonic feature of thought processes, judgmental values belong to the disciplines and deeds of the political and judicial social systems (politicians, barristers, police, judges), pedagogy, religious ministry, and parenthood. It has nothing to do with analysis, begging for its "negativation".[6] To the analytic couple there remain other actions: the analyst must try to apprehend and propitiate an environment furnishing awareness of some unconscious features of the patient; the patient must decide if they are debits or credits (Bion, 1979, p. 154). The analyst must not furnish driving lights to the patient's conducting of his or her life, but rather help the patient to live his or her life in agreement with the same patient's own lights; the analyst must help the patient in the discovery of what his or her lights are (Bion, 1965, p. 37). Psychoanalysis is an *organon*, not a *canon*.

In examining the analyst's attitude, there is a need to attain abstinence from self-importance which unwittingly flows into self-dismissal. In other words, there is a need to discipline oneself from phantasies of self-importance. Also, there is a need to exert the most powerful discipline possible of the analyst's personal interests, which have to be distinguished from his or her instinctual need to contribute to the welfare of others and to be available to care.

Abstinence from judgment and acting out are expressions of a "capacity for compassion". More than a positive dimension as quoted above, as seen by Bion in his original first Grid, it also qualifies in its negative dimension, a blank, a locus-where-something-may-be-placed. It represents a danger with some types of patients: "a capacity for compassion is a source of admiration and therefore envy in an analysand who feels incapable of mature compassion" (Bion, 1965, p. 143).

Psychopathic and delinquent personalities under the prevalence of desire and pleasure (which includes inflicting pain on other people), neuroses (meaning prevalence of memory) and psychosis (meaning prevalence of omnipotent and omniscient understanding), which are as a whole equipped by self-feeding autistic cycles of greed⇔envy, run into the obverse road (hate of analysis). The analyst's state of mind is under scrutiny in that which puts analysis at risk:

> Developments of memory that are inevitable to the psychoanalyst are ... the primacy of pleasure–pain (in contrast with reality or truth), and "possession" with its reciprocal, fear of loss; all have been acquired in close association with the senses. The impulse to be rid of painful stimuli gives the "content" of the memory ... an unsatisfactory quality when one is engaged in the pursuit of truth O ... An analyst with such a mind is one who is incapable of learning because he is satisfied. [Bion, 1970, p. 29]

Perhaps the ultimate presence of judgmental values can be exemplified by the analyst who thinks and says about a given patient: "This is an interesting case", and its corresponding negative: "This is a patient who cannot be analysed" (or is "difficult to reach"). Any analyst can vouch that he or she cannot analyse one patient, or cannot reach some parts of another; this differs from an attitude of issuing a "death sentence" whose underlying factor is a sheer lack of self-responsibility and professional commitment. All faults resulting in the failure of the analytic treatment would belong uniquely to the patient.

The n-dimension Negative Grid must also have *no slavishness to appearances*: sensuously apprehended appearances—material reality in Freud's parlance—have their initial function in human perception, as a step towards the quantum leap into the other existence of the same reality, psychic reality. The latter is immaterial: it uses (as a kind of door or window), but transcends, what is sensuously apprehensible. Unknown, or *unbevußt*, life in itself has a continuously variable and transient state. Tolerating this mutative transient state manifested in different forms enables one to detect that which does not vary (the invariant). This corresponds to seeing a pattern emerge (Bion, 1980, p. 11).

The description of few features towards a multi-dimensional Grid hints at future amendments from other researchers of psychoanalysis. If their particular contributions could be made under the scientific vertex, in other words, if they are based on and return to experience, with no devotion to flights of rationalised or narcissistic imagination (even if highly palatable), they will be useful to patients and analysts alike.

Notes

1. See Volume 1, Part II for examples of reversal of perspective.
2. See Chapter Seven on Epistemology.
3. See Volume 1, Part II for a glimpse of reversal of perspective in analytic sessions.
4. Reproduction is one of the criteria for stating whether or not something is scientific, according to Popper (1959).
5. This may be due to the relatively short span of time since Freud's discovery of psychoanalysis. One may wonder what the reaction of early mathematicians or artists might have been to criticism made one hundred years after the inception of those disciplines. Even the exercise of criticism was not developed enough in this time. It had to wait until Kant; and even after Kant, it is not properly practised due to insufficient psychoanalytic development in dealing with primary narcissism, which came much later.
6. Please see Volume 2, Part I.

PART II

FREE ASSOCIATIONS AND FREE-FLOATING ATTENTION

CHAPTER FIVE

Freie Einfälle: the verbal irruption of the unknown

> The erudite can see that a description is by Freud, or Melanie Klein, but remain blind to the thing described.
>
> —Bion, 1975, p. 11

The concept *freie Einfälle* was translated by "free associations". A practising psychoanalyst may be seen, analogically, as a kind of translator who goes beyond literary analysis. He or she may conjoin the description of the semantic domain entailed by its formulation in the German language with his or her clinical experience, trying as far as possible to reach its numinous counterpart. Words usually attempt to describe their counterparts in reality, but the written experience falls short of it. Experience and clinical experience in psychoanalysis may improve this pretension.

Language, German language, Psychoanalysis

Bion observed that language is a human development whose functions do not encompass the expression of feelings or emotions (1977c). Voltaire insisted that the human gift of speech was used to hide and dissimulate truth. Freud (Sandler, 1997, 2001), who came from the Enlightenment and from the Romantic Movement, also observed this, but improved the observation of the polarised insights of his antecedents: "to hide" also means "to reveal".

Conversely, some employ language to pursue the elucidation of something truthful underlying it (Bion, 1970, p. iii). This requires the gift of seeking truth and an ability to go beyond the concrete and the sensuous unavoidably embedded in each thought, each uttered or written word. As an example one may take the word "dog". It encompasses much more than the image, visual or acoustic, would furnish. The platonic class "dog" refers to any and every thing considered a dog; it confers an impossible-to-define "doggishness", which allows for living experience. In the same sense, what could be said of a still more living, specific phrase such as "little dog", when a single adjective can evoke powerful infantile feelings? Some disciplines demand a careful use of language in order to cover the realm of truth as it is.

Is it an impossible task? The realm which we nowadays call "mind" was known by different names in earlier eras: spirit, soul, personality, self, ego, character, and others. Its ultimately unknown nature challenges our perception of its transcendent permanence. As a matter of coherent consequence, this realm is ultimately ineffable: it not only challenges, but is beyond the human ability to name it. Irrespective of failed attempts to name it, such a realm corresponds to that of the Platonic forms, the numinous realm, or unconscious.[1] Each one may pick one's choice; again, a number of names have been proposed over time. As "mind", its object of study is ultimately unknown at least as far as its naming is concerned, for both are ineffable. In other words, it is refractory to verbal formulations, as a built-in feature. Chris Mawson introduces the question "when is a free association not a free association?" (Mawson, 2002).[2]

In contrast with scientists, lawyers and ministers of religion, other people who made intensive use of language to earn their living—poets, writers, journalists, ghost writers, publicists and demagogues—did not develop technical language and kept using colloquial language. With time their language also ranged into peaks of florid ornaments which bordered on pedantic fashion with the same intent—to draw near to "O". The Romantics returned to colloquial ways. Poets achieved artistic qualities, if art can be regarded as having this goal, to approach "O". Through symbolic forms whose hallmark was their compacted complexity, *poiesis* acquired the status of a queen among peer-arts, such as music and concrete-plastic constructs such as sculpture and painting. Languages, after all, are made with symbols, which can be understood (after Gombrich, 1959) as representations that mean more than themselves, if concretely regarded. What can be seen beyond or after the sign and attains a symbolic form (after Cassirer) reaches feelings and emotions in a sensitive audience. Mathematicians and other scientists also worked through sophisticated symbolic systems with the purpose of representing and communicating some realities that they purport to apprehend; the symbol systems effectively correspond to their counterparts in reality.

Unfortunately, due to some tendencies linked to features of human thinking processes[3] in many scientific fields and disciplines, as well as in the philosophy of science, epistemology and, incredibly enough, in art criticism and philosophy, the symbolic systems have evolved to jargon—especially when they resort to neologisms. Neologism is often the only way to make clear something which had no previous verbal formulation to serve as a communication tool, but its "jargonified drawback" is ever-present, depending on the audience or the onlooker who will read it. It is considered, in this book, that jargon not only results in superficial, flawed apprehension but also favours banality. In the religious field, it is expressed by questions about the Vulgate.

It seems to me that some languages are particularly developed in the expression of human happenings, deeds and especially mental activities: for example, the German and Russian languages. By mental activities, we mean psychic reality as defined by Freud (in *The Interpretation of Dreams*) and the attempt to express it through words. It includes, therefore, the naming of emotions, affects and feelings. The emphasis on the German and Russian languages does not detract from any other languages, which are more widely used all around the world. For example, as regards the powers of a colloquial language, English has become a real universal "second language", fulfilling expectations that Zamenhof thought could be attributable as to his own imagination when he proposed Esperanto.[4] It seems that all languages put a kind of plasticity at the disposal of their users, especially poets. Turning back to German and Russian, it seems that those languages offer even more developed ways in terms of this plasticity and malleability: they enable each user to build words in a shape, mode, tone and rhythm that seems not attainable or possible in other languages. Again, this is not to be regarded as a competition about the communication powers of languages; the confrontation is not in the kind of comparison, but as an assessment and appreciation. What interests us now is that some languages make some terms and expressions instantly "valid" with no resort to neologisms. This means that they attain much more precision in their communication powers to the extent that they diminish their accompanying penumbras of meaning and fuzziness in the boundaries of definition. A proof of this was Freud being recognised in 1930 by the judges of the Goethe Prize for his contributions to the German language; another is the existence of a prize whose range of interests included this kind of contribution.

Therefore we may use as a means of access to the semantic field and communicative powers of a specific term, free associations, its original formulation in German, *freie Einfälle*. This formulation in its original form seems to be able to approach the numinous realm of the unconscious.

Perhaps it would be opportune to use the German counterpart of the verbal expression "unconscious": *unbewußt*. Both mean "not known", or "unknown". What happened (and it usually does happen) to make an overused term lose its communicative power is ultimately unknown, but there are some observations that help this attempt to find out what happens. As we have observed, the fact that it becomes banal blunts its communicative strength. Such terms seem—just *seem*, because it is part of hallucinosis—to acquire a life of their own. People deal with them as if they were entities. Words belong *in part* to the material world—they flow through wave movements in the earth—and are, to a certain extent, materially concrete: they can be sensed and captured by devices such as microphones, amplifiers and loudspeakers. But such amplifying modes cannot turn them into living entities outside the human realm. Audibility cannot be confused with livability. All of this has profound mechanisms, dealt with in other chapters and illuminated by Freud, Klein and Bion: the ever-present human capacity to hallucinate all the time. Regarding words as "living entities", like Frankenstein's monster, confers on the words some anthropomorphic features, and the words seem to the onlooker to acquire a life of their own. This occurrence was dealt with in many ways, especially after the inception of cinema, but first by theatre, where gifted authors intuitively used the audience's ability to hallucinate in order to create a special environment to construe the drama. Some people—including actors—mistook the farce and acquired in hallucination the character's ... character. As far as our term "free associations" is concerned, its banal and widespread use debased its meaning, moving it further from its original German root. The root of *unbewußt* (unknown) is *wissen*, which means "to know": for example, in *Wissenchaft*, "science", which means looking for, and becoming aware of, knowledge. The Latin languages, from which part of the English language derives, indicate a common root for the word "science" (*scienza* in Italian, *ciência* in Portuguese, *science* in French). Therefore, this chapter will use a dual-track method of study: the original German term and clinical experience to know something about the term "free associations". After all, Freud used the German language as one of his means (or tools) to discover psychoanalysis, so this choice cannot be too far wrong. We have some other evidence to justify this choice; if the above quoted seems not to do so, more was published elsewhere (Sandler, 2000b). Its inclusion would lengthen the present text excessively as well as just being a diversion.

Psychoanalysis and free associations

Freud established some parameters to tell whether or not a given activity is psychoanalysis. We will focus one of those parameters, which seems to express the scientific-poetic function of the mind, and shares (with the dream work and processes) the nature of the unconscious: free associations. Another necessary parameter was the need for the personal experience of undergoing an analysis. In fact, this is a *sine qua non* in order to get a hint about concepts and conceptions in analysis.

There is no substitute for the experience of personal analysis to furnish illumination (but not explanation) in order to achieve growing knowledge of what "free associations" are all about. The knowledge is the same as that of skills in life: they are grasped instantaneously but may take time to acquire—for example, a child who sees adults walking but still cannot do the same. Like analysis, it has kinships with scientific and artistic skills. Without this experience, one falls into "flights of fantasy" disguised as rational explanations. On the other hand, there is still a hope that written texts may help those who have experience in analysis to make verbal constructs that help to make things more explicit. If it is true that the German language is more adapted to expressing emotional experiences, resorting to it in a free associative way is another aid to getting nearer to the experience and further from just talking about it.

The principle of psychic determinism

It does not seem feasible, at least me, to talk about "free associations", Freud's fundamental method in psychoanalysis, while disregarding the principle of psychic determinism. Together with the need for clinical experience, there are some difficulties in grasping the *ethos* of "free associations" that seem to lie in considering this principle. Alas, clinical experience is not amenable to being acquired from a written text like this one.

The work of James and Alix Strachey and Joan Riviere made a formidable attempt to transport psychoanalytic concepts into the English language. The generosity of their "public service" can be compared to the magnitude of contempt and doubtful criticisms to which it has been subjected in later years.[5] Melanie Klein's observations about innate or environment-induced and cultured, self-feeding cycles of envy and greed towards the feeding breast may help to understand those attacks—including the commercial interests of publishing enterprises. Some exceptions confirm the rule, as exemplified by the attempts of Dr Ilse Grubrich-Simitis, a recipient of the Goethe Prize. Perhaps a useful way to acknowledge Strachey's contribution is to quote his careful, synthetic and lucid introductions, such as the one about psychic determinism:

> There was another fundamental belief of Freud's which could be convincingly supported by the examination of parapraxes—his belief in the universal application of determinism to mental events. This is the truth which he insists upon in the final chapter of this book: it should be possible in theory to discover the psychical determinants of every smallest detail of the processes of the mind. [1960, p. xiii]

This constitutes the practical, rather than theoretical, rule of anything in psychoanalysis. In nature and science anything has a function; like them, the determinants of psychic determinism have as their bases beauty, simplicity and function.

Provided that the patient has no serious neurological decay, nothing that he or she utters in a session lacks function. It can be detected and then submitted to reflection and communication. No warranty that such a task is wholly possible and total can be implied. Nature has an immense quantity of fact whose function is hitherto unknown. Human ignorance about specific functions of Nature does not serve as evidence of their non-existence; conversely, they may be used to stimulate scientific or artistic research and creation.

As soon as it was discovered, the principle of psychic determinism became a target of misconceptions and distortions, in a manner that can be likened to Einstein's principle of relativity. One of these misconceptions is to affiliate it to positivism, after a concretised, hasty and superficial apprehension of the concept (Sandler, 1997). The principle of psychic determinism assumes importance to the extent that its determinants are unconscious. Therefore, they have no causality included; the determinants are conveyors, or pointers to the unconscious processes of mind; they are modes of access to the unconscious processes in the same way that dreams are; and they serve as proofs of their existence. One knows that Freud nourished interest in proving the existence of the immaterial facts of mind to the positivistic scientific establishment (Freud, 1901, p. 239).

There is a need to emphasise this point: there is no "unitarian", "univocal" causality involved in the concept. The term "pointer" is used in dog breeding for those specimens specialised in pointing where the hunted animal flies, hides or otherwise is.

The *purposive ideas*, a basic foundation of the whole of psychoanalysis, have aleatory origin and are naturally selected in the unconscious. After having been formulated, they are endowed with the unconscious goals and pursue them in their developments. These developments are hinted on the surface of the phenomenal facts. These phenomenal facts manifest themselves both in real life and in a psychoanalytic session—which is a representative sample of real life. They contain embedded information about the original goals, even though they are usually presented in a fragmentary form. Bion's theory of transformations and invariants helps here: the "unconscious goal" suggests a given invariant; the "surface phenomenal facts" are the transformations around the invariant. They correspond to that goal and not to anything else. In this sense there is "determinism"; the idea is determined by its unconscious goal. Freud's conception of psychic determinism is an attempt at the possibility of making scientific assessments about something real: to see facts as they are, beyond their chaotic and fragmentary presentation, and beyond their pseudo-rational presentation.

In Freud's time, there was an interest in the "association experiment", an attempt to formulate an experiment in a scientific form that could elicit free associations, introduced by Eugen Bleuler, Carl Jung and Franz Riklin, starting from Freud's observation. They construed a pattern of terms and then asked the patient to associate something to them.

> I demonstrated that a whole number of actions which were held to be unmotivated are on the contrary strictly determined, and to that extent I contributed towards restricting the arbitrary factor in psychology. I took as examples slight failures of memory, slips of the tongue or pen, and the mislaying of objects ... small actions which are performed apparently by chance ... revealed ... as "symptomatic actions" linked with a hidden meaning and intended to give unobtrusive expression to it ... Once one has accustomed oneself to this view of determinism in psychical life, one is justified in inferring from the findings in the psychopathology of everyday life that the ideas which occur to the subject in an association experiment may not be arbitrary either, but determined by an ideational content that is operative in him. [Freud, 1906, pp. 104, 105]

Freud observed that it was possible for the analyst to stay in constant contact with psychic reality through searching for its manifestations. He calls "arbitrary" that which today makes for the relativist and idealist defence of a little learned theory of chaos. It is the hallmark of hermeneutics and post-modernism. In this tendency, a free-for-all, or *laissez faire* interpretive action prevails. One may discern a "postmodernistic chaos" and mathematical chaos: the former harbours arbitrariness; the latter has an underlying, mathematically calculable, hidden order. The former abhors probability; the latter characterises it. The functioning of the mind and the mind as it functions, that is, as it goes on functioning. Things happen as they happen in any probabilistic event: if, and when, and where a real fact did occur, this fact may be experienced, observed and, at least in part, evidenced; after having occurred, it is wholly determined, quite independent of its undetermined origin.

As soon as the dice are thrown and a given number is obtained, its undetermined nature ceases to exist. Freud's psychic determinism means *the mind exists*. There is no reference to causes. Even if the term "arbitrary" may open a flank to strictly linguistic interpretation recalling probability, it involves causality.

> I cherished a high opinion of the strictness with which mental processes are determined, and I found it impossible to believe that an idea produced by a patient while his attention was on the stretch

could be an arbitrary one and unrelated to the idea we were in search of. [Freud, 1910a, p. 29]

As you already see, psychoanalysts are marked by a particularly strict belief in the determination of mental life. For them there is nothing trivial, nothing arbitrary or haphazard. They expect in every case to find sufficient motives where, as a rule, no such expectation is raised. Indeed, they are prepared to find *several* motives for one and the same mental occurrence, whereas what seems to be our innate craving for causality declares itself satisfied with a *single* psychical cause. [*ibid.*, p. 38; Freud's emphasis]

Among so many texts one may quote from Freud, in this one too a serious objection can be raised against those who see "positivism" in Freud—who does not talk about *causes*, but about *motives*, which have the meaning of factors and functions. On causes, he observes an *innate craving*, which can be seen in his other texts as a religious belief, the climax of solace before the basic state of human helplessness. There is an anxious, non-analytic (or anti-analytic) satisfaction in *finding* isolated causes. Among his steps beyond positivism, Freud seems to be one of the first to pinpoint what would later be called "multifactorial analysis", now a common method of research in mathematics and medicine alike. This also has to do with scholars who pose as idolaters but are actually iconoclasts who deprecate Freud and label him a positivist (for example, Fulgencio, 2000). It is no coincidence that the same scholars regard Freud as the initiator of the dubious activity of post-mortem psychoanalysis, that is, the analysis of people long dead. A non-hermeneutic reading of Freud's psychoanalytic exercise about the life of Leonardo da Vinci, or Woodrow Wilson, may enable the reader who has some training in—rather than simply information about—psychoanalysis to regard those works in the same way that a musician regards the practising of scales. Leonardo's life helped Freud to construe psychoanalytic hypotheses, rather than theses: "We are left, then, with these two characteristics of Leonardo which are *inexplicable* by the efforts of psychoanalysis: his quite special tendency towards instinctual repressions, and his extraordinary capacity for sublimating the primitive instincts" (Freud, 1910b, p. 136; my emphasis). The idolater-iconoclast reader misread the whole paper about Leonardo as "explicable". Psychoanalytic texts, in my experience over more than thirty-eight years as a teacher and conductor of seminars, show that the mental processes initially described in dream work and later as the ego's defence mechanisms—namely, repression, reaction formation, transformation to the opposite and denial—are much more common in readings than is often noticed.

Freud outlined in this text a fact later expressed in more precise terms by Bion: the *same* mental happening admits *several motives*. Freud knew precisely the notion of the tandem movement between Contingency and Necessity,[6] in what he called the "complemental series" and the "aetiological equation", that is, the description of factors which converge to fulfil aetiological requirements. This permeated the whole of his work, from the early drafts on Hysteria up to the study on Moses and Monotheism: for example, Freud, 1895, p. 149fn; 1939, p. 73; also the two later introductory lectures from 1916–17 and 1933–36). To extract only a few quotes may do injustice to his insights. Taking into account that this is not an exhaustive review, so let us try just to illustrate the issue:

> The apportioning of the determining factors of our life between the "necessities" of our constitution and the "chances" of our childhood may still be uncertain in detail; but in general it is no longer possible to doubt the importance precisely of the first years of our childhood. [Freud, 1910b, p. 137]

> What occurs to the dreamer in response to the dream-element will be determined by the psychical background (unknown to us) of that particular element. [Freud, 1916, p. 109]

The determinism is not a *cause* in the unconscious, as an isolable fact compounding it (which would make it extricable from the unconscious), but rather an event *due to* the nature of the unconscious. In other words: not a cause *in*, but *by* the unconscious. It is intrinsic rather than extrinsic; its vector starts from the unconscious and goes to dreams, symptoms, phenomenal manifestations, etc. Immediate questions arise: what determines the unconscious? Freud's observations isolate the instincts and repression of them. Again, what determines them? The eternal struggle between the two principles of mental functioning: pleasure/displeasure and reality. Also, in a simultaneous mode, the instincts are biologically determined, rooted in the survival of the species. In other words, determinism is easily found in the psychic life. Before they were determined, all was chaos and probability (chance). From the moment they arose by unconscious, unknown and unknowable choice—that is, as soon as the human species emerged, there follows a determinism of functions. The same example can be seen with quantum particles: as soon as energy is liberated, quantum mechanics determines what and how this energy is. Therefore one may discern two kinds of determinism (Sandler, 1997). The first is *Determinism of Causes*, linked to illusions, hallucinations and delusion; it is also linked to the illusory concept of time independent of space (see Part I on the multi-dimension Grid). The second is *Determinism of Functions*, which are real and have the concept of functions as their *raison d'être*. The concept of function is better studied by mathematics, physics and biology; Freud brought it to psychoanalysis and Bion (1962) unearthed it.

Psychic determinism seems to belong to the latter type. Therefore, a further question imposes itself: what is the function of psychic determinism? It has a nature-linked function, in the sense of a creative action; like nature, it seems to be turned to perpetuating itself. The creative action of psychic determinism can be represented as a cycle:

... indeterminism ⇨ determinism ⇨ indeterminism ⇨ determinism ⇨ indeterminism ...

The creative product of psychic determinism is free associations.

Freud's psychic determinism brings with it the germ of a renewed indeterminism, to the extent that free associations in a session of analysis are always a trip into the unknown; free associations are our ultimate working tool. Probability is a natural fact in both the human and animal (animate) and the inhuman (inanimate, not alive) realms. Probability was perceived, apprehended, studied and used by mathematics, constituting a remarkable and important (in terms of further creative development) discovery of this discipline. It was soon adopted as a formidable means of knowledge in other fields such as genetics, physics, economics and technological sciences. Jacques Monod's genetics uses it; and probability happens to be in the individual mind's functioning. Natural selection can be found in the individual mind; through the term "Intuition", Natural Selection enables realisation of something that was named in a cloudy way which could serve as indicative of its presence, such as Leibniz's "monads", Descartes's "corpuscles" and Locke's "percepts". As occurs in the universe as well as in life above Earth, those "units" (which could be called "thinkers") will survive to the extent that they prove to be adapted to reality *as it is*.

The powerful armoury and high tonnage in muscle and bone of dinosaurs at first proved useful to the point of making those living entities dominant on the face of the Earth. But their greatest advantage became their worst disadvantage. What determined this was a probabilistic, indeterminate, unexpected, sudden natural fact—as natural as was the millions of years of development of those reptiles. First the former advantage proved to be wasteful. Then it proved to be self-murderous. External reality, as it was, changed. Polar ice melted: the origins of this are still the subject of discussion and do not matter now. What matters is that the origin was itself probabilistic. The renewed reality became incompatible with the former reality as well as with the internal—genetic—reality of the dinosaurs.

At that time there were some extremely small creatures that could be viewed by the dinosaurs—if the dinosaurs had a mind—in the same way that we regard harmless worms. Today they are regarded as the ancestors of primitive hominids, whose existence, again, was due to probability. When polar ice melted, they were destined to be the fittest to survive. Some centuries later, the heirs of the primitive hominids construed a theory that saw what had happened as a deluge.

The same kind of probability that determined—after its occurrence—the survival of the fittest carries on occurring in human minds. There is no scale of time devised to measure this occurrence in each human mind; an instrument graduated in milliseconds would be hopelessly weak, as if one wished to measure an ant, which demands a rule graduated in inches, with a device graduated in miles. Perhaps free associations (understood as a cycle, to and from, a tandem movement between determinism and indeterminism) occur in quantum time, or perhaps infra-quantum, perhaps impossible to measure, if one considers the progress in neuro-transmitters.

Survival of the fittest refers not to "strongest", a distortion which was abhorred in theoretical terms, as in Gumplowicz's "social Darwinism", which emphasised the sensuous-concrete aspect (material reality), implying a denial of the psychic aspect of reality.[7] Fittest means truthful or approximating to truth. Anything that was devised or fabricated by our mind, engineered by our rational powers, hides irrational powers that underlie what is thought of as rational, in the same proportion, but pass unnoticed, enhancing their effects. Hume observed that logic is psychologically necessary: in other words, reason (here understood as the exercise of human rational power) is demanded by the psyche to justify (explain, convince, advocate) its actions and pleasurable interests. Conversely, there are thoughts created by a kind of imposition by reality and truth over our mind (and in this sense not engendered by it) and nourished by pleasure and desire. They are created in their form, but are not creations in their link to truth, which happens whether we desire it or not.

Truth is understood here in the sense of containing both love and hate (Bion's sense of truth):[8] attempts to approach reality with forbearance and the patience for trial and error, intuition and respect for oneself, and personal smallness and fallibility. Free associations are possible under the constant conjunction of these factors, and this allows us to intuit what is useful at that specific moment.

Free associations, becoming, being at-one with oneself

I suggested[9] that any analyst's basic posture should include an ability to tolerate paradoxes with no hasty attempts to find a resolution. "Free association" is the name chosen by the first translators who produced the *Standard Edition*, James and Alix Strachey and Joan Riviere, with Freud's approval, which respects this tolerance. To be "free" and to be an "association" entails a paradox so obvious that, like all obvious events, it is usually not noticed. The "transcreation" (a term coined by Haroldo de Campos) from *freier Einfall* respectfully conserves the *ethos* of the German term. In other words, it refers to an action which is simultaneously *free from* and also *associated to* something. At one and the same time it is free and it is linked. The free associative processes tell us the same history told by married (or sexual) couples. The two members of a sexual couple are free to be themselves, and at the same time they are associated (linked) with no loss of their individuality. The Ancient Greeks' "combined figure" when the "supreme creative act" (Klein), or procreation, is occurring is brief, much like a Higgs boson, and results in a third, soon-to-be-free individual person. The mind's evolving free associations bring in themselves an individual's paradoxical state of "being and becoming", or immanence and transcendence. Nevertheless, like any translation into a foreign language, it falls short of fully conveying the meaning of the original. Freud was aware of this; out of what could be seen as arrogant prejudice, he was fond of the English language and the achievements of British culture. In his earliest lectures on psychoanalysis, given to the American public in 1909, he resorted to paraphrases in order to avoid the pitfalls involved in available translations:

> The German word here is *Einfall*, which is often translated "association"; but the latter is a question-begging word and is avoided here as far as possible, even at the price of such long paraphrases as the present one. When, however, we come to *freier Einfall*, "free association" (though still objectionable) is hardly to be escaped. [Freud, 1910a, p. 29]

One of many possibilities to gain awareness about the meaning of the German term is to be reminded that free associative activity constantly conjoins mind and imagery. Freud was at first perplexed about the possibility of the mind's ability to form images, and this is a remarkable motive for his study of dreams. After his initial puzzlement, he turned the issue to a good account, especially when he described some factors in it, abandoning pretences to explain it. Freud called this image formation "regression", a verbal expression and definition almost forgotten today. This compact formulation of thinking was published in item B, chapter VII of *The Interpretation of Dreams* (1900).

We need some definitions to distinguish free association from verbal turbulence. Clinical practice allows for the observation of two types of social interchange of words: senseless verbal turbulence and meaningless verbal turbulence. Both have as their main feature rationalisation in the thinking processes. Both are driven by the pleasure/displeasure principle. Both result in the spending of many years—sometimes decades—in the activity of maniacal or sub-maniacal "word production", mostly talkative and imbued with either undirected (senseless verbal turbulence) or directed (meaningless verbal turbulence) *ad hoc* meanings. No analysis can ensue from these juxtaposed individual minds, even though social "friendships" with business-like interests may. The "senseless verbal turbulence" always has logical thinking behind it; it is easily done, and obeys the principle of "saying what one has in one's mind", or "saying what one thinks". Disguised as sincerity, it corresponds to a lack of sphincter education. Many patients—and, alas, colluding analysts with no sight of that which goes under the heading of manifest content—praise manifestations typical of the pleasure/displeasure principle, full of denied and split narcissism, and fuel situations regarded as "containment" and "good enough mothering".

Despite the exaggerations of "Bionians" and "Winnicottians" (a special reading utterly different from what Bion and Winnicott wrote), these travestied forms of containment and good enough mothering lack the basic compound of the real thing: frustration and eventually some pain felt. The underlying real situation indicates mutual seduction, which has a sexually pleasurable intent and foundation. Other factors may complicate the situation: filling a workday schedule, whose real motivation could be the need for survival, is contaminated by vanity or similar traits of the professional, who favours mutual eulogy. Sometimes, a psychopath enters into the flow; also, difficulties in discerning latent contents. In the end, the idea is that anything that comes into the patient's head means, *a priori*, free associations. But the prevalence of the pleasure/displeasure principle provokes enslaved, not-free disassociations; they are clung to and amalgamated with desire.

Klein observed phenomena which, for the want of an available name, she called projective identification. It is a mental hallucination that frees the mind from itself, extinguishing the self-*arbitrium*, or personal responsibility for a mind of one's own; it empowers the mind's unconscious phantasy of being able to expel mind itself. This observation illuminated the fact that undisciplined and disordered ejections of words—to which Bion added the observation that speech fulfils the function which could be expected from a missile, or cannot be discerned from flatus—differ from free associations.

Free associations, as Strachey said, are something related to the designated issue, that is, determined (Strachey, 1955). Free association emerges from the unknown, and as regards its form, it is initially undetermined. Bion's observational theory about transformations helps here to detect more precisely where indetermination and determination reside.

An experienced psychoanalyst from earlier times, Dr Frieda Fromm-Reichmann, received analysis from Sigmund Freud but had to migrate to the United States, where she later worked with Dr Harry Stack Sullivan in the famous William Alanson White Institute. She dedicated herself to treating people diagnosed as schizophrenics; and emphasised formally the avoidance of Bleuler's and Jung's "associative experiment" with those patients. According to Dr Fromm-Reichmann, the material issued allowed no interpretation at best. At worst, the experiment could be lead to a psychotic crisis. In my view, Dr Fromm-Reichmann had her particular way of seeing that she was not dealing with genuine free associations. Instead, she was witnessing a stimulus to hallucination and delusion, where anything unreal is possible, with no links, not even small ones, to reality. Scrutiny of free associations allows discrimination if the analyst's free-floating attention dispenses with countertransference, collusion or flights of fantasy. Countertransference can be detected and dealt with in the analyst's personal analysis.

Life and free associations

What we usually call "Life" can be regarded as the real, albeit immaterial counterpart of "survival", which in its turn is the predominantly sensuous-concrete counterpart of "Life". That is, both are the same existence, albeit in different forms. Human limits to perception and apprehension (or approximations to "O", coupled with added obstacles such as the features and functions of speech) preclude an accurate enough statement about what this "same existence" is, other than stating that it is the same and possesses an existence.

Lack of maturity has consequences in that which we call life; something so obvious that it should not merit such a statement. It is debatable whether this lack occurs in some people or classes of people, except when one has the opportunity to study individual cases. From this observational vantage point, lack of maturity may mean lack of coupling between mental and physical death; as Bion noticed (in *A Memoir of the Future*), there are people who cannot wait until physical death comes and decree their own mental death before. Fanaticism and slavery to any establishment usually indicate this almost mindless situation even if physical survival continues. This kind of maturation is seen in analysis. From this vertex and conditions of observation, mental maturation can be put in the following terms:

Firstly, it means that some degree of apprehension and coping with the limits to one's omnipotence, greed and envy may be conducive to the apprehension of the depressive position and its attendant emotions, which includes a renewed dive or paradoxical return to the paranoid-schizoid positions; the cycle continues, as long as physical survival lasts. Secondly, it means facing the unknown—a "renewed newness"—getting in touch with both day and night dream work (Freud, 1900; Bion, 1959a, b, c, pp. 44; 50–59; 63), which means an unconscious self-knowledge, the sufficient enough bridge to reality as it is. This "unknown" in real life assumes both infinite and definite forms, limited just by each person's needs and opportunities. For example, seeing a friend again or making new friends; waking up and beginning a new day; sleeping.

Schopenhauer and Nietzsche named—with the awfully poor restrictions on any naming—the "libertarian force" that gives *élan* to the mystery of life *Wille*; Freud called it *Trieb*, an instinctual life and death movement. Darwin apprehended its presence in all living species. It resides in spermatozoa and ova. Another transformed counterpart of it is present in the ineffable and incalculable energy concentrated in Hawking's and Penrose's black holes, as well as in each conversation between patients and analysts. Which has only one difference in its purpose—and consequently, in its function—*vis-à-vis* any conversation between two people: it is a scrutinised conversation, with a constant gauging from unconscious to conscious and back, primarily and predominantly at the service of one of those two people, the patient. Briefly: both members of the analytic couple exert and freely associate their feminine intuition and masculine potency to "choose" under the "libertarian force" a renewed free association. The term "renewed" seeks to be precise; it is both "new" (in form, being transformed) and "not new" (in carrying a mental transcendence until it is there; or invariant).

Let us return to Darwin's evolution of species. Originally having a biological investigation and method, it gained a transdisciplinary reach, having focused and described something real and valid for many other disciplines and levels of observation. It is true for mental functioning as described by Freud, as well as for the ontogenetic mental development of children. Under the psychoanalytic vertex, Darwin's survival of the fittest applies to those who can cope with desire and tolerate frustration, being able to face up to the principle of reality.

Also included in Darwin's description is a kind of historicity which can be called a "moving process" that carries on unfolding unless mindlessness or physical death ensues—as life goes on. To catch a free association, one enables or switches on something that can be, for the want of a better name, one's "internal artist". In other words, one switches on one's own artistic function that exists (albeit to different degrees) in any human being. The "catching" happens when one gives up one's soothing belief in what is already known, what has already occurred, what is already placed. The giving up refers to the belief; one cannot give up what is already known, for one cannot abandon that which does not exist. Under the aegis of the pleasure principle, one longs for the future and only the future, always "planning" non-frustrating projects. Conversely, the principle of reality imposes itself, sooner or later, to show that things are as they are. They can be apprehended up to a point, and if this apprehension is good enough, things and no-things are amenable to be used and thought, albeit unconsciously.

In the first situation, anything that can happen will happen, albeit transformed or even distorted. This statement can be seen as belief in destiny, such as occurs in religious thinking. But "can happen" just indicates a state of possibility, ruled by the laws of probability. Freud emphasised one of his achievements from Charcot, the possibility of waiting until a pattern could obtrude and be observed. Are free associations a most fundamental principle of human thought and therefore of mental functioning? Perhaps it was not a coincidence that they were advanced and possibly discovered years before the other two principles of mental functioning, the principle of pleasure and displeasure and the principle of reality. They are encompassed by the later principles, but Freud never changed his ideas about the "fundamental rule", the principle of psychic determinism.

The second situation is that, paradoxically, anything that may happen may also not happen—not ever. This paradox differentiates this situation from destiny.

When we talk about "natural selection", "$E = mc^2$", "black holes", concerning observations about life on Earth and about the great universe, and when we talk about "unconscious", "free association", "unconscious phantasy", "paranoid-schizoid and depressive position", concerning psychic reality, we use descriptions endowed with a synthetic nature that accounts for the complexity of the fact described. To construe those formulations, a work of geniuses (at least, geniuses in verbal formatting), a compacting action occurs.

The compacting feature of scientific communication that conveys its counterpart in reality at a glance to a trained audience is acknowledged in mathematics. Analysis deals with it in its everyday practice. Psychoanalytic constructions must be delivered in concise, terse and brief packages, spoken in a custom-tailored language that proves to be adequate for each individual patient. Understanding is called to the language used in interpretation (or construction) but not to interpretation itself; that must be apprehended through insight, which is partially unconscious. Free associations, *freie Einfälle*, do this compacting work, synthesising that which flows from the unconscious. Without free associations, the flow would be chaotic and disconnected, or, worse, connected by formal logic, which masks and makes more difficult the detection of chaos. The non-chaotic presentation keeps the chaos continuing unchecked. This always will depend on the analyst's analytic capacity and intuition, which can be developed. Some analysts hurriedly conclude that the patient cannot issue free associations, which is not true and leads to the judging mistake (easily made by those who fall victim to phantasies of superiority) of "non-analysability". Even a liar cannot be put into this category; his analysis will be restricted to the pointing out of his lies. Usually liars cannot undergo the suffering of analysis without resorting to a destructive, violent outcome, resolving between suicide and homicide. Free associations in these cases demand to be found elsewhere, including the careful conjoined scrutiny of non-verbal communication. In this case, patients struggle to furnish logical reports, or focus on a given issue that they feel would be "important for a psychoanalysis", or "important to the psychoanalyst".

Another variant of this state of affairs is to stay around a seductive explaining issue, with utterances like "My analyst said this and that about this and that", or "I have been working with this issue since the last session (or month or year)", and so on. Feigning collaboration, they feed collusion and display hate for the unknown, psychic reality, creativity. In short, they hate their free associative capacity. Bion puts the issue synthetically: "Thus far and no further" (*A Memoir of the Future*, vol. I; please see Volume 2 Part III).

Collusion from the analyst with this kind of talk indicates desire for involvement in logical networks, a condition akin to anti-platonic philosophy. Collusion precludes the development of free associations; psychoanalytically, it also means shared hallucinosis.

In this sense I proposed two concepts to encircle the analytic posture and the creation of a fertile soil for free associations under the responsibility of the analyst. These terms describe the same thing that Freud called "neutrality" and Bion called discipline of memory, desire and understanding. In any human individual, every attempt to approach truth is accompanied by its obverse, that is, an attempt to move away from truth. A groups being the sum of many individuals, the acts of groups multiply the acts of individuals—sometimes elevating them to a logarithmic scale. Therefore, as far as the history of ideas in Western civilisation goes, there are episodes when the pursuit of "truth-O" (Bion, 1970, p. 9) is successful, only to be followed by the contrary movement, equally successful. There are many indications suggesting that this group's "to-and-fro" cycle follows the movement between the Positions, PS⇔D, as described by Klein in the individual mind. Therefore, the surge which characterises the free movement between the Positions can be seen as a tendency to establish "understanding", the hallmark of the K link (Bion, 1962). When there is a freezing in one position or the other, hampering or precluding free movement, there is a tendency to misundestanding, or being under the aegis of the minus K link (see Part I of Volume 2 in this series, the Realm of Minus). If we focus our study on the fate of Freud's observations, the achievements of his contributions in approaching truth are being subjected to continuous misunderstanding. A very common one is the attempt to mix or degrade Freud's theories with the positivist religion as exposed by Auguste Comte.

My first concept, probably already known to the reader who has had the patience to carry on reading into the third volume, is the ability to cope with paradoxes without any hasty efforts to resolve them. The second is the analyst's "propitiator-propitiatory" posture: an amiable, collaborating effort to furnish the minimal conditions for analysis. Definite transdisciplinary analogies can be seen between, on the one hand, Bion's conception of "reverie", Harold Searles's "facilitating environment" (1960) and Winnicott's "good enough mothering" in analysis; and, on the other hand, the efforts of physicists to construct particle accelerators such as the Large Hadron Collider at CERN in Geneva, with their cold neutron depth capture that profiles impurities of subatomic particles. Perhaps future researchers into the human mind will take into consideration progress in quantum physics (Penrose, 1994; an informative text dedicated specifically to psychoanalysts can be found in Sandler, 1997).

If and when—these are fleeting moments, like a flash of lightning which reveals everything for an instant, as Poincaré poetically pointed out—the psychoanalyst tolerates the anxiety of not hastily attributing abrupt meanings, enslaved by the sense and meaning imposed by the patient's consciousness, helped by his or her own *a priori* and *ad hoc* patterns, he or she will see that something transpires from the unknown. It was underlying, buried archaeologically, as Freud intuited very early about the unconscious.

Still resorting to analogies with modern physics, a scientific discipline whose discoveries were contemporaneous with psychoanalysis—even if without mutual recognition and collaborative development—the many possible ways (transformations) manifested by the verbal reports issued by patients during their analytic sessions, some disconnected matters and issues, seemingly weird and inviting us to discard them as soon as they appear, repose over stable "phase space".[10] Usually they are prone to present themselves in a compulsion to repetition; many times they indicate some real fragments of that specific person, shareable with no other entity, such as fingerprints. In this atmosphere, which can be seen as rarefied, the analytic couple makes close contact with a "non-linear dynamics", which behaves, in a swift and overly fugacious instant, as a regular cycle, before falling into a probabilistic chaos. This situation can be seen in a cross-level or cross-disciplinary way, observed in the great universe through quantum physics, and in mental functioning through psychoanalysis. Melanie Klein (and Bion's notation of her description) marked it under the name of the tandem movement PS⇔D. Klein discovered this in 1946, after twenty years of psychoanalytic research; physics could come to it, after fifty years of relativistic and quantum physics analysis, during the 1980s. Freud furnished its forerunner with his observations (still subjected to misunderstanding and pseudo-controversies) under the names life and death instincts.

The dimensionless networks where fugacious multi-dimensional free associations sprout during an analytic session are safe havens from rational logic (as seen in the formal logic of Euclid, St Thomas Aquinas and Descartes), from the spatial locations that facilitate belief in cause-and-effect, predictive relationships, as well as from the split between mind and matter that profoundly marked the time before Darwin and modern genetics, before psychoanalysis and before relativistic and quantum physics and chemistry. A safe rule of thumb guideline could be: the more we feel that the communication issued by the patient is formally logical, the further we are from the unconscious. The term "feel" attempts to be precise; it must be distinguished from "being real". Conversely, the more the communication embodies the free associative germ, the closer we are to the unconscious.

Abhorrence of free associations

Fear of free association is equivalent to a phobia, as Green observed in the analysis of a young man. He proposed a "phobic position" underlying the definition of free associations. Leaving aside the attribution of a "position" (which may or may not be likened to Klein's definition of the Mental Positions and would require a specific discussion to clarify), it can be understood that his proposition is of a negative or minus—"phobic"—antithesis to the positive thesis "free associations". Its coherence with the minus or negative field is elicited by him in the same paper (Green, 2000) and in later developments, which put it into that very setting (*cadre*; Green, 2002). The phobic position may well be a particular case of abhorrence of the unknown, or resistance to the *Unbewußt*.[11]

Unauthorised incursions in the German language

Ein, as a single term, may mean "in", "into", and "piercing", as well as "one", an arithmetic connotation. *Fallen* may mean "to fall" (as in English), and it may also indicate a kind of living irruption. A pictorial image—under the clinical vertex—would be "fall" as that time of year when leaves fall naturally from their originating trees.

Freud pointed out early on the to and fro flux between unconscious and conscious. Bion revived the conception, already used by Freud, of a "contact barrier" between the two systems. Something "falls" from the unconscious to the conscious, *in a probabilistic mode*; "*ein*" endows it with a unique and single form, for it is this association and not any other which has acquired a still probabilistic-guided form in the conscious, in order to be thought, communicated and—hopefully—forgotten. Its German double-word expression furnishes in a straight way the associative sense (vertex, like a vector, rather than meaning) "the (single) falling one". The determinism refers to the link of an image or its representing image ("word representation", after Freud) in the unconscious system. It is the only one possible in that fleeting instant. Probability occurs in the form rather than in the content, or probability makes its previous action in transformations, in the immanence, rather than in the real transcendence, or invariance, or in the numinous realm of the unconscious (not-known, *unbewußt*). The laws of probability exert a function analogous to *bricolage*, the anthropological formulation of Lévi-Strauss (1962).

Clinical experience helps us to realise that the sense of the term "association" is not restricted to thoughts associated to other thoughts in a logical manner. If logic prevails, it already belongs to the individual strata and merits interpretation, associated with other observations.

In the German language, logical thinking[12] is better indicated by the use of terms such as *Assoziation*.

Clinical experience in real analysis furnishes the intuition needed to apprehend the dream-like nature of free associations. The association occurs first as an unconscious act and again when a free (or as free as possible) movement occurs between unconscious and conscious and back, through the contact barrier.[13] The word *Einfall* attempts to describe both an unconscious principle and functioning and also a function of consciousness, bridged by a fleeting and incomplete awareness that serves just to utter the free association. As with the dreamer who cannot know his dream but can utter its manifest contents, the freely associating person cannot know what the sense of the association is, but can utter its analogy of the manifest content—unwittingly, because when it is uttered, it is already returning to the unconscious. Consciousness is here understood (as it must be understood in any psychoanalytic text) as corresponding to Freud's hypothesis: the sense organ to apprehend psychic quality (chapter VII, items C, D and F, *The Interpretation of Dreams*).

The issue of free association cannot be studied using a philosophical, semantic, linguistic, literary criticism, literary or even alphabetical vertex. As Bion warned in *Transformations*, alphabetised transformations cannot serve. They provide explanations, logical, rational understanding of the associative connections which come from the observer's imagination or previous formulation applied over the many words and phrases issued and emitted by the patient—but not from the facts. As mentioned above, the German term that better describes those self-feeding flights of imagination and rational intelligence is *Assoziation*. The source of free association, *freier Einfall*, the *primus inter pares* concept in psychoanalysis, the fundamental rule of psychic functioning, is the psychoanalytic clinical experience.

Here and now

Free associations are not discursive or speech associations. They are a living and lived association in the here and now of the session; they are a kind of unconscious emanation experienced once and no more in the analytic "third ear" (Reik, 1948), occurring intuitively in the ultra- and infra-sensuous realm or whatever it may be, outside the senses but depending on them as a port of entry.

Analytic function was always emphasised by Freud, as regards the environment that allows the patient to have their *freie Einfälle* as well as the imperious need to interpret (or construe around) them—this is a condition of their carrying on. This point was made crystal clear in his post-1937 papers, especially in "Constructions in Analysis". Free associations come forward as a scientific judge of the validity of analysis, as its proof or refutation, later described (albeit in incomplete form) by Lakatos[14] in the field of philosophy of science. Like life, they belong to a fragile and rare species and require a safe haven to be kept alive.

Attention to minute and unnoticed details, Necessity and Possibility (Volume 2, p. 136) seem to be factors in keeping them going. Experience shows that if the analyst converses with the patient in such a way that both are unwittingly paying intense attention to nothing in particular—as Parthenope Bion Talamo once said—this special, non-social conversation and talk flows almost unencumbered—to the degree that it is possible for both components of the analytic couple. The Patient's free association, thanks to its counterpart in the Analyst, his free-floating attention, flows from the unconscious to the conscious, as well as from what the patient says to himself and to the analyst, and vice versa.

This is a description of the most fundamental tool hitherto known in the psychoanalytic clinic. The two first volumes of this series as well as earlier chapters of this book include attempts to illustrate the use of this tool, but its sense and eventual usefulness are dependent on the analytic experience or intuition, and the benevolence, of the reader.

The continuing use of free associations in Freud's work evolved within the evolution of the psychoanalytic theory in his lifetime; the unconscious nature of it can be seen in its embryonic times, in his "Studies on Hysteria" (1895), in its inception, in "The Interpretation of Dreams" (1900), and continuing in "The Dynamics of Transference" (1912), "Repression" (1915b) and "The Unconscious" (1915c). Unlike some theories (and like others, such as Oedipus and dream interpretation, which proved clinically successful through their reproduction), it resisted the wear imposed by the true testers of pseudo-scientific findings, time and "cultural" space. Free associations appear in the late works of Freud ("Analysis Terminable and Interminable", "An Outline of Psychoanalysis", "Constructions in Analysis"), where they explicitly acquire their function of empirical validation or refutation of the scientific status of the analyst's views. The state of mind of the analytic couple must be kept as free (*frei*) as possible, but at the same time "linked" or "associated" to that which exists in psychic reality, or *is*. *Freie Einfälle* share the same nature of latent content (please see Volume 1).

The German term *Einfall* allows further investigation encircling the sense, or vector of its direction. It is a flux or flow bounded in the thinking person when it can exert its own introspection. Free associations are born from what the person is in reality and contribute to his or her becoming (Bion, 1965). To catch and visualise their sense, whose provenance is given by clinical experience, one may resort to another German term, *Einfühlung*. This term provides the individual realm that is a hallmark of psychoanalysis. It may convey a state described by Bion as being at one with oneself. My own investigation, as far as it could go, shows three authors who used this term, which helps one to apprehend what a free association is all about: Freud and Ferenczi, who used the term *Einfühlung*, and later, Bion, who wrote in English, adjoining, as he usually did in his theoretical contributions, the expansions of Klein regarding the depressive position: "at-onement" (Bion, 1970, 1977; Sandler, 2005). The scientific importance of this concept in analysis, the "fundamental rule of analysis" was proved by the test of time and space.

Verbal formulations and what they cannot reveal

A disclaimer: this chapter does not propose to replace or reform verbal formulations in any language, and has no pretension to judgmental superiority of any kind. Terms which were chosen by their continuous and widespread use, even if they allow criticism, must not be replaced by the whims of individual researchers, by the risks of vanity and confusion. Moreover, some terms recommended on the grounds of precision or even erudition are rejected by common usage resulting from familiarity. Some due or apt criticism may help the apprehension of the counterparts in reality which terms consecrated by their very use pretend to reflect—an unexpected fringe benefit of their imprecision.

As is the case in any free association.

Notes

1. Please see Part III on Epistemology and Truth. The relationship between Plato's ideal forms, the numinous realm and the unconscious as discovered in practical use by Freud was discussed in Sandler, 1997.
2. See Volume 2, Chapter Ten on intelligible beta-elements.
3. Please see Volume 2, Chapter Ten (anti-alpha function) and Part I (the realm of Minus), as well as Part III of this volume (Epistemology and Truth) to dwell on the mentioned habits of thinking, especially the sensuous-concrete syndrome.
4. This is true about this very text—my own native language was Portuguese, even though in my original family home other tongues were spoken and taught in some way.
5. "Transcreate" is a neologism proposed by two brother poets, Augusto and Haroldo de Campos, who also made translations into the Portuguese language. The former wrote a version of Joyce's *Finnegans Wake* and Carroll's *Alice Through the Looking Glass*; the latter wrote a Portuguese version of Genesis, translated from Hebrew, among many other works.
6. Please see Volume 2, Part III.
7. See, for example, Bracher, 1969. One of its offshoots was Nazism; Samuel Huntington's "clash of civilisations" displays its continuous force, in other forms. It aroused many debates and took at least ten years to be realised as truth; discussions on it can be found in *Foreign Affairs*, September 1993 (Palm Coast, Florida).
8. Please see Part III on Epistemology and Truth and Volume 2, Chapter Eight on Binocular Vision.
9. Sandler, 1997, 2001, 2003 and in this work; please see the chapters about the Minus realm (Volume 2, Part I), Truth (Part III of this volume) and Binocular Vision (Volume 2, Part III).
10. The definition of phase space may be found in Part I.
11. André Green's contributions on free associations appeared in Volume 1.
12. If it can be described as thinking in the analytic sense at all, because it corresponds to rationalisation, a psychotic mechanism illuminated by Freud in Schreber's case. It characterises no-thinking.
13. The mechanistically charged associations or encumbered non-associations correspond to what Bion called the beta-screen (Bion, 1962; review in Sandler, 2005).
14. Imre Lakatos died before completing his work. Other researchers before him, such as Rudolf Carnap, attempted to approach the same goal.

CHAPTER SIX

Free-floating attention: the personal factor

ROLAND It doesn't matter it is a man or a woman—the condition for breeding animate objects is the warmth generated by decay. If decay did not betray its presence by its stink, no ovipositor could find a suitable source of warmth.

ROBIN The ovipositor would have to have a nose.

P.A. Certainly; humans find it difficult to recognise and reconcile an evil smell with creative activity, whether it is producing children, blow-flies or ideas. There are both good and bad smells. A cheese can be fermented and that, to me, is unbearable, but the cheese is good. So are durians.

—Bion, 1979, p. 511

Some in the psychoanalytic movement are—unwittingly or not—dazzled by fashion, "the cunning livery of hell" (Shakespeare, *Measure for Measure*, III i). The unavoidable consequence is a casualty: bury the Classics (Bion, 1975, p. 9; Green, 1995, 2000; Sandler, 1997, 2001; reported by Kulish, 2002).

The Classics—who cares? Destined to be one of them, Italo Calvino did care early on (quoted by E. H. Sandler, 2001). Goethe, an early adherent of the Romantic *Sturm und Drang*, saw as a drawback how fashionable it was and soon departed from the movement. He remained highly critical of the Romantics, regarding them as sick. Superficiality is an unavoidable consequence of fashion. Goethe was fated to be a star rather than a comet; he preferred to be labelled a Classic.

Western civilisation revived the Classics, at least from the Renaissance; the revival reached its acme in Enlightenment times and began to decrease after the Romantic Movement. This revival made possible the discovery of psychoanalysis by Freud (Sandler, 1997–2003). More specifically, the later (but not out-of-time) renaissance of the Classics occurred in post-Reformation British and Prussian space-time, with an influx of Eastern (Slavic and Jewish) contributions. The Romantic Movement decayed into Romanticism, detected by Goethe at an early stage, with growing political leanings.[1] It turned against the Classics, in the wake of an irresistible attempt to revolutionise anything that *was*. "Revolution" advertised itself as a creative impetus, proposing new forms. In fact it did not propose, but imposed through going against timeless beauty and truth; not content with modifying immanence according to the moment, it wanted to deny transcendence, and with it the "arrow of time". It did not realise, or in some cases simply denied, that the "arrow of time" (a term borrowed from Eddington, 1933) was, in itself, timeless. Revolution was doomed to perpetuate its own forms, disguised as a "wholly transforming" activity. Its most emblematic example was and still is totalitarianism, sprung from and breeder of murder: the kernel of revolution. Like greed, which today dominates the financial markets, revolution has its psychic motivations (even if not exclusive). As such, those motivations and factors demanded to be put into the unknown, or unconscious, to be allowed to act with no conscious hindrances or obstacles. Awareness of Murder and Violence which equips it, in the end: murder of truth and life, was denied for some centuries. The fall of Nazism and later of Stalinism ended the denial, but not their presence, which continues in other forms. Some outstanding revolutionaries, such as Arnold Schoenberg, had second thoughts—sometimes almost too late—and realised that they had become immersed in a mistake. To "be against" whatever it is can be likened to adolescence: in this case, abhorring the infant idealisation of earlier "renaissance". Revolution pleases the narcissistic personality; followers of it made projective identifications of its own narcissism. The iconoclast has an idol-maker in his heart (please see Volume 2 Part II and Part III of this volume to scrutinise outstanding psychic factors in it).

The detailed study of the movements between the paranoid-schizoid position (with its attendant omniscience and omnipotence) and the depressive position in the history of ideas in the Western world was proposed and reviewed elsewhere, as regards the birth, threats to and maintenance of psychoanalysis (Sandler, 1997, 2001, 2002, 2003). In the psychoanalytic movement, which was wrongly seen as revolutionary—could "evolutionary" be a better term?—there was the unwitting aping of "revolutions". Accusations of idolatry could obfuscate the perception, but could not impede the glimpse of the paradoxical, transcendent numinous realm of the unconscious, "O": timeless truth.

Bion was not a revolutionary. This may be seen as my personal view, expressed elsewhere (for example, Sandler, 2005). Nevertheless, such a view cannot be fairly regarded as a mere individual opinion, as it is substantiated in hard evidence: Bion's own repeated written manifestations expressed in unequivocal terms. Those terms are "reader-proof", that is, impermeable to personal interpretations. Little learning, coupled with idolisation and worshipping always contributed to the still fashionable vision that Bion could vindicate the revolutionaries' banner (any revolutionary needs an idol and its banners). The worshippers' claim is that Bion "invented" a "new analysis" which was bound to make "classic analysis" obsolete. He left unequivocal disagreement with this view; this permeates his whole work and can be seen from 1959 to 1979, the year of his death. For example, his failed attempts to elaborate a renewed theory of dreams, dismissed after 1960, and his half-hearted *entrée* into the fashionable countertransference bandwagon (see Bion, 1965 on the use of theories recognised as insufficient until a new one could appear, and 1958–1979, p. 377 on worshipping and on "whereabouts a little niche could be occupied by ourselves"). Klein was also not immune to being put into this role by so-called "followers", especially after her death. Nevertheless, Klein's and Bion's real example, seen in their writings, was a non-idealised profiting from the classics. They expanded from Freud's work in a way that proves their respect for his achievements.

The group, whose sense of well-being derives from hallucination (Bion, 1965, p. 129), often does not welcome the classics, especially after the advent of "'revolutions". Freud, Ferenczi, Klein and Bion stand out in the analysis as those who profited from the profound ethos of so many classics that a listing demands whole books. Kant was continuously worried about idealism and he himself revived the Greek classics; like Beethoven, Mendelssohn revived Bach; we now have to revive Freud, Ferenczi, Abraham, even Klein and Bion, removing from them especially the tombstones of adoration. Bion used the metaphor of "Vixere fortes ante Agamemnona multi" (Horace, *Odes* IV: 9) to describe that which I propose to see as the eternal burial of the classics. Some people dig them up and revive them, which seems to have a Phoenix-like ethos.

Ideologically minded historians came to see the development of science as an eternal denial of transcendence. They unavoidably favour immanence. Correcting one's points of view and one's views with the aid of new data that were hitherto unobserved—the development of science—differs from using these facts at the service of hate for truth. As long as the human being carries on existing as is known today, there *are* timeless truths, such as mothering, Oedipus, the wheel, hepatocytes, human love and hate, death, $E = mc^2$. The relativistic post-modernist philosophers and truth-dismissing epistemologists, together with others who cannot be confused with them, such as Derrida, had a serious intention: they wanted to be rid of "essentialist" philosophies. But many, such as Popper, Kuhn, Deleuze, Lyotard and Foucault, refuelled unchecked idealist hermeneutics, the essentialist "No"; perhaps they are just chroniclers of deviations of science. They mistake the deviations for the real thing.

Are the two naïve expressions of the persistent difficulty of grasping the non-sensuous ethos of the "dynamic unconscious"? There is an adhesion to Freud's pre-psychoanalytic times: both an idea that life is just desire and its fulfilment (and the accompanying avoidance of pain) and a belief in the "trauma episteme", a positivist cause-effect fallacy. From there to invitations to throw away both the metapsychology and the concept of psychic reality (Arlow, 1996; Kohut, 1984; Modell, 1981) it was just a matter of taking an unavoidable step.

One possible view of classics is that they can function as "refinding-providers", as Delacroix said about the geniuses, for "the first and immediate aim … of reality-testing is not to *find* an object in real perception which corresponds to the one presented but to *refind* such an object" (Freud, 1925). Ferenczi, recognising a classic of his own lifetime, was the only author I have ever read who quoted this observation of Freud, who vindicated Kant's project of a scientific psychology that could respect the numinous realm (Sandler, 2000). Bion had both sources to hypothesise about the pre-conception of the breast (Bion, 1961b, 1962). Hegel's observations underlie Winnicott's paradox that encircles the issue: the infant creates the breast and simultaneously it is already there (Winnicott, 1969). Is it by tolerating the paradoxes of refinding and of the pre-conceptions that the personal factor meets its ends?

The personal factor

Freud observed the existence of a "personal equation", asking:

> Why do you choose to except your own mental processes from the rule of law which you recognise in other people's? When you have attained some degree of self-discipline and have certain knowledge at your disposal, your interpretations will be independent of your personal characteristics and will hit the mark. I am not saying that the analyst's personality is a matter of indifference for this portion of his task. A kind of sharpness of hearing for what is unconscious and repressed, which is not possessed equally by everyone, has a part to play. And here, above all, we are brought to the analyst's obligation to make himself capable, by a deep-going analysis of his own, of the unprejudiced reception of the analytic material. Something, it is true, still remains over: something comparable to the "personal equation" in astronomical observations. The individual factor will always play a larger part in psychoanalysis than elsewhere. [Freud, 1926]

This observation is common sense in real science today. Due to the popularity of post-modernist ideas, there was a misunderstanding of the Lockean concept of common sense; it was mistaken for commonplace. But it is not always noticed that Freud's finding in psychoanalysis preceded that in physics by a few years: Freud did it in 1900; Einstein in 1905 and Heisenberg made it more explicit in 1926. The participant observer in physics measures interferences in quantities of quanta after bombarding sources of matter/energy with known quantities; in analysis, the participant observer can equally ponder on interferences of the reality sensuous and psychic (Bion, 1970) of both members of the analytic couple. A detailed transdisciplinary study of psychoanalysis and physics, which includes my proposal of the concept of "participant observation", is published elsewhere (Sandler, 1997).

The fact that remains, put into shorthand, is that the analyst's personality influences his perceptions. Hume (in connection with his disagreements with Rousseau) observed that with this idea, it would be impossible to distinguish the thinker from the madman. The underlying rationale is an internal concordance between ideas, making logically coherent systems of ideas; this sharply differs from Espinoza's and Kant's concordance between ideas and reality (the correspondence theory). To a psychiatrist, it is striking to see in philosophy postures that he has become accustomed to seeing in narcissistic and paranoid psychosis. Bion once observed that the psychotic patient becomes baffled when the laws of natural science do not obey the laws of his mental functioning (Bion, 1956, 1957, 1977).

The "personal factor" shows that the observer interferes with the object observed. In the history of the psychoanalytic movement, the issue was only taken up by Sándor Ferenczi. To know at least part of those interferences, and how do deal with them, is decisive in analysis due to the fact that the object of study and the method of studying it are the same—the human mind. Amid the analyst's views, are there some which convey more about himself than about his patient? Does the "personal factor" differ from countertransference? "It seems absurd that a psychoanalyst should be unable to assess the quality of his work" (Bion, 1970, p. 62). Have you settled those questions? If so, your patients and you are a lucky bunch indeed.

Reality

The broadness of the perception that we human beings have of our sense of our own reality was enlarged when Freud observed a paradox: psychic reality and material reality are two different forms of the same existence (Freud, 1900, p. 620). Are there personal *realistic* ways to deal with "real realities" (Locke, 1690) that in their turn are not personal?

Oedipus furnishes an example that is paradoxically personal and non-personal: Oedipus is an invariant of the human race. If the psychoanalytic posture demands toleration of paradoxes without attempts to solve them, this situation can be analogically dealt with through the aid of the concept of "bio-analysis" and "organic mathematics" (Ferenczi, 1920, p. 191; 1926, p. 367, 370, 379). Is the regard for truth inborn (Bion, 1958–1979, p. 247)? Does one who strives to make approximations to truth have to be "at one" with oneself (Bion, 1965, p. 37)? Does psychic reality shelter psychic non-reality? Are the personal factor and reality friends, strangers or enemies?

The abolition of the personal factor

Some people tenaciously split and enshrine material reality at the expense of psychic reality. Kant observed "naïve realism": the idea that the human sensuous apparatus (the five basic senses) can grasp reality. He also said that the senses do not err, due to the fact that they do not think. Ferenczi extended this: "Sense organs are better mathematicians than the ucs (less personal)" (1920, p. 191). Naïve realism is in the mainstream of that which is today known as positivism, which flourished in the "fallacy of the neutral observer" (Adorno et al, 1969). It denies the psychic reality.

The enthroning of the personal factor

Others do the obverse: they enshrine psychic reality at the expense of material reality. There ensues the idea that there is no reality at all to be apprehended, no real truth at all to bother with. For the world is just a creation—"construction", the post-modernistic relativism calls it—of the human mind. This doctrine's dismissal of truth as a philosophical or scientific issue had a soothing consequence: the belief that scientific observations are ever-disposable stuff. Disguised as Kantian criticism, it enthrones irresponsibility; it was heralded by Pontius Pilate, a hand-washer. In the 1970s this belief evolved to an explicit authoritarianism: science "is" the product of peer groups who politically reach "paradigms" and thereafter those elected paradigms were doomed to disposal. In this way the whole idea of science is fated to go into a waste bin; there would be no transient glimpses of truth. I propose to call this tendency "naïve idealism". According to it the imposition of the "personal equation" rather than its knowledge is all that one may aspire to attain. It seems that art may, in some cases, be more scientific than a self-styled science. One may compare this posture with Keats's formulation: "Beauty is truth, truth beauty,— that is all/Ye know on Earth, and all ye need to know" (Ode on a Grecian Urn).

O tempora, o mores

There is hard evidence that the classics did not refrain from dealing with the numinous realm of the unconscious, "beauty-truth". But its features enraged the naïve realist and delighted the naïve idealist.

The former denies this realm; the latter uses it to believe in a "created reality"[2] that denies the existence of the empirically real "out there". Is the dismissal of the classics a factor in the flourishing of the naïve realist and the naïve idealist in the psychoanalytic movement? The classics help us to grasp the effect of infantile omnipotence in difficulties of knowing the sense of reality (Freud, 1910b, Ferenczi, 1926, p. 366; Klein, 1946; Bion, 1961b, 1962). The naïves reinstated infantile omnipotence: the realist in the schizoid sense, the idealist in the paranoid sense. Hate for truth and psychoanalysis is old wine in new bottles: it comes, vanishes and periodically returns under novel names, profiting from forgetfulness (Freud, 1933).

The naïve realist lingers on in the "cause-effect" Cartesian episteme in the guise of oversimplified, highly speculative models that try to concretise Freud's contributions: neurophysiology, neurochemistry and now neuroscience. It denies the immateriality of psychic reality.

Ferenczi described naïve idealism under the label of "ultra-idealistic solipsism" (Ferenczi, 1926, p. 373). Freud called it "nihilism" (Freud, 1933, p. 176). Through a dangerous mix of little learning (Sokal & Bricmont, 1998; Callinicos, 1997; Norris, 1997) and idealism, Heisenberg's principle of uncertainty is being turned by many in the psychoanalytic movement into a "principle of ignorance". Einstein's relativity—which shows that at least one fact, namely, the speed of light, was amenable to be truthfully observed as it is, quite independently of the position of the observer—is debased into a blind "relativism" which legalises the individual opinion. There is an "absolute truth statement": truth does not exist; imagination construes reality. Reality would demand to be deconstructed and "metaphorised". There is a paradox demanding tolerance: the mind cannot be known wholly but it exists and may be in part apprehended in transient, intuitive, living glimpses. The legalisation of the individual opinion enthroned the analyst's feelings as if they were arbiters of knowledge, the clue to the emotional state of the patient.

The naïve realist bypasses the intuition of latent contents and clings to manifest contents; he performs a blind search in the external reality hoping to stumble on new discoveries. The naïve idealist bypasses reality in an attempt to disembody human nature. Both deny the possibility of a "pursuit of Truth-O" (Bion, 1970, p. 29, 31). To the naïvely idealistic professional, psychic reality is felt as "too little". The patient's reality is not relevant, with the rationalisation that it is ultimately unreachable. The analyst becomes the focus in the session, as in the kind of patient who is so successful in his exercise of projective identification that he "has no problems other than the existence of the analyst himself", the analyst's opinions, beliefs, interests and so on (Bion, 1957b, p. 88). To the naïve realist, psychic reality is felt as "too much". He seems to want to extinguish the personal factor, and with it the "elasticity of the analytic technique" emphasised by Ferenczi. We will dwell on this "elasticity" below. The naïve idealist wants to enlist it in order to turn the elasticity into complacency, making the analyst's imaginative powers, feelings, and individual opinions indistinguishable from parthenogenesis, hallucinated imaginations of the individual mind. Both deny that real creativity depends on a matching pair able to match *differences* (Sandler, 2000).

> TWENTY-FIVE YEARS We all make mistakes. Knowing what I know now I could certainly not choose to be intelligent. Wise perhaps, but not intelligent.
> SEVENTY YEARS That's something you can pat yourself on the back about. I cannot honestly say I feel wise.
> TWENTY-FIVE YEARS Perhaps your honesty is overdeveloped—more pathological than benign.
> SEVENTY YEARS No, I don't think so. In real life it gets worn off as fast as it grows.
> FORTY YEARS You are too personal, Twenty-five. You've learnt that from P.A. He is always being personal.
> FIFTY YEARS Not personal—specific.
> P.A. I have great respect for the individual. Do you think that is wrong?
> FIFTY YEARS No, but it is not in keeping with the growth of the Herd. I can see P.A. will be in serious trouble if the Herd develops faster than he does.
> P.A. If the development of the Herd is incompatible with that of the individual either the individual will perish, or the Herd will be destroyed by the individual who is not allowed to fulfil himself.
> [Bion, 1979, p. 30]

The meeting point of both naïves imperils the individual; mentally speaking, he is immobilised by already known ideas. The dogmas, transference, compulsion to repetition, *Weltanschauungen* crush him. It is the anti-Enlightenment and anti-Romantic posture. This point was made painfully real by that peerless no-thinker who in his ignorance excelled in a sinister mix of dead machinery (naïve realism, Marinetti's futurism), false science and authoritarian idealism.

Forgetting the classics

To what extent do we forget the classics due to the prevalence of the idea that one always creates thoughts over the idea that we have at our disposal thoughts without a thinker? The latter can be apprehended in the same way that one inhales oxygen that floats in the air. Otherwise "the personal factor" is confused with ideas of superiority, rivalry, and irritable search for originality—both in the session and in the psychoanalytic movement. I suppose that if life instincts prevail, *to improve*, *to extend* and *to use* happen to be. If death instincts prevail, their negative counterparts take charge: respectively, *to replace, to denigrate* and *to extinguish*. Self-criticism turns into criticism of others.

Both naïves attempt to replace psychoanalysis with extraneous models that fall back on a psychology of the conscious. As a matter of consequence both naïves deny infantile sexuality; there is a diminishing concern to analyse and report analysis of Oedipus and unconscious phantasies, and less interest in developing the work on dream processes, and especially in the two fundamental rules of psychoanalysis (Ferenczi, 1928, p. 88), free associations and the analyst's personal analysis.

The personal factor and reality

Bion, who observed the paradox that truth is the food of mind but mind hates it, lived during a time that he saw as the dawn of oblivion for psychoanalysis, focusing on the internal wars against it. He noticed that politically-minded members of the psychoanalytic movement devoted themselves to unreal controversy, but were just a "beating into the air"; that Freud's emphasis that children were sexual was denied (Bion, 1975, p. 11); and other seminal issues subjected to unfair decay. External, or social doubts carried on arising, as had occurred during Freud's time: Winnicott tried to warn about the price of disregarding psychoanalytic research (Winnicott, 1965). If Santayana's observation that a group which does not knows its history is condemned to repeat it is valid, and if Marx did not err in observing that history occurs first as a tragedy and repeats itself as a farce, the study of the classics in psychoanalysis is a real need.

Together with Freud, Abraham and Ferenczi can be seen as classics who highlighted issues such as the sense of reality, the infantile omnipotence that denies it, and the scrutiny of the "personal equation":

> Nevertheless, there has been, and still is, a great deal in psychoanalytic technique which has created the impression that it involves a scarcely definable, individual factor. This has been chiefly due to the circumstance that in analysis the "personal equation" has seemed to occupy a far more important place than we are called on to accept in other sciences ... The second fundamental rule of psychoanalysis [is] the rule by which anyone who wishes to undertake analysis must first be analysed himself. Since the establishment of that rule the importance of the personal element introduced by the analyst has more and more been dwindling away. Anyone who has been thoroughly analysed ... will inevitably come to the same objective conclusions in the observation and treatment of the same psychological raw material. [Ferenczi, 1928, pp. 88–89]

The personal equation, invariants and transformations

The scientific status of analysis is at stake; the personal factor marks a quest for invariants amidst multifarious transformations (Dirac, 1932; Bion, 1965).[3] If an envious person, or a generous person, or a "spoonerist" person (Bion, 1962, p. 1) is analysed by different analysts, the envy, generosity, "spoonerism", or whatever, must emerge in some way or other, sooner or later. The patient's personal factor is his *quality*, which makes him himself and no one else. The analyst's personal factor, like his fingerprints, will determine the timing, the depth, the opportunity and the sensibility, the ways, ruder or tenderer, whatever it may be. The matching of the analyst's and the patient's personal equations may or may not allow for the patient to become who he really is. There seems to be a delicate paradoxical balance: we issue personal views on that which is not personal (for it is "already there", reality internal or external) and will not be affected by views (for it is as it is). The *invariants* are person-dependent from the patient's vertex but they are not from the analyst's. In contrast, the *transformations* are always person-dependent. One must achieve a quantum leap over that which is personal, but in order to do this, it is necessary to know as much as possible about the personal equation—to be ourselves in a living way, in a continuous becoming. The nature of this paradox has qualities of the sense of truth (Bion, 1961b, p. 119) that is achieved when one tolerates the paradox that the object that is loved and the object that is hated are one and the same object; and its manifestation in the area of knowledge, that the object that is known and the object that is unknown are one and the same object (Sandler, 2001).

The forthcoming death of the analyst's analysis: a case of Peeping Tom?

Today, the personal equation is increasingly coming under scrutiny *outside* the realm of personal analysis. Is it scientific or sexual curiosity? A whole congress of the IPA was dedicated to examining the "analyst's mind", in the peculiar setting of a floor discussion with thousands of people attending. Confessions of countertransference—a fact that appalled Klein—are nowadays *de rigueur*. André Green issued a passionate warning of the dangers involved in both facts. But who can show that this warning was followed by renewed interest in the analyst's analyses? Instead, recommendations to *lower* the number of sessions earned popularity and due recommendations (Green, 1993). Dr Jean Laplanche, in his 1997 visit to Brazil, stated publicly that in France the analyst's analysis lasts for two years but the same person spends fifteen years in supervision. The proceedings of the meeting were recorded.

Elasticity and improvisation

Can a symbol represent things other than itself (Gombrich, 1960)? Musical authors said that music was not their creation, but rather came from a Muse. How could Furtwängler and Schnabel, according to many, maintain alive the "O-Beethoven" that others could not? I suppose that real interpreters are able to respect their personal equation without allowing it to distort the "invariant-Beethoven", thus glimpsing transiently the "O-Beethoven". Johann Georg Hamann, the now forgotten professor of Kant, wrote:

> Oh for a muse like the fire of a goldsmith and like the soap of the fullers! She will dare to cleanse the natural use of the senses from the unnatural use of abstractions, by which our concepts of things are just as mutilated as the name of the Creator is suppressed and blasphemed. [J. G. Hamann, quoted in Smith, 1960]

How not to blaspheme "O", the analysand's psychic reality? Through knowing as far as possible when and how the personal equation transforms the analyst's dream and the dreaming of the session (Bion, 1958–1979, p. 39) into narcissistic hallucination (supportive, authoritarian, pedagogical and suggestive therapies). The paradox to be tolerated is: our interpretations are *and* are not ours. The insight stems from the patient: "I am suggesting an aim, an ambition, which, if I could achieve, would enable me to be deliberately and precisely obscure; in which I could use certain words which could activate precisely and instantaneously, in the mind of the listener, a thought or a train of thought that came between him and the thoughts and ideas already accessible and available to him" (Bion, 1975, p. 204). How can this be done?

There is no ready-made formula for something that demands decades of experience; Ferenczi left us a synthetic attempt: "oscillating between introspection and object observation". He named it "utraquism" (1920, p. 190); this name did not stick. Ferenczi's "elasticity", derived from Freud's "tact" (Freud, 1926, p. 220; Ferenczi, 1928, p. 89), is far from the improvised makeshift or lack of care. It is close to the jazz player's improvisation. It is not promoting changes in the analytic setting which merely sponsor complacency, a common misunderstanding (Borgogno, 1999), but rather in a sense of respecting the reality of that patient as it *is*, and not as we want it to be. This allows the analytic couple to evolve. Lack of it leads the session to flicker in the empty shells of Procrustean *ad hoc* theorising and *a priori* patterning. We may allow ourselves to evolve with the patient, within him and within ourselves, as the expedition into the unknown of each moment unfolds, passionately lived as if it were the last moment of our lives.

One may allow this mystery to be as it can be. *Muss es ein? Es muss sein*, Beethoven wrote on the manuscript of his String Quartet no. 16 (op. 135). That paradoxically encompasses what is universally human and, in a certain sense, "known": the two principles of mental functioning, Oedipus, PS⇔D, and other formulations close to "O". The illusion of parthenogenesis develops into the real creativity of a couple

(Sandler, 1997b). One must develop a capacity to make participant observations, not falling back into the fallacy of the "neutral observer" (Adorno, 1969). What changes are the forms (transformations): in philosophical parlance, the immanence. The prefix "trans" express their nature: they are transient sensuously apprehensible appearances, the multifarious *something* that emerges on the spur of the manifest contents of a dream, being dreamt in the session or reported as night experiences, the "stripe in the coat of the Tiger" (Bion, 1975, p. 122), the resistances that paradoxically betray and simultaneously hide that which is the *some* in the *thing*, that calls to be intuited "elastically", the invariant, the transcendence, that which calls to be nurtured and patiently waited for, that evolves, that becomes, that can be experienced and lived but cannot be understood.

The *some* is one arm of a diapason; the *thing* is the other half of the pair. Let us try our hand at a "Lewis Carrollian" mathematics proposed by Bion and forecast by Ferenczi (Bion, 1965, p. 153; Ferenczi, 1920). Elasticity in the technique allows for detection of transformations whose evolving around the invariant enables the analytic couple to approximations close to "O". In a musical transformation, the creative couple creates an instant *singing = some + thing*. Celibidache and Zuckerman knew it was doable but not recordable. The couple creates an instant son/daughter, Oedipus, the new that is also old due to its heritage passed on to the new. New = the unknown that evolves into an adult. In analysis, it is the insight in the "here and now", or transformations in "O", the numinous realm that can be intuited, apprehended and used but not known—one cannot sing potatoes (Bion, 1965, p. 148). Ferenczi and Bion maintained that analysis is an investigation into the unknown, the stuff of the unconscious. Both used the same term: one must be "at-one", have *Einfühlung* (Bion, 1965, p. 146; 1970, pp. 33, 89; Ferenczi quoted by Borgogno, 1999, p. 144).

The unconscious is not amenable to be harnessed by rational thinking. It is beyond imagination; it cannot be put into words. I observed that many regard dreams as if they were *the* unconscious. But a dream is *the royal road to* the unconscious processes of the mind (Freud, 1900). To think that the unconscious can be wholly known denies the definition of it; it makes Freud a contradictory author in his own terms. I think that the analyst in a formal sense construes the latent content; *he or she formulates verbally* something that already *is* in the manifest content, that appertains to the patient.[4] We risk becoming the brokers of the imaginary. The avoidance of the unconscious seems to make many in the psychoanalytic movement themselves fall back into a phenomenological, academic psychology of superficialities and symptoms. Abhorrence of the unconscious leads to adaptive, ego-oriented psychotherapies, as if the whole issue of adaptation could be seen as adaptation to an external environment, indistinguishable from behaviourism. Today's "intersubjectivism", which consciously or not leaves aside its Husserlian origins and is presented as if it originated from psychoanalysis, is the most recent transplant of an extraneous model, aping the "existentialist" transplants so fashionable in the 1950s. Are they "tales full of sound and fury, signifying nothing", to quote the Bard? It is no surprise that today psychoanalytic training does not receive the interest it once enjoyed among young professionals from the medical field and the encircling social environment. Nowadays, many people refuse to look for analysts. It is of little use to the practising analyst to resort to easy reassuring and alleviating explanations, such as blaming modern social engineering which is profit-oriented, consumerist, materialist and globalised, or some of its variations, such as the deleterious activities of pharmaceutical laboratories, or more careful appraisals, such as the perception of the extinguishing of the Guilds. Hungarian analysts persisted under the iron fist of the pseudo-communist state. Perhaps a psychoanalytic posture would be: "what did we do to get ourselves into this situation?" Or, putting it in harsher terms: how many of the officially certified members of the psychoanalytic movement (I use the term after Freud, 1914b) are practising "real analysis" (I use the term after Bion, 1977b and 1979)?

A personal equation in two movements

The impossibility of describing the misery, suffering, waste of time, distrust, terror and destruction that seem to encircle Albert's life makes me long for a form of communication with colleagues that could include an acoustic medium. The working through of Albert's paranoid phantasies can be seen in the evolution of his musical performances at the piano, as well as his growing awareness of his capacity to hallucinate. We met when he was 38; he had seen many psychiatrists from the age of five, hardly spending more than a few months with each one. They included a child analyst. The last one, by sheer coincidence a professional whom I saw in the condition of a severely deluded and drug-addicted in-patient in the mental hospital where I worked twenty years before, borrowed money from Albert's father, and became drunk at their home after dining with them at the invitation of Albert's father. The same happened with a famous local maestro with whom Albert tried to study music, who, according to both Albert and his father, felt humiliated by the material wealth of Albert's family. Albert interrupted his analysis with me four times, seeing me as his father's envoy; but as work proceeded, the transference phantasies lessened, and three years ago he decided to take responsibility for coming, rather than coming at his father's behest. He comes with the seriousness of a scientist. A self-taught scholar who never completed any formal training, Albert is also a *Menschenkenner*, gifted with intelligence, honesty, personal integrity, sensibility, concern for truth and capacity to love that I have never seen before or since in 32 years of practice. Seems too good to be true? The other side of the coin is that he is skinless, utterly vulnerable, and had unfortunate familial conditions that enhanced Oedipal homosexual phantasies. His analysis demanded an elasticity and mutual forbearance that I had not experienced before, closely resembling that of child analysts. I had to be able to play with him with his adult-like toys, and actually to see his father in some sessions. Through mutual projective identification, both Albert and his father vehemently denied that the father came. But he kept on coming, and Albert kept on bringing him. He was providing me the opportunity to see a "child" begging for a "mother" (me) who could protect him from a father better described by the myth of Saturn. Albert's mother left home when he was 13; she had already left a first husband and progeny. He hated women and invariably had turbulent relationships that often ended with the girls enraged, slapping his face. He had over the last ten years avoided any contact with women, and returned to look for them after one year of analysis. His father is an extremely intelligent, self-taught, self-made man who survived two wars and achieved admirable financial success. He seems to have "stolen" the progeny from a fragile mother and created the omnipotent idea in them that he could be both father and mother—better than any mother, raising them without pain and also with almost every possible expectation of perfection. Albert's younger brother marched resolutely to drugs and delinquency. Greed was nourished through the idea that they should be perfect in their imperfection, thus attaining the better of two worlds. Let me show now what my words cannot depict: the evolution of Albert's homosexual phantasies of superiority in musical terms and the rescuing of the real artist he is, after he had given up any hope of becoming a pianist twenty years earlier under the pressure of both his internal and external father. He sought out a very famous and highly regarded professor, who accepted him. He has bought a grand piano and thanks to his multi-technical abilities, which include the management of computer software, is also making transcriptions of long-forgotten Brazilian masters. How could we reach this point if our personal equations and elasticity were not at play and at stake all the time? This has nothing to do with the setting, which is strictly analytic.

Analysts' individuality ... or personal analysts?

It is commonplace (alas, not common sense) that nowadays there are pushes towards and favouring of the enshrinement of personal facts about the professionals in analysis, focusing on the analyst's confessions of so-called "countertransference". That denies the influence of the analyst's unconscious—a fact strongly emphasised by André Green in his comment on Theodore Jacobs's institutional paper at the 1993 IPA Congress in Amsterdam. Bion (quoted in previous chapters of this book) tried to clarify this point, which comes at least since the Enlightenment's defence of the individual, epitomised by the phoenix-like resurgence of medicine after it had been condemned to death by medieval Roman Catholic policies, as happens with the apprehension of truth. The question is: as an infantile reaction, emphasis was put on individualism, or better, personalistic features mistaken for individual. Narcissism breeds individualism and authoritarianism. In analysis, there are no external enhancements to our senses, be they mechanical, electronic, or (in the future) biological or quantum-based. The only tool at the disposal of the analyst is his own mind and intuitive experience coupled with the patient's mind and intuitive experience. Some good enough analogies could be the skills of the chef and the surgeon, even though they have at their disposal some mechanical and biological tools in their practical activities. Misunderstanding about the analyst's personality confounds its possible manipulation and apparent management in the individual transformations due to his personal, individualistic outlook and judgmental values, with his good enough apprehension of invariants originating from the patient's outlook. If the latter coincide with the analyst's invariants—and some of them would perforce coincide, for patients and analysts are human beings—this has no importance whatsoever in the "here and now". The freer an analyst is to exert his truthful individual being, the less personalistic he will be. The same misunderstanding expresses itself in another manifestation, which is a complication of the first one: the conundrum about the "analyst's neutrality". It means discipline of memory, understanding and desire, or emphasis on the personal analysis of the analyst.

The great authors of psychoanalysis developed their contributions—beginning with Freud—through their individual gifts, inclinations and experiences, which determined the range of their apprehensions. Again, "individual" in their case made a quantum leap over "personal", acquiring a generalised—which means scientific—value which encompassed specific (personal) cases. Oedipus, envy and greed, transitional objects, hallucinosis, the dead mother syndrome (respectively, by Freud, Klein, Winnicott, Bion and Green) sprang from individual experience. "What you have inherited from your fathers, earn it in order to make it yours."[5] Is the personal factor the resulting synthesis of this paradox?

Notes

1. The political leanings also persist to our time; they gave rise to social experiments oriented by ideologies and were the origin of the psychoanalytic movement, distinct from but sometimes confused with psychoanalysis proper. This debasing had already obtruded through Rousseau, in the birth of the Romantic Movement. The academic classifications based in time are flawed, but are still usually used as a first guide for the novice. Both Enlightenment and Romantic Movements persist to our days, if considered in a more truthful space-time dimension.
2. Please see the section *A psychoanalytic vertex: two naïvetés* in the next chapter.
3. Please see Volume 1 Part II for Bion's proposals on Invariants and Transformations.
4. Please see Volume 1 Part I.
5. "Was du ererbt von deinen Vätern hast, erwirb es, um es zu besitzen" (Goethe, *Faust*, Part I Scene 1).

PART III

EPISTEMOLOGY AND TRUTH

CHAPTER SEVEN

Psychoanalysis and epistemology: relatives, friends or strangers? Paranoid-schizoid features in the paths of psychoanalytic practice

> Theory may be necessary to represent the similarity between people separated by race, religion, language and distance, measured in terms of or by physical time and space. Our concern is how this "domain", usually left to be dealt with by geniuses, is to be managed by ordinary humans. Nietzsche says a group must produce or find a genius; how is it to recognise and preserve it when found? Is the human "mind" the sense organ that could be adapted for the purpose? Can Freud's theory of consciousness be extended to the whole human mind and the object of its attention to whatever lies "beyond"?
>
> —Bion, 1977b

I am thought searching for a thinker to give birth to me. I shall destroy the thinker when I find him. I am the Odyssey, the Iliad, the Aeneid. I prevented Mars from destroying me but I ate away Mars from inside, from outside so he died. He is a memory and a desire: I am the eternally alive, indestructible, indispensable, adorable. I am the force that makes the books. My last triumph is the Mind.

> The mind that is too heavy a load for the sensuous beast to carry. I am the thought without a thinker and the abstract thought which has destroyed its thinker Newtonwise, the container that loves its content to destruction; the content that explodes its possessive container.
>
> —Bion, 1975, p. 38

It is usual to state that Bion's contribution to analysis included epistemology. It may be a redundancy. Psychoanalysis, like any science, has its own universe of discourse to state, display and communicate itself, to meet the need for exposition of its *nous*. We live in a post-Aristotelian "metaphysics"; his example practically forced any science to form part of theories of knowledge, or epistemology in its most commonly used meaning. Verbal or other symbolic formulations (such as those occurring in mathematics, physics and chemistry) which are used to communicate science share the nature of epistemological practice. Science and its universes of discourse are "epistemological-per-se", as a continuing practical activity. Metaphysics, as a name, was born from an editor of Aristotle who had to lump together his non-physical essays. So he named the chapter "that which came after physics"—concerning a way to think about the earlier studies. Aristotle tried to meet, at least in part, a human need: the "urge to know". Freud upgraded the status of this urge many years later to the epistemological instinct, emphasising more its nature of "human need". As an analyst who took truth as a built-in feature of his work, Bion was concerned with epistemology—like Freud before him. This may justify the inclusion of a chapter on epistemology heavily influenced by Bion in a practical book.

I will try to couple the epistemological view of psychoanalysis to the psychoanalytic view of epistemology: a mutually fruitful collaboration with neither predominating. There is some evidence of the epistemological nature of psychoanalysis; that epistemology was a non-medical forerunner of psychoanalysis when it paid attention to truth and mind; that psychoanalysis was born as a way out of an age-old conundrum, idealism versus realism, a resilient difficulty in grasping the non-sensuous ethos of the mind which divorced science from humanities (Berlin, 1956), imperilling both; and finally, that the sweeping reverberations of this issue in our movement part us from Freud's fundamental contributions, a main factor in our so-called "crisis". May we learn from the epistemologist's tragedy in order not to repeat it as a farce? Bion's *A Memoir of the Future* and Sir Isaiah Berlin's work inspire the following psychoanalytic history of ideas about knowledge made by an analyst, addressed to analysts. It includes a hypothesis on the researcher's state of mind.

What is epistemology?

Epistemology is the study of knowledge, justifying theories about it and obstacles to it (perceptual, psychological, and socio-political). It deals with perception and thought processes. *Episteme* is a piece of knowledge; *doxa* is the discourse about it. Both equip the *philosophy of science*, the critical examination of scientific theories and methods, including searching for and gathering data, communication (verbal or not) and, especially, refutation (which includes evaluations of results). Those very terms suggest the similarity of the problems faced by the epistemologist and the psychoanalyst.

Those activities seem to have such a kinship that philosophy was often regarded restrictively as the study of the Mind and sees analysts as intruders; and psychoanalysis, the study of the Mind par excellence, is often regarded as philosophy, losing its practical and scientific ethos. During the last two millennia, philosophers have been cyclically concerned and unconcerned both with Truth and with the "Mind" and its functioning. It has been variously named "Human understanding", "Spirit", "Soul", "Personality", "Character", and "Psychic Reality", after Freud. On the one hand, for some researchers it is a condition of the very existence of philosophy; on the other hand, in our times these attempts have been criticised for "psychologising" philosophy. This happened cyclically at least since Hume's contributions to epistemology. Bion pointed out that the philosopher "falls back defeated when the factor of emotional impulses obtrudes. This will, I am sure, be very ably denied. That is my point: it is the function of philosophy to deny it" (1947). Eight years later, he amended this to: "what is not so easily appreciated is the immediacy of the impingement of the problems with which the philosopher of science is familiar on the mental phenomena that modern psychoanalytic methods make overt" (1958–1979, p. 9). Both scientific and psychoanalytic regard for truth flows to an unprejudiced and non-partisan view which can manifest itself as an integrative view, detailed in the following pages.

Similarities: epistemology is to knowledge as unconscious is to mind

Internal objects, instincts and their psychic equivalents (unconscious phantasies) are the luminescent blind man's stick for one's life, amenable to be likened to "epistemes", the ultimately ineffable, non-sensuously apprehensible, transcendent underlying guidelines to knowledge. Beginning with Freud, psychoanalysts of genius were aware that the psychoanalyst's task is sometimes combined with that of a kind of epistemologist.

It is necessary to exclude the post-modern tendency which relies absolutely on relativism, for reasons we shall review soon. This obliges a mere artisan-reproducer like me to pronounce their names in reverence and awe, not for peremptory adhesion to projected Authority or blind religious adoration that compose the deadliest enemies of science and psychoanalysis itself, but as an acknowledgment of their contributions to this specific integration between psychoanalysis and epistemology. After Freud, I think that Sándor Ferenczi, Ernest Jones, Melanie Klein, Edward Glover, Donald Winnicott, Harold Searles, Wilfred Bion, Roger Money-Kyrle, Theodor Reik, Eliott Jaques, John Wisdom, Karl Menninger, George Klein, André Green and James Grotstein were able to maintain the "epistemological posture" and contributed in an original way to it.

Epistemology seems to me a kind of ancestor of psychoanalysis. I suppose that Gaston Bachelard was an early thinker who noticed this, albeit in a reversed way, probably due to his lack of clinical experience.

Psychoanalysis seems to me a vindicating phylogenetic introjection of some cyclically forgotten insights on truth, mind, life and nature. It integrated the Renaissance/Enlightenment and Romantic movements' unearthing of ancient Greek and Cabbalist *cognitio dei experimentalis* (Scholem, 1941; Yates, 1979; D'Arcy, 1930). This Latin expression was a synthetic phrase of St Thomas Aquinas; nowadays we may replace *dei* with Kant's Noumena, or Science, or Art, or Bion's "O". In other words: dealing with Truth and Mind through disciplined, living formation of interpretive intuition, free from the brokerage of reason and senses. Plato's "Ideal Forms" (the realm of noumena) and his metaphoric work of the Demiurge (the phenomenal realm) seem to me early formulations of, respectively, psychic reality and material reality (Freud, 1900) as well as of latent content and manifest content. Those formulations are metaphors. It is debatable whether Freud's verbal formulations or any scientific formulations are exclusively metaphors too, despite the fact that any successful verbal formulation has a metaphorical power. I suppose that a dazzling interest in language can hamper the realisation that some verbal formulations are closer to experience and in this sense less purely metaphorical in the figure of speech sense. This statement can resemble Heidegger's suggestions, but my intent is closer to Goethe's work and the Frankfurt School's development of Heidegger's work.

Non-sensuously apprehensible transcendences and timeless realities, "Ideal Forms", establish the artistic realm of Science *and* the scientific realm of Art. *Both seek basic elements and make timeless generalisations that encompass individual cases.* They glimpse aspects of the ultimate *unknowable but existent* "intuitable" reality *as it is* through symbolic non-verbal (e.g. $E = mc^2$) and verbal formulations (e.g. Oedipus). It would be useful to differentiate these ideal forms from philosophical concepts as regards their having a counterpart in everyone's life. They demand to be intuited and apprehended rather than to be rationally understood. If, as Bion observed, real analysis is real life, a consequence of this is that psychoanalytic basic and elementary concepts, such as the two principles of mental functioning, or Klein's formulations on paranoid-schizoid interplay, would be among the closest the human being was able to come to the *noumena*. Like any scientific schemes or models (Kant, 1781; Freud, 1940, p.191; Bion, 1962, p. 79, 1963, p. 2, 1965, p. 127), they must transiently outline their counterparts in the *already existent* reality.

Some researchers—who adjoined empirical field work to thought and were known as scientists—had shown the need to distinguish what *is* from what *is not*, or real from unreal, or true from false, through intuiting *paradoxical pairs*. In-depth research on this concept can be found elsewhere. Nevertheless, a passing précis of the foundations of the ideas of Western civilisation can be included here. They have been put forth in an explicit mode at least since Aristotle; St Thomas Aquinas adapted them to some needs and interests of the Roman Catholic Church; they were further developed by Descartes, whose ideas came to be organised by Auguste Comte under a system of rules which he named positivism. Before Comte those ideas were already put into practice by scholars and practical researchers in physics, chemistry and biology, from Harvey and Kekulé to Ernst Mach and Alexander Graham Bell. Those ideas furnished limited, but successful measures for actions in the material, non-living realm, such as the design and construction of mechanical and electrical contraptions. This development (or negative development) attempted to split matter from mind, and among many other tendencies, tried to impose the task of approaching truth through what can be named an "internal" method of formal logic. They were researched using a method which can be seen as "rationalisation", based on deduction and induction. This method selects parts that are dismembered from a whole. It believes in the law of the excluded middle; it deals just with contradictions and is good at resolving them. Nevertheless, the knowledge obtained by this method is limited, because it abhors the existence of paradox—a feature of living systems. To qualify as "internal" means: with no reference to counterparts in reality that correspond to the thought-rationalisation. Conversely, other thinkers, such as Plato, Spinoza, Pascal, Shakespeare, Bacon, Locke, Hume, Hamann, Kant, Maimon, Herder, Goethe, and in later days, Einstein, Planck, Bergson and Bion, were among those who looked for the coincidence between concepts and objects through observation and intuition about a whole. The intuition about the whole can be made by models and analogies, but it cannot be made directly; from this intuition the need to tolerate paradoxes arose (Sandler, 1997–2003, *A Apreensão da Realidade Psíquica*, vols. I–VII). Some parts of this research also appear in previous chapters of this book as well as in Volumes 1 and 2.

Psychoanalytically speaking, the issue appertains to the realm of perception rather than of morals: [True/False] and [Reality/Hallucination] would be synonymous. The sign/means "and" [True/False] or [Reality/Hallucination] must be regarded as paradoxical, inseparable pairs. Under the vertex of dogmatic, authoritarian morals, the realisation of the existence of [True/False] is precluded. Authority is born from belief, and the path to consolidate it is paved with an attempt to remedy by adopting morality: True (or Reality) is replaced with Right and False (or Hallucination) is replaced with Wrong. The consequences in the realm of thinking processes are, firstly, denial that Truth and Reality do exist; secondly, attacks on perception of Reality and on linking of objects; and thirdly, due to the fact that the very existence of paradox is denied, there is a splitting of the inseparable pairs.

All of this results in the added belief—a cancer-like situation which grows infinitely—that the pairs, now debased and hyper-tuned, can be separated, obeying the law of the excluded middle: instead of the paradox of [True and False] there would be Right *or* Wrong. Plausible schemata, pure delusion cannot be discerned either from reality or from dreams—which, by the way, keep links with reality. Delusion is a jigsaw rationally built under Euclidean logic, made from hallucinations (which means, in classical psychiatry and academic psychology, that one has sensuous perceptions with no external object) and hallucinosis (in psychiatry, the presence of hallucinations in a personality otherwise preserved). What Aristotle called the *nous* turned into a psychoanalytic task: it is obtained by consciousness, "the sense organ for the perception of psychical qualities" (Freud, 1900, p. 615). It demands an interplay between conscious and unconscious that allows the mind to think about itself through "binocular vision" (Bion, 1962; please see Volume 2, Part III). Transference, projective identification and narcissism may be regarded in the clinic as epistemological errors. Freud realised the hallucinatory nature of transference (1912), and Klein, of projective identification (1946), even though the psychoanalytic movement as a whole produced unequivocal expressions of resistance towards what they showed, and thus threw off their "babies" (or empirically creative research) and nourished what was just the placenta, furnishing a Frankenstein-like "life" to models and pure hallucinations clothed in psychoanalytic words. Thus they cannot see the hallucinated phantasy-nature of transference and projective identification. Bion emphasises this in *A Memoir of the Future*: the erudite can know that a text was written by Freud or Klein, but remain blind to the thing described (Bion, 1975, p. 9).

Differences

Psychoanalysis amended the need to apprehend the truth of outer reality with the apprehension of the self's truth, inner psychic reality. The scientific, caring, medical concern towards suffering *individual* people leads *practical humanistic utility* to the condition of epistemology, turning it into a matter of interest (Sanders, 1986), albeit divested, as Freud, Bion and Winnicott showed, of illusory curative powers. Real Medicine never had them, as any experienced surgeon, clinician or patient knows. The Enlightened/Romantic's regard for Nature and Reality *as they are* enabled Freud to go—I think for the first time in the history of Western thinking—beyond the Principle of Pleasure/Displeasure, eliciting the existence of a Principle of Reality; an epistemological statement by itself. Dispensing with conscious rationalism, the Romantics go beyond the sensuously apprehensible façades; non-mystical Intuition and Living Experience equipped their thrusts into the unknown. Like any classification, the label "Romantic" has some limitations; one may find a "romantic ethos" in Spinoza, Bacon, Kant and Goethe, who refused to be put into that category.

The discovery of the Principle of Reality unites detractors and crypto-detractors (those disguised as defenders) of Freud's contributions. Both usually attribute to Freud the novelty of having "invented" the unconscious. This is false; Plato knew about it, and at least since Kant the same verbal term has been used extensively. This is true in almost all of the French and the German Romantic Movement. Freud led practical utility at the service of individuals to this already known reality.

The same applies to the alleged "invention" by Freud of the human proneness to satisfy desire. In the 1960s, the "hippie" movement as well as self-help literature put Freud's effigy on banners and flags with the inscription "make your instincts free", or the like, as the road to happiness. Conversely, the principle of Pleasure was also known to Hobbes, Spinoza, Descartes, Locke, and Kant; if Freud really brought a novelty, it was the eliciting of the Principle of Reality at the service of individuals. No one could deny its presence in prose and poetry since Greek mythology and theatre, as well as in Shakespeare's "tragic" plays; in that sense, they could be described as "realistic plays". The psychoanalytic movement is plagued by those fashionable but hasty attributions of originality, denying Bacon's apt observation that all novelty is but oblivion. The concept of unconscious phantasy is usually attributed to Melanie Klein, but it is Freud's. She explored it clinically, better than anyone before or since. The same occurred with the concept of thoughts without a thinker, which was attributed (by Meltzer and Thorner) to Bion. In fact it was proposed by Descartes, in the *Discours sur le Méthode*, even though he dismissed it as absurd; Bion rescued it from the darkness of rationality.

Romantic achievements could—and sometimes were—put at the service of knowledge of groups, as usually occurs in literature and philosophy, mostly in terms of warning to be aware of some conflicts; this is usually seen as a social service of those disciplines. But it did not serve individuals, and this could be a factor that gave birth to psychoanalysis, out of necessity, in the light of medical interest in individuals. Psychoanalysis extracted real immaterial facts from the paradoxical, timeless/transient realm of the unconscious, that sojourn of human truth and untruth. Freud endowed the bare bones of philosophical generalisations with a living experiential ethos. His practical vertex, born from clinical reality, does not "talk about" but "is" and "suffers". Where explanatory, absolute, positive truths were he allowed the "negative" nature both of the unconscious noumena and of the numinous realm of the unconscious. This research encompasses the realm of minus, or negative, as emphasised in analysis by Bion and later by Green (Bion, 1962, p.95; Green, 1986, 1997); Grotstein also implicitly encircled the issue as he approached a form of knowledge of the until then forbidden numinous realm (1981, 1995, 2000, 2007). Please see an expansion of this in Volume 2, Part I if this work. In daily practice it means grasping—as John Donne did before the advent of psychoanalysis—the due value of frustration, or the need not to be enslaved by pleasure and desire. Analytic practice added to this nonhedonist evaluation the need to be careful and thus acquire a good enough discipline over any surge of desire to interpret, understand and cure patients.

Psychoanalysis may well be an epistemology of lie; the lies construe the hallucinated false self[1] one describes to oneself. Through encircling, eliciting and naming lies, it strives to paradoxically enliven, via free associations, truths or germs of truth—the eternally bred "germens" so feared by Mephistopheles in Goethe's *Faust*. In Poincaré's metaphor, free associations are the mind's selected facts that give coherence to hitherto separate facts.

Psychoanalysis turned the Socratic "know thyself" into *"becoming* oneself through knowing one's truth *and* untruth" (Bion, 1965, p. 148 ff). It rescued the mind's ability to tolerate paradoxes. This "double-tracked" (Grotstein, 1981), art-and-science root of psychoanalysis is, in itself, an epistemological paradox that demands tolerance to be used, but not understood or resolved.

> The permanently therapeutic effect of a psychoanalysis, if any, depends on the extent to which the analysand has been able to use the experience to see one aspect of his life, namely himself as he is...It follows that a psychoanalysis is a joint activity of analysand

and analyst to determine the truth; that being so, the two are engaged—no matter how imperfectly—on what is in intention a scientific activity. [Bion, 1958–1979, p. 114]

Our roots: an epistemological-psychoanalytic fable

A primitive hominid listens to the cry of a helpless miniaturised being resembling himself. Was knowledge born when he tolerated the loss of his pleasure-giving partner and paradoxically linked her to the acoustic stimulus of pain, replacing the desire-fulfilling act with the thought of a need-meeting emotional experience, namely, the supremely creative relationship (Klein, 1932)? A phylogenetic introjection of humankind's "urge (or desire) to know" (Aristotle; Kant, 1781, p. 415) depends on one's genetic endowment—the "epistemophilic instinct" formulated by Freud. This hypothesised phylogenetic introjection can be analogically compared to the embryo steps which compress hundreds of thousands of years of human maturation in a gestational period of something in the environs of nine months. That is, it occurs in the compacted span of one lifetime—just as the human embryo passes from a fish-like existence to a biped mammal reality. Linked to survival, it prompts efforts to apprehend reality *as it is* (Bacon, 1620, Boswell, 1791). They developed through a spectrum of increasingly "de-sensified" abstractions, beyond signs. First came pre-verbal, predominantly sensuous Art: Music, Painting, Sculpture. There followed verbal modes: Myths, Prose/Poetry; later on, Theatre. Philosophy ensued, forecasting the path of the youngest sophistication, Science (Kant, 1781, p. 408). Some (Descartes, 1637) tried to establish a science founded on rational concordance between ideas creating self-feeding rational schemata and jargon. This allows for the "rational manipulation of symbols" referred to by Whitehead and later brought to psychoanalysis by Bion. Both idealists and positivists suffer from that: Kuhn, Lakatos, Feyerabend and Rorty represent this tendency—a serious mistake that still hampers in an authoritarian way the free exchange of ideas. Kuhn's ideologically oriented "paradigms" proved to be fashionable in today's periodicals in the guise of "peer review"—a network of political, personal and psychological friendships and "fiend-ships". This was evidenced by Sokal and Bricmont's denunciation of post-modernism's abuses, when they exposed Professor Andrew Ross to a scandal (1998). Nevertheless, truth and its investigation continues not to be fashionable in the philosophical world; scientific controversy is abhorred, replaced by "pro" and "anti" manifestations that have kept Professor Ross's role as a publisher undisturbed in some quarters.

Other researchers such as Locke (1690), who differentiated between "verbal reality" and "real reality", and Hume (1748), who inspired especially Kant (1781, 1783) in his warnings on "verbosity", observed that with this criterion it would be impossible to distinguish the thinker from the madman. Skilful doctoring of internal logic mimics real science and is not conducive to discoveries. At best it builds circularities, furnishing illusory *a priori* credence to Deduction and *ad hoc* credence to Induction.[2] Kant's, Hempel's, Penrose's, Einstein's, Heisenberg's, Planck's and Schrödinger's criticism of deductive methods can be useful to the reader: deduction is a kind of heuristics, that is, a linguistic or psychological device that makes the *presentation* of certain mathematical issues and facts more convincing or interesting. Centuries later, the perception of logically irresolvable antinomies (Kant, 1781) elicited the need for intuition, sensible or not, to overcome built-in limitations of logically positive rationalism and reliance on the senses. *Real Science demands coherence between ideas (concepts) and experience (empirical objects of study)*. It is necessary to *distinguish* but not to *split* the immanent *methods* of study from the transcendent *objects* of study. Aristotle did it, as advanced on the first page of this chapter. He linked the methods to what came to be known as "metaphysics", a name given by his editor, referring to the ordinal position in the printed form of those studies that "came after (*meta-*) Physics". Therefore, a non-concrete issue received a concrete, sensuously apprehended denomination that in its turn came to define a non-concrete realm! The Myth of Babel, one of the manifestations of the prohibition of knowledge, strikes in unexpected quarters. Later, Kant was able to further this differentiation, establishing the realm of Philosophy with more clarity than before. I will leave aside the rivalry between disciples and masters which marked the relationship of Aristotle and Plato, Leibniz and Newton, Kant and Hume, Kierkegaard and Hegel, much to the detriment of the progress of knowledge. Obviously, those thinkers had no opportunity to undergo the suffering of a real analysis, which affords some ways to be aware of rivalry and greed, functions as well as manifestations of clinging to the paranoid-schizoid position. Real life offers a chance to get some insight about these human occurrences. Biographies are not a very trustworthy account, but there is no other way than a scrutiny of the existing biographies of those thinkers. This allows us to infer—a mere inference with all the drawbacks, first pointed out by Hume, of this type of reasoning—the *hypothesis* (with no chance of empirical confirmation, those persons being long dead) that they were prone, in various degrees, to these human features. Probably much more in Hegel and Kierkegaard, less in Hume, and a middle road, peppered with maturity as years go by, in Aristotle and Kant.

In the psychoanalytic field, the object and the method are the same—Mind itself. One observes Mind through Mind. The same overlapping of methods and objects occurs in other scientific disciplines: physicists observe Matter and Energy through interference and bombardment by known quantities of matter and energy.

Freud rushed into Plato's numinous realm that Kant elicited but feared to enter. The former's awareness of the observer's interference with the phenomena observed unfettered psychoanalysis from the omnipotent illusion of the neutral observer. I find it useful to use the term "participant observation", which is already used in anthropology. Freud and Planck were able to do it in their scientific disciplines, with no knowledge of each other's work. Both intuited constants of Nature. Both faced the same kind of reaction from the establishment. Psychoanalysis, like modern physics, knows some data on the observer and measures what happens when those known data of the observer interfere in the unknown data of the observed.

Beating positivism at its own game, Freud's pure empirical science—respect for clinical facts—enabled him to dispense with his initial logical cause-effect explanatory episteme. A huge transdisciplinary integration of Shakespeare, Enlightened Medicine, the Romantic *Bildungskraft*, Goethe's *Naturphilosophie*[3] and Schopenhauer's *Wille* allowed him to formulate some mental functions "inhabiting" the unconscious, a timeless numinous realm of unknown: the two principles of mental functioning, the dream as the epistemological tool of the mind to self-critically know itself, the three basic instincts (life, death and epistemophilic), and primary narcissism.

The epistemophilic instinct, discovered by Freud in his observations of children, was researched in more depth by Melanie Klein. With the exception of some hypotheses by James Grotstein, who at least from 1995 did much work endowed with a daring quality (for he challenged "established absolute truths" forbidding research into "O", considered un-researchable by its very definition), few other authors have explored the epistemophilic instinct.[4] Dr Grotstein suggests a "truth drive", which seems to me an opportune reminder, adapted to our present times, as well as an attempt to expand some theoretical implications of the epistemophilic instinct (Grotstein, 2004).

At any rate, as regards clinical consequences, the original discoveries of Freud and Klein stand. To the extent that one must perceive; and that maturation means this perception being put to use in order to enable one to reach some kind of compromise with one's own inner, biologically dependent, most profound and elementary needs. One may quote the need to eat and to drink as operations for survival. They are expressions of the paradoxical pair death and life, seen by Freud as instincts. At a certain point in one's life, echoing the development of humankind, as always occurs with the ontogenetic/phylogenetic chain, one must come to terms with one's urge to know: the epistemophilic instinct. The epistemophilic instinct expresses itself in the ways humanity has developed to perceive and grasp reality *as it is*, which includes the experience of what it is not. It is a paradox that demands tolerance, composing the stuff of *unconscious phantasies*. Mathematics and some branches of science (such as chemistry) have used this method since time immemorial, in proof by contradiction (*reductio ad absurdum*) and the detection of an unknown chemical component through known reactions with known reagents.

Profiting from Vico, Hamann and Herder's historicism, but different from Heidegger's, Freud unearthed Oedipus, unconscious phantasies (the psychic equivalents of instincts) and internal objects. Freud's epistemological approach, his knowledge of the emotional stance of the analyst, allowed him to describe some of the interferences this participant observer makes in the phenomena observed. The underlying episteme of Klein's, Bion's and Winnicott's work is an introjection of Hegel's insights on the "*gist* experience" that turned Kant's dialectical antinomies into pairs of *living, ever-moving* opposites. Not in a *warring*, but rather in a *creative* way. Thus Klein elicited the interplay of the Positions and some paradoxical contents of unconscious phantasies; Winnicott tolerated the paradox of a breast that was created *and* was already there. Bion's epistemology of psychoanalysis first attempted to validate the analyst's interpretations using the achievements of neo-positivism, finely distinguishing the various types of psychoanalytic objects, elements, transformations and their "truth-value". Later he amended this with a "pursuit of Truth-O", "O" being his symbol for the numinous realm. Their methods were purely psychoanalytic.[5]

Above all, they avoided an "activity which is only a more or less ingenious manipulation of symbols" (Bion, 1975). Bion, like Freud, warned about endangering psychoanalysis with "a vast paramnesia to fill the void of our ignorance" (Bion, 1976). Freud, Klein, Bion and Winnicott relied on common sense to detect constant conjunctions, rushing into the realm of trained intuition that Freud feared to make explicit. Theirs was a "language of achievement". In doing so, they apprehended daytime dream work and expanded the micro-observation of the free associations in the living here and now of the session. Like Freud, Bion used myths as scientific "fact-finding tools" that elicited transcendent "invariants".

A psychoanalytic vertex: two naïvetés

It proved difficult to realise the ethos of the Forms that reunite Mind and Reality. Moreover, making available failed and ultimately misleading names—Mind, Matter—to "see" them proved to be more an obstacle than anything else.

Two questions arise. One was put by Bion and the other is a consequence and expansion of it. Firstly, is Mind "too heavy a load for the sensuous beast to carry" (Bion, 1975, p. 46); and secondly, is Truth—the frustrating and paradoxical reality as it is—too heavy a load for the desiring beast to carry? For the "Two Great Splits" constitute wars against knowledge: a splitting of immanence from transcendence; and, as a matter of consequence, the splitting of matter from mind. As in any Mindless war, the first casualty was Truth. Truth-and-paradox-abhorring expressions of the Two Great Splits further impoverished research; a splitting "Or" replaced the integrative "And": matter or energy, mind or body, psyche or soma, psychic or material, right or wrong, cause or effect, crazy or normal, pain or pleasure, known or unknown, good or bad, penis or breast, mother or father. Epistemologically speaking, I propose to name the expressions of the Two Great Splits "Naïve Realism" (after Kant) and "Naïve Idealism". Both aim at Absolute Truth and abhor basic paradoxes. Kant boldly criticised both "pure reason" and its negative counterpart, "blind idealism". He had a fair experience of idealism and profited in part from it. One can notice his ambivalent feelings about experience: sometimes he emphasised its importance and sometimes he downgraded it. Kant was not able to be a scientist, and his brief career as such produced some wild flights of imagination or flights of fantasy (warned against by Bacon, when one got far from observed experience), such as the idea that the wind that blows in the North Sea was cold because it had to cross the Ocean. His work leaves a margin to be taken in a split way and both naïve realism and naïve idealism are an integral part of his inheritance, as important as his warnings against them.

I think that those splits underlie the often commented and sometimes lamented attitude to divorcing Science from Humanities (Berlin, 1977). They were initiated by Aristotle, furthered by St Thomas Aquinas, Maimonides and Avicenna, and deepened by Descartes and Comte. Conversely, this tendency was countered by Spinoza, Goethe, Freud, Planck and Einstein.

This splitting history of ideas demands more study, as regards their consequences in probably all human endeavours. Social movements such as the so-called "materialisms", like consumerism (too much interest in the accumulation of material comforts or of physical wealth), have been studied by psychoanalysis under the aegis of mother-baby relationships (Bion, 1962), where the breast's solace, warmth and love may be confused with concretely seen milk. This is at least one psychic origin of the split. The study of the same fact can be made in social and philosophical manifestations or levels, which express the same psychological situation. This can be seen in the fate of Plato's and Aristotle's work. Both were seemingly wasted and doomed to oblivion for many centuries. A powerful factor was linked to some "secular" (that is, linked to deluded sources and warranties of physical wealth) interests from the political-religious establishment. St Thomas Aquinas, regardless of his formidable contributions to the realm of human perception of reality, was a thinker who can be held responsible for deepening the "First Great Split in the War against Knowledge" (namely, the split between mind and matter), due his partisan involvement with the Roman Catholic Church. He used Aristotle's insights to favour certain religious interests that put knowledge into a dead end of subservience to the blind authority of the Holy Scriptures. The Platonic realm came to be a privilege of God and His ministers. Avicenna and Maimonides also did this in their respective cultures. Robust minds, such as Descartes, were prey to the sense-based realism that favoured rational, deductive/

inductive schemata. A by-pass to the blind subservience to authority, which extensively damaged the human attempts to gain knowledge, had to wait many centuries, for the men of the Siècle de Lumières, whose hallmark was honesty and concern for life and truth. Spinoza, Bacon, Locke, Hume, Diderot and, above all, Kant were able to escape from the Thomistic-Cartesian trends without falling back into Wolffian dogmata or Leibnizian idealism. Darker times were to appear as a reaction to their achievements, only to resurface again from time to time as novelties that were only unrecognised remembrances, a fact noticed by Sir Francis Bacon.

Naïve idealism

Naïve idealism constitutes an omnipotent *disregard for Truth*. As a habit of mind, that of the unthinking, it produces untruthfulness as described originally by Thomas Payne. Its aftermath is mindlessness, if a factor is psychopathic traits, a commitment to cynicism, or extreme hate for truth. In its origin, before those degenerating transformations on the path of a crescendo in unthinking, it typifies primitive people, children and psychotics. It nourishes the belief that *reality is a construction of the mind, a product of individual or group-shared imagination*. Naïve Idealism is a denial of a "reality out there" (Gardner, 1989) or "thoughts without a thinker" (Bion, 1962, p. 110–111; 1963, p. 35) waiting to be apprehended. It is displayed in the most mortally destructive mass phenomena of all times, the Nazi and the Stalinist totalitarian states.

Many educated citizens of the Western world grew suspicious of Romanticism, with their lives too deeply affected and carrying the heavy burden of the actions of self-styled Romantics and their typical enthusiasm. Feminine surrender was mistaken for Mindlessness; Search for Truth was replaced with Owning the Ultimate Truth. As Niehbur, Russell and Bion (among so many others) pointed out, a direct outcome of German Idealism (best expressed by Fichte) was Nazism and Stalinism. As in any delinquency (as opposed to psychosis), they knew exactly where truth was, in order to avoid stumbling into it accidentally. Therefore they intuited the danger that psychoanalysis and science posed to them. Rationalism emerged as concretised Consumerism, another enemy of Science and Art. All abhorred reality to the extent that they made explicit promises of sense-based fulfilment of pleasure. A Paradise in Heaven was replaced with a concrete *Lebensraum,* or Paradise on

Earth for workers with consumer goods (greed fulfilled), where the bad (frustration felt as pain, equated to badness) is denied.

Reality, Spirit, Psyche, Truth, External, Internal, as well as many of their expressions such as Mind and Body, are coarse verbal caricatures that fail to grasp the counterpart in reality that they purport to describe. They express much more the impossibility of naming the realm of "truth" and "reality", of what *is*, than anything else. Metaphors, Symbols—in poetry or mathematics, for example—and even Jargon are unsuccessful and disposable, dated periodic attempts linked to culture and age, that try to refresh our insights on the unfathomable and ineffable (albeit existent) "reality", but they do not even reach the status of caricatures. Artistic ways to apprehend and communicate reality were made possible through the use of symbols—a paradoxical epistemological tool, for they mean more than themselves, as Gombrich observed. Symbols therefore offer a very good example of the need not to separate transcendence from immanence; symbols carry transcendence on in their concrete immanence. They are the bricks that bear both Science—Mathematics—and Literature. A perennial problem seems to be distinguishing objects and methods of study, *episteme* and *doxa*, without splitting them.

Myths are an example: full of metaphoric symbolic imagery whose reliance on sight retained its dreamy power—for dreams are a built-in epistemological tool of the human mind, powerful and compacted depictions of realities. Symbols demand formative training and intuition. They built Mathematics and Science and the Mystic tradition, a claim of direct contact with reality. They can be debased in the concreteness allowed by a superficial, imitative pseudo-learning. Insights facilitated by symbols created by men of genius are turned into systems, rules, dead schemata established by disciples, worshippers and followers. Symbols are regarded as if they could allow a hermeneutic approach, with idealistic and imaginary interpretations linked to *a priori* theories. Even dictionaries of symbols were created. Dreams are analysed without resorting to free associations and in the light of a preferred theory, not in the light of the patient's psychic reality.

Hitler, who was fond of repeating his imitations of the banal, popular writings that composed his little knowledge, often said: "Imagination is the basis of knowledge".[6] Both began as a destruction of thought, knowledge and respect for reality and truth (Cohen, 1992). That which the philosopher knew as "subjectivism" or "idealism" came to be known in psychiatry and psychoanalysis as hallucination, delusion and hallucinosis, with prevalence of projection and projective identification. In our field it is represented by the staunch defence of hermeneutics[7] that enthrone anti-scientific, generalisation-loathing explanations of meaning that are not amenable to verification; the staunch defence being part of the problem. Idealism puts man as a god-like creator of the universe. If one can cope with paradoxes, it is not surprising that in the contributions of a religious man like Bishop Berkeley, which was heavily criticised by Kant, there would be no things, only ideas.

The same ideas were cyclically revived. In the twentieth century's disillusionment it acquired the form of regarding false science and its social fakery as real science. Numinous Forms were gradually denied with a reasonable rationality, as all reasons are: how could something unknowable be formatted? What was being denied were approximations towards what was ultimately unknowable, but could be infinitely and infinitesimally approximated, as well as the intuition (and sensible usage) of its existence. In the last third of the century, it came in the guise of post-structuralism: an attempt to reduce science to ideology.[8] It was revived by this century's intelligentsia, who mistook false science and its social fakery for real science; the numinous realm of Forms was gradually denied. The eulogy of hallucinosis came to its peak in today's financial and economic problems of inexhaustible stocks of nothingness and greed and misuse of future planning, bringing with them neologism like "leverage", or the curious, but sadly revealing name of "securities" which are based on non-guaranteed or even existent goods; of future markets of commodities, currencies or anything, and so on. They were preceded by the search for created unnatural epistemes called "paradigms". Science would be politically reached agreements of peer groups, who pick a paradigm disconnected from the reality of facts other than the very agreement.[9] Bion tackles the issue in a dialogue:

> P.A. Quite; I do not see why an infinitely small biological particle being whirled round the galactic centre on a speck of dirt—called by us the Earth—should, in the course of an ephemeral life that does not last even a thousand revolutions round a sun, imagine that the Universe of Galaxies conforms to its limitations.
> PAUL The laws of nature are only the laws of scientific thought.

ROBIN It is readily assumed, filled with meaning, that these colossal forces "obey" these laws as we obey social conventions. [Bion, 1977b, pp. 11–12]

Lack of scientific training condemns those thinkers to be truthful chroniclers of false science. Cooked into a Pilate-like dismissal, truth would be a non-scientific, non-philosophical issue (Rorty, 1982). The latest version of this lack of common sense (Locke, 1690; in analysis, Bion, 1958–1979, p. 10–22, 23, 123) couples hate for truth with praise of desire: it is the "post-modern" advocacy of an analysis of discourse and metaphors. It privileges the signifier over the signified, dealing with words in an unobserved anthropomorphic/animist way, as if they could generate meaning autonomously through their interrelations.[10] It culminates in a legalisation of individual opinions, a "readings-über-alles" posture that praises wish-fulfilling imagination as the only truth to which people may aspire. Freud's developments beyond the pleasure/displeasure principle are dismissed; therefore, the underlying psychoanalytic episteme of this "psychoanalysis" is a pre-psychoanalysis Freud, dazzled with wish-fulfilling, harking back to his cocaine days. Fuelled by "little learning",[11] today's idealism fails "to grasp the nature of relativity...the fact that it includes paradox" (Bion, 1975, p. 80). It disfigured Freud's bisexuality and Einstein's relativity into relativism[12] and Heisenberg's Principle of Uncertainty into a "principle of ignorance". It confuses the ultimate *unknowability* of "O", the noumenon, with its *non-existence*, and denies the possibility of a transient glimpse of it. The failure to realise the non-sensuous realm of noumena splits and overvalues a "mind" that is hallucinated and disembodied, a slave of desire. To split the principle of reality favours the principle of pleasure/displeasure; a wish-fulfilling, all-powerful imagination is enshrined. The naïve idealist condemns us to a poverty which is a travesty of self-attributed richness, "individual imagination". Psychoanalysis indicates that Real Creation demands a matching pair—imagination and reality, male and female. Blind, conceptless pseudo-intuitions abhor reality and facts other than the dictates of the individual parthenogenetic creation. The idealistic analyst becomes baffled when the laws of natural science do not obey the laws of his mental functioning. Schiller's *sentimetalisch* forecast the naïve idealist: "his observation is forcibly pushed aside by his fancy; his sensibility by his ideas".[13]

Naïve realism

Naïve realism constitutes the warring reaction against idealism: a disregard for Mind (and Life). Positive "Science" believes that reality can be adequately apprehended by relying on concretising human apparatus: the senses and conscious rationalism[14] that privilege phenomena over noumena. Empirically intuited underlying Elementals are replaced by an attempt to extract roots as in primitive mathematics; reality is felt to be reachable through depicting causes, predicting effects, locating things in the Euclidean-Cartesian model taken as a reality. It denies that reason is at the service of passions.[15] It seems to be impossible to intuit the transcendent negative nature of Forms, which was emphasised by Bion, Grotstein and Green. The Noumenon, "O",[16] is concretised into seemingly positive immanences. Today's fashionable naïve realism in the psychoanalytic movement fails to observe that the reproducibility (Hempel, 1962, Popper, 1959) of analytic phenomena depends on intuition of their numinous realm, of their non-sensuously apprehensible, non-concrete nature, rather than a belief in an axiomatic neutrality of the observer, the begetter of a reification of methods (Adorno et al, 1969). Positivist concretised neurobiology once "located" the Id in the Limbic System, not realising that both are models of reality rather than realities. The quantification of flattened standardised "clinical" data obtained through conscious filtering reduces them to their sensory manifestations. Naïve Realism works well in the material reality, providing "a framework which seems to have facilitated the development of knowledge, but the element of growth appears to have escaped formulation since it resembles maturation" (Bion, 1975, p. 87). The naïve realist condemns us to mental poverty full of empty concreteness. He concretises states of mind, in a phenomenon linked by Bion to the psychotic's state of mind (Bion, 1953, 1956, 1962, 1963, 1965, 1975), dealing with the animate realm using methods more suited to inanimate objects. One advocates that Reason is superior to *Wille*, the nature-bound origin of instinctive intuition. Freud, helped by Judge Schreber's writings, was not fooled by "rationalisation" (Freud, 1911). Instead, he discovered this mode of mental non-functioning or non-mental functioning, which tended to mindlessness clothed with the full finery of the intelligent mind.[17]

Nevertheless, the animate realm, of which medicine and psychoanalysis are part, is where and when an indivisible matter/energy space/

time happens to be. The naïve realist becomes perplexed when the laws of the natural mind do not obey the laws of his pre-patterned castings. His myriads of disordered, intuitionless, rational, plausible concepts are devoid of insight, of elemental key-concepts and invariants. His denial of Truth resembles the naïve idealist's paradigms; he imagines a *disposable science* that can be "falsified" (Popper, 1963). Both naïves collect erudite advocating paramnesias, marking the return of psychoanalysis to conscious psychology. "Meaningful" is replaced by "many meanings" stemming either from the analyst's imagination or from the analysand's manifest contents. For example, instead of investigating a particular way of non-development of Oedipus, one can focus on the presence of "solidarity" or "kindness", and so on.

The analyst who tries to transplant this model forgets, ignores or denies that it has not worked in real science at least since Einstein and Planck. Again and again an Ur-pre-psychoanalysis is favoured, its basic episteme being a belief in the cause-effect traumatic theory.

Truth is beauty, beauty truth[18]

Is personal analysis and analytically trained intuition, learning from clinical experience, doomed to be replaced by fashionable "paradigms" transplanted from other fields? Can the romantic suffering of a passionate intuitive experience (namely, personal analysis and analysing others) be replaced by erudition (rational learning of psychoanalytic theory), or by disordered flights of imagination, or by quantification? Or is it time to return to a purely psychoanalytic, empirically clinical view? Freud and Bion recommended apprehension of the state of mind of the researchers: ourselves in the first instance. Both Freud and Bion studied the researcher's state of mind; Freud did this in his psychoanalytic conjectures around Leonardo's work and Bion dwelt on the positivist and the philosopher's ideas on scientific method, as well as on geocentric ideas. My conclusions stem from a few decades of continuous practice of analysis. Some of the clearest data come from the analysis of a Physicist who loathes Einstein's expansions of Newton, two artistically minded housewives, two engineers, a banker, four candidates for entry to analytic societies, a nuclear chemist working on a nuclear weapons project, two musicians and three medical doctors. I include my own difficulties in grasping what seems to me the psychoanalytic ethos, as seen in my own analysis and a comparative study of these data with the work of great thinkers, published elsewhere (Sandler, 1997–2003). This can be put into the movement between PS and D in the history of Western civilisation's ideas about mind and truth.

A basic source of error seems to me to be subservience to desire and pleasure, which manifests itself as a mix, in varying degrees, of hate for truth and love and a sensuous-concretised contempt for mind and life. Not tolerating that the real breast *differs in a frustrating way* from the breast that is desired (or perhaps needed) may be the basis either of naïve idealism—one hallucinates the ideal breast—or of naïve realism—one concretises the breast that cannot deliver solace or, if it does, the solace cannot be experienced due envious narcissistic and paranoid endogenous traits and "forced splitting" (Bion, 1962). Therefore both kinds of naïveté are expressions of immobilisation in the paranoid-schizoid position. The interval between the real breast and the desired breast, the no-breast, can produce thinking, due to the action of the epistemophilic instinct. The realm of the negative is tolerated. If this is the case, loss and real-life difficulties are not introjected as hostility, but they are introjected as the facts as they are; the person symbolises the breast. Greed and envy in a narcissistic personality can be coupled with the perception that a real breast existed but is irretrievably lost; hate for truth can thus be turned into delinquency (Winnicott, 1966). The psychotic cannot perceive the truth and hallucinates; the delinquent knows where the truth is just to avoid stumbling into it inadvertently.

The sense of truth

Shakespeare's manner included the placing of the most seminal, perceptive observations about human nature into seemingly minor characters. As with the Bard, there are still contributions by Bion which remain unobserved. Even Bion's scholars do not pay attention to what is in my opinion a remarkable advancement made through psychoanalytic findings to epistemology and scientific research. After Klein, in 1961 Bion suggests an entropic state achieved when one realises *that the object that is loved and the object that is hated are one and the same object* (Bion, 1961b, p. 111). He coined the term "sense of truth" for this act.

The sense of truth deals with antithetical pairs and their outcome, including the most profoundly unfathomable mysteries of creation, life and nature, as they are—a thrust into the unknown, beyond preconceptions. Lack of it is expressed by desperate, concrete attempts at ownership of a hallucinated "absolute truth". I propose to extend it to the realm of knowledge: one tolerates that *the object that is known and the object that is unknown are one and the same object*. The sense of truth (with a kinship to Berlin's sense of reality) allows for what I have been suggesting throughout this work as being a basic psychoanalytic tool, forming its own ethos: the tolerance of paradoxes without hasty or forced attempts to solve them.

It is difficult to evaluate how any relative lack of this tolerance of paradoxes damages the appraisal of clinical cases—and real life. In this case, Religion replaces Research; Prescription replaces Description; Morals replace Comprehension; Representation replaces Presentation; Understanding replaces Apprehension; *ought to be* replaces sympathetic apprehension of that that which *is*; False Compliance and Collusion replace *"At-one-ment"*. The patient learns about analysis but remains virgin of it. True and false are not seen as distinguishing between reality and hallucination, but are mistaken for right and wrong. *The psychoanalytic endeavour is equated to adaptation to a given pattern*: skilful, brainy adaptation to some *a priori* psychoanalytic theory or moral, cultural cure; always external, rather than internal adaptation of the self to the true self.

The splits we reviewed in this chapter are expressions of loathing paradoxes and the unavoidable, forced attempts to resolve them. The naïve idealist and the naïve realist cannot discover real elementals that appear in paradoxical pairs, *both in theories and in the here and now of the session*, in the patient's utterances. They are blind to the embedded transcendent truth that endows a theory of its "science-ness" due to its all-embracing generalising/particularising power; this truth is neither the patient's nor the analyst's creation; those paradoxes endow an interpretation of its value. How can one experience the quantum qualitative leap represented by intuiting insightful latent contents, "paradoxical truth-O"? The idealistic practitioner, or witchcraft apprentice in the psychoanalytic movement, clings to imagination and violent feeling as the basis of knowledge; the realist, or our movement's "contraptioneer", cannot go beyond manifest contents.

Both analyse discourses, not realising that psychic reality includes psychic non-reality too. Both mistake the condinuous hallucinatory activity, a negative counterpoint to the apprehension of reality, for "phantasising/dreaming", dismissing the latter. The idealist overexaggerates it and the realist sees is as pathology.

Some do not split and do not concretise or exaggerate the feelings, such as a gifted little girl of five who was fortunate enough to find a real analyst.[19] In her third year of analysis she said: "It is easy to draw a teddy bear. You must have a teddy bear, pay attention to it and then imagine it a little bit."

Notes

1. A truthful concept by Donald Winnicott (for example, 1958). During a seminar in a course on the apprehension of psychic reality (later published in book form) that constitutes the foundation of the present chapter, a practising analyst asked: "Is psychoanalysis the naming of our lie?" (Miguel Marques, 1997, personal communication). The association with Poincaré's selected fact, brought into the psychoanalytic movement by Bion (in *Second Thoughts* and *Cogitations*), was made by a gifted and attentive (as the young usually are) Portuguese student of psychology during a conference given by me in 2004 in Lisbon, at the kind invitation of Dr Eduardo de Sá, Federico Pedreira and Maria Luiza B. Vicente. Unfortunately, I could not trace his full name after the conference.
2. See Hume on induction and Popper on *ad hoc* pitfalls (Hume, 1748; Popper, 1959).
3. And his forebears, today almost forgotten: Hamann and Herder. One must include Schiller and Heine too. See the origins of psychoanalysis in those authors in Sandler, 2001a, b; 2003.
4. I have had the opportunity to exchange ideas and experiences with Dr Grotstein since his first visit to Brazil in 1983, especially as regards Kant's contributions, as well as some obvious (albeit never explicitly expressed) links between the three basic instincts and the three first links (H, L, K) described by Bion.
5. Expansions on Freud and Kant, and Klein and Hegel, may be found in Sandler, 2003.
6. Quoted in Cohen, 1992, Lüdecke, 1938, and Trevor-Roper, 1953. It may be unfair to quote non-scientific books expressing self-propaganda and arrogant, opinionated ideas such as Hitler's (the two latter books) together with Peter Cohen's film, which was based on hard research, but since they were consulted for this chapter, it may be useful to indicate them to the reader.
7. As in the work of Gadamer and Heidegger.
8. The post-moderns came from the excesses of structuralism; see Lévi-Strauss (1950), Althusser (1967, pp. 200–239), Feyerabend (1975, 1978),

Foucault (1963). One may quote the easy, superficial and simplistic statements clothed in fashionable epistemological wording that stated: psychoanalysis is a Victorian practice; the same false episteme contradictorily underlies the statement that it was a Jewish-Bolshevik idea.

9. Thomas Kuhn introduced this as an agenda for a disposable science; Karl Popper and Imre Lakatos had overt political quarrels with Kuhn, wisely realising his totalitarian idealist view. See Kuhn (1970), Rorty (1982, Chapter 6), Lakatos (1963–4), Lakatos & Musgrave (1970).

10. In psychoanalysis, Ricoeur's textualism and the adaptations of Lyotard. Derrida's textualism must be distinguished from this; he had a genuine, albeit eclectic, interest in truth (See Ricoeur, 1977, Derrida, 1966, Lyotard, 1979, and appraisals by Norris, 1997, Nozick, 2001 and Williams, 2002). I personally believe that those authors distorted Bachelard's and Derrida's work, lacking their care for reality and truth. The praise of individual readings can be seen in Gilles Deleuze, Michel Foucault and Bruno Latour.

11. Perhaps Gilles Deleuze was one the best examples of this trend.

12. Many tried to repair the damage already done, including Einstein's own failed attempts, and later Eddington, Russell, Hawking, Penrose and Sokal (see specially Norris, 1997). No cyanoacrylate can repair a finely entwined eggshell of knowledge broken by idealistic omnipotence.

13. It will be noticed that I use the term "naïve" in the same sense that Kant, Cassirer and Bachelard used it; this differs from Schiller's usage (1795).

14. That debased Rational into Rationalism.

15. On Logical and Psycho-Logical needs, see Bion, 1965, p. 75.

16. Bion's notation for the numinous realm (Bion, 1965, 1970, 1975).

17. It is popularly said that Freud invented Oedipus and the unconscious, which is wrong (and he never claimed that, though he claimed to have given them a practical use): they have been known since the Ancient Greek and Romantic philosophers and poets, as my own and other people's research has shown. Conversely, Freud's discoveries are usually buried, like infantile sexuality, the principle of reality and the extension of what he called "rationalisation" or omnipotence of thoughts (the latter is described in "Totem and Taboo").

18. Keats, *Ode on a Grecian Urn*: "When old age shall this generation waste, / Thou shalt remain, in midst of other woe / Than ours, a friend to man, to whom thou say'st, / 'Beauty is truth, truth beauty',—that is all / Ye know on earth, and all ye need to know."

19. Dr Ester Hadassa Sandler, who treated this girl and furnished the illustration after reading this chapter.

CHAPTER EIGHT

Truth

> And finally we must not forget that the analytic relationship is based on a love of truth—that is, on a recognition of reality—and that it precludes any kind of sham or deceit.
>
> —Freud, 1937a, p. 248

> Reality has been deprived of its value, its meaning, its veracity to the same degree as an ideal world has been fabricated…The "real world" and the "apparent world"—in plain terms: the fabricated world and reality…The lie of the ideal has hitherto been the curse on reality, through it mankind itself has been mendacious and false down to its deepest instincts—to the point of worshipping the inverse values to those which alone could guarantee its prosperity, its future, the exalted right to a future.
>
> —Nietzsche, 1888, p. 4

Are there any facts that at least partially justify the spending of time, life and, according to some people, money on them? I think that if there are, they would include the empirical substratum of psychoanalysis that is the clinic.

One may take a partial descriptive statement, which has the advantage of being simple, to depict an analytic clinical situation: one puts oneself to truthfully listen to what someone else has to say (slightly modified from Bion, 1979). No wonder, because psychoanalysis is a development, a kind of "offspring" which displays its "heredity" from medicine. The same description serves well for medical practice, which also includes some material statements. Clinical practice confers, in theoretical terms, scientific status to psychoanalysis. In practical, real-life terms it confers its strength: its reality-value, or truth-value. Clinical experience demands "participating observation" of real facts as they are, quite independently of reaching them wholly, permanently or not.

As may have occurred in the findings included in Volume 2 Part I, I can be accused of ignorance, or perhaps pretentious or opinionated dismissal of the whole body of polemical discussions under the umbrella of what is known as the philosophical contributions. Truthfully, conscious or unwilling commitment to what I view as a decayed romanticism (meaning the established or institutional, inanimate movement which extracted life from the Romantic Movement) had descended to the ignominious position of defending untruth in denying the possibility of knowledge and processes of knowing. Revolutionaries of all species won the day—sometimes measured by year or decade—erudition was mistaken for wisdom; schooling was seen as unnecessary, mistaken for education; superficial autodidactic "training" replaced a disciplined way of getting in touch with truth. The results of this are just opinionated ignorance, or "little learning", a dangerous thing according to Alexander Pope.

I think that it is possible to get at least transient glimpses of partial aspects of facts which are not psychoanalytic facts or physical facts but are just facts, where—and when—matter and mind cannot be artificially split. Though it is only a flash between two long nights, this flash is everything. Trained intuition (experientially acquired, or sensible intuition, as Kant called it) can have weird appearances to the sizeable number of people who are seduced by external appearances and the commonplace—which is often mistaken for common sense. On the other hand, other people are able to observe that "though this be madness, yet there is method in't" (*Hamlet*, II ii). By intuition we understand the apprehension of reality as it is with no interference of rational thinking. Freud—as well as his contemporaries in German culture—called intuitive people *Menschenkenner* (he did not consider himself part of this group).

We saw in the previous chapter that some people deny any possibility of intuiting and respecting facts as they are, independently of one's (or our, considering the human species) ability or possibility to apprehend them. Once upon a time, philosophers dealt with truth and mind; this is no longer true in our present days. Perhaps, in an unknown time, phoenix-like, the equalisation of natural facts, truth and reality may return to philosophy's nest. Out of necessity, today (as with some species of birds) truth takes refuge in other, more hospitable and safer environments, such as psychoanalysis, physics and mathematics, and artistic forms such as music. As a patient who was a born pianist, who had suffered one of the supreme untruths (un-naturally noxious as any unnatural action is) to which one may be submitted—to be abandoned as a child by an un-mothering mother—told me, "Music is where I found more truth than in any other endeavour known to me in life".[1] Beethoven, who wrote *Muss es ein? Es muss sein* on the manuscript of his String Quartet no. 16 (op. 135), is quoted as saying: "I love truth more than anything". Anyway, keeping a psychoanalytic vertex does not dismiss the philosopher's achievements in the human history of ideas, which would equate to ignorance. It just makes psychoanalysis a phylogenetic heir to them, when the great "systems" or "totalisations" attempting to sum up "the whole" made by the greatest philosophers were not subjected to the contempt of nowadays.[2]

Perhaps it is timely to define what we mean by "facts as they are" in this book. The verbal formula is borrowed from Francis Bacon, and was used through many centuries, sometimes ambivalently (as in Kant's work), sometimes in more definite terms (e.g. by Dr Samuel Johnson). Facts cannot be wholly known or formulated but can be intuited and used. They belong to space-time as discovered by Einstein, so any formulation in terms of either just space or just time fails to give a full description. Facts possess a kind of beauty given by their truth, as in Keats's poetry; in philosophical terms, they are durable because of their transcendence. Facts as they are belong to the realm of Truth. In this sense they can be equated to Reality.

Truth cannot be regarded alone. Like anything in Nature, its appearance depends upon a couple[3] and can be scrutinised through a relationship with its opposite (but not opposing) counterpart (or antithetical pole). The antithetical counterpart of Truth is Lie. Disclaimer: "Counterpart" does not mean "Alternative". The verbal formulation more apposite for scrutinising it would be Truth⇔Lie. It is more cumbersome to put in written form but it is more precise as well; in any case, for the sake of brevity, when we write Truth, we mean [Truth⇔Lie]. Other commonly applied names, which may be seen as synonyms, are Reality (or truthful apprehension of facts) and Hallucination (untruthful, for objectless perceptions). Therefore the sign that marks a movement (growing and its obverse) would be [Reality⇔Hallucination]: each is conducive to the other under an "eternal", living movement as long as individual or group life still exists. This corresponds to the movement between the Positions described by Klein and the movement between the conscious and unconscious systems described by Freud. Both movements were made more explicit by Bion's graphic notation, the double arrow.

Still using the advantage furnished by verbal formulations, we may distinguish Truth (or Truth⇔Lie) from that which can be called "*The Truth*". The former is a "hetero" pair formed by two observational counterpoints. The latter is a belief of having attained "Absolute Truth". It is a single entity which is not the fruit of observation but rather of morals. Psychic determinants belong to the realm of narcissistic traits, typical of the paranoid-schizoid position. Its non-coupled, un-related mode endows it with a "homo" nature.

Truth appears to be important to philosophers, mystics, scientists, visual, acoustic and verbal artists and to any human being who attempts to enjoy a life worthy of this name. I use the verb "enjoy" not in its sense of pleasure but rather in the sense of "undergoing the benefit of an experience", pleasurable or not. The lungs of the human species profit from relating (through exchange) with the oxygen in the environment—in this sense, lungs respect their own and external reality. Therefore truth does not seem to me a strictly philosophical issue. Philosophical experience is not inimical to analysis despite the fact that they differ in terms of practical utility. Philosophers are fond of stating that philosophy has none. Philosophy is older than psychoanalysis; when philosophers dealt with Truth and Mind, their problems were the same ones that the practising analyst faces (Bion, 1958–1979, p. 125; 1962). So any experience gained could be—and in Freud and other authors was—profitably used.

I personally cannot profit too much, except as a counterpoint, from the currently prevailing trends in philosophy when the issue is truth. They took the name "post-modernism"; to put it mildly, the philosopher seems to have given up any attempt to search for Truth, or "apprehension of reality", as I propose to call it. There is a widespread denial of the very existence of truth, and therefore of science, which is usually seen as ideologically-oriented, as Althusser always insisted. What seems to me to remain unobserved in post-modernists is a renewed, disguised idealism (or subjectivism): there are insistent claims that reality does not exist at all, for it is "constructed" by the human mind, as in Deleuze and some of Foucault's contributions. Truth seemed important to those authors, when we consider the efforts they made to deny it. Sometimes a kind of "relativism" is used to prove those ideas, even though its basis, half-learned quantum theory and relativity, proved to be at least controversial, as some authors, like Sokal, pointed out.

Our time may reflect an old love-hate affair the human being maintains with Truth. There is confusion over moral superiority and the election of one "side" (truth or lie) as superior, knighting it (who, after all, is entitled to be the pope or emperor or dictator who knights?) "Valiant of truth" (or lie) like Meltzer's dream or, later, Gawain (Meltzer, 1988, 1989). The way may be exemplified by Nietzsche, who, in Freud's view, knew himself more than anyone before or after him: "on many occasions he said that Nietzsche had the most penetrating knowledge of himself of any man who ever lived or was likely to live" (Freud, quoted in Jones, 1955, p. 385).

The relationships of psychoanalysis, and much more, of Freud and Bion with Nietzsche have been studied by many authors, but as far as my research goes, with no implications other than philosophical—which is equivalent to saying with no practical or empirical or psychoanalytic implications, even though they were indicated by Freud. That is, these implications and alliances had been subjected to an equally strong oblivion, under the myths of prohibition of knowledge or truthfulness, or achievements in approaching truth (Thorner, 1981):

> The theory of repression quite certainly came to me independently of any other source; I know of no outside impression which might have suggested it to me, and for a long time I imagined it to be entirely original, until Otto Rank showed us a passage of Schopenhauer's "World as Will and Representation" in which the philosopher seeks to give an explanation of insanity. What he says there about the struggle against accepting a distressing piece of reality coincides with my concepts of repression so completely that once again I owe the chance of making a Discovery to my *not being*

> *well-read*. Yet others have read the passage and passed it by without making the Discovery, and perhaps the same would have happened to me if in my young days I had had more taste for reading philosophical works. In later years I have denied myself the very great pleasure of reading the works of Nietzsche, with the deliberate object of not being hampered in working out the impressions received in psychoanalysis by any sort of anticipatory ideas. I had therefore to be prepared—and I am so, gladly—to forgo all claims to priority in the many instances in which laborious psychoanalytic investigation can merely confirm the truths which the philosopher recognised *by intuition*. [Freud, 1914b, pp. 15–16; my emphasis]

Bion extended the hallucinated nature of memory, which is usually mistaken for truth; nevertheless, police and justice systems as well as professionals dedicated to history learned to mistrust memory, or at least to try to resort to methods of refutation in order to verify it. It seems that psychoanalysis, having Nietzsche as a kind of forebear who interfered in the history of ideas in Western civilisation and "nourished" both Freud's and Bion's outlook, finally provided a way to scrutinise how emotional facts biased memory. Thus a "selective memory" was elicited, which created selected memories full of vested interests as regards the influence of the principle of pleasure and displeasure—at the expense of the principle of reality.

Freud mentions a quotation from Nietzsche's *Beyond Good and Evil* which he heard from one of his patients, later known as the "Rat Man", adding that no other person could portray the phenomenon and its psychological basis in such a complete and remarkable way, that is, emphasising the influence of affect on memory and truth:

> "I did this," says my Memory. "I cannot have done this," says my Pride, and remains inexorable. In the end—Memory yields. [Nietzsche, 1886, quoted in Freud, 1909]

One cannot state that Freud was wittingly or consciously influenced by Nietzsche, aside from the influences from his patients and from colleagues such as Rank:

> Nietzsche, another philosopher whose guesses and intuitions often agree in the most astonishing way with the laborious findings of psychoanalysis, was for a long time avoided by me on that very

account; I was less concerned with the question of priority than with keeping my mind unembarrassed. [Freud, 1925, p. 60]

But the unconscious cultural milieu that formed both Freud and Nietzsche cannot be dismissed. Bion's notion of Nietzsche, also seen in a non-erudite but nevertheless in a certain sense scholarly (or serious) way can be demonstrated by his tolerance of paradoxes and the value he placed on the realm of minus, as I have stated. Nietzsche wrote in a mode than can be regarded as metaphorical as well as resorting to parables. It is less explanatory, convincing and allowing—to some readers—a straightforward way to direct insight. Even though to other readers this way may sound heretical, and even authoritarian, it resembles Bion's wish, enhanced in *A Memoir of the Future*, that one could "use certain words which could activate precisely and instantaneously, in the mind of the listener, a thought or train of thought that came between him and the thoughts and ideas already accessible and available to him" (Bion, 1975, p. 190).

> What is great about human beings is that they are a bridge and not a purpose: what is lovable about human beings is that they are a *crossing over* and a *going under*.
> I love those who do not know how to live unless by going under, for they are the ones who cross over.
> I love the great despisers, because they are the great venerators and arrows of longing for the other shore. [Nietzsche, 1883]

> The man of knowledge must be able not only to love his enemies but also to hate his friends.
> Now I bid you lose me and find yourselves; and only when you have all denied me will I return to you. [Nietzsche, 1888]

> Perhaps no one has ever been sufficiently truthful about what "truthfulness" is. [Nietzsche, 1886]

Not very unlike Kant, Nietzsche can be seen as ambivalent, furnishing quotations just as a pursuer of "O" and a defender of idealism, and those written doubts and earlier positions were coined by truth-haters as the definitive aspect of his contributions. There is a tendency for a sizeable number of readers to take part of a work as if it were the whole. This impressionistic observation merits a quantitative study. A specific mode of doing this is to quote the earlier position of a great author as if it were the whole of his or her contributions. In doing this, the reader denies the author's development—which, if the author respects the facts as they emerge, can amount to changing many of his or her previous theories, and in some cases whole theoretical constructions. A most telling example of this is Freud's theorisation about the instincts. Taking a part as if it were the whole is a special kind of splitting, and corresponds to Freud's, Bleuler's and subsequent psychiatrists' observations about a hallmark of what is now seen as psychotic non-thinking. This was best illuminated under the psychoanalytic vertex by Klein (1946), Fairbairn (1952) and Bion (1953, 1956, 1957). This chapter cannot go on to detail Nietzsche's contributions, but I will just emphasise his discovery of ways out that warrant a kind of truthfulness as a psychic attitude. Bernard Williams had classified this kind of people, whom I see as solipsists, idealists and relativists, as "deniers" who "often claim the inheritance of Nietzsche" (Williams, 2002, p. 13; a review of them appears in Allison, 1977; they also claim to represent a "new Nietzsche", which could be completed by an "old Nietzsche", the paradox of the interpreters or "readers"). A favourite quotation among the "deniers" is based on a young Nietzsche's musings in *On Truths and Lies in a Non-Moral Sense*:

> What then is truth? A movable host of metaphors, metonymies, and anthropomorphisms; in short, a sum of human relations which have been poetically and rhetorically intensified, transferred and embellished, and which, after long usage, seem to people to be fixed, canonical and binding. Truths are illusions we have forgotten are illusions; they are metaphors that have become worn out and have been drained of sensuous force, coins which have lost their embossing and are now considered as metal and no longer as coins. [Nietzsche, 1873][4]

In a late work, *The Antichrist*, Nietzsche writes:

> Truth has had to be fought for every step of the way, almost everything else dear to our hearts, on which our love and out trust in life depend, has had to be sacrificed to it. Greatness of soul is needed for it: the service of truth is the hardest service. For what does it mean to be *honest* in intellectual things? That one is stern towards

one's heart, that one despises "fine feelings", that one makes every Yes and No a question of conscience! [Nietzsche, 1888]

But compare it with the "ur-psychoanalytic" tone, later amplified by Freud and expanded by Bion, written in *The Gay Science*:

This unconditional will to truth—what is it? Is it the will not to let oneself be deceived? Is it the will *not to deceive*? For the will to truth could be interpreted in this second way, too—if "I do not want to deceive *myself*" is included as a special case under the generalisation "I do not want to deceive". But why not deceive? But why not allow oneself to be deceived? [Nietzsche, 1882]

The deniers prefer to eliminate other parts, such as Nietzsche's unabashed final admiration for the ancient world due to its inventing the "incomparable art of reading well…the prerequisite for a cultural tradition for a uniform science", with its "sense for facts, the last-developed and most valuable of all senses" (*The Antichrist*, 1888). An admiration shared with Ruskin (1865), the rescuer of classics. This scientific awe produced Nietzsche's warning about Enlightenment-bashing in England: he thought that Hume and Locke should not be the object of contempt because of their having been "taught to sacrifice desirability to truth, *every* truth, even a plain, bitter, ugly, foul, unchristian, immoral truth… Because there are such truths" (*On the Genealogy of Morality*, 1887). The relativists, post-modernists and their like prefer to omit that Nietzsche surmounted through maturity the adolescent formula more typical of his earlier studies; as regards this book and Bion's contributions, it was when Nietzsche was able to put truth into the realm of hallucinosis: "The antithesis of the apparent world and the true world is reduced to the antithesis 'world' and 'nothing'" (*The Will to Power*).

If the classifications of non-thinking can be made by resorting to the two "naïves", realist and idealist, the former falls into a limited sensuous error while the latter takes the side of untruthfulness and attempts at self-deception. Theirs is enslavement to the principle of pleasure and displeasure, which supports no unconditional valuing of truth. This is seen in different modes, but with the same result, by realists, who treat truth as a cheap good (such as money in the economic crisis of 2008), and by idealists, who deal with it as a disposable waste. In this sense, they take not "a new Nietzsche" but "an earlier and younger Nietzsche" and mistake him for a mature thinker. Some people, like Nozick (2001), are not as harsh as others such as Norris. He concedes to the relativists and idealists the benefit of doubt more appropriate to philosophers like Derrida, who respect truth with no hate. Such a doubt hallmarked the German philosopher and many others—a possible, if dangerous, way towards truth. This can be seen in adolescents, if one takes the psychoanalytic vertex.

It seems that there are stumbling blocks when one tries to search for truth, amounting to the construing of a taboo in the very attempt to pursue it. During some epochs those obstacles are regarded as amenable to be dealt with even within known limitations linked to our sense apparatus, the human equipment to apprehend and tolerate truth.

I suggested elsewhere that Psychoanalysis is one of the heirs of both the Enlightenment and the Romantic Movement. After the Renaissance's brave attempts, they finally rescued the Truth in Ancient Greek and Jewish (cabalistic) achievements in science, art and human reality. The Enlightenment and the Romantic Movement produced more powerful apprehensions of reality—"truth-O" (Bion, 1970)—than were ever made before or since. They had a specific purpose: being beneficial to the individual human being. It is not a mere coincidence that the revival and formidable development of Science and Medicine in particular was typical of those times. The quest was a search for truth devoid of religious dogmas and authoritarianism, a respect for facts and natural facts as they are (Samuel Johnson's letter to Langton, quoted by Bion, 1958–1979, p. 114).

Some of the hereditary traits of Psychoanalysis that are linked to the Romantic emphasis can be subsumed by the word "passion". The Romantics disclosed the need to take into account the emotional experience as regards apprehension of truth. Philosophy had problems with this task when it resorted to formal logical, rational, conscious thinking in its attempts to approach truth. Academic teaching puts some authors from the Enlightenment in the dustbin of rationalism, reducing them to Empiricism (British or not), something that acquired the status of a dirty word in the Structuralist and Post-Modernist relativism. But it can be just a one-sided and incomplete learning that denies Diderot's passion-unlocking dialogues, Locke's forays into intuition, Hume's attempt to display that reason is a slave to passion, and the influence of passion in the work of Kant.

In the cross-roads of rationalism, idealism and the platonic realms, there were the somewhat ambivalent attempts of Kant, who would not deny the existence of the noumena but forbade any attempt to investigate them; some of Kant's teachers, such as Hamann, pointed out his timidity. This adventure was made in later times by Freud, Planck, Einstein, Klein and Bion. They formulated insights into the numinous realm, forays into the human truth as it is. The transient and unavoidably incomplete glimpses obtained, which are far from apprehending the ineffable whole of the numinous realm, could not justify not making the attempt. Apprehending "O" (Bion's notation for the numinous realm), in the sense of a transient intuition of its existence, demands "becoming" rather than knowing (Bion, 1965).

Individually, some philosophers did not hold back from the task. But those who succeeded paid a price: sometimes remarkable, like Socrates and Giordano Bruno, whose murders were linked to their attempts. Others had their work debased, assimilated into banality and reviled. A common denigrating reaction against attempts to get closer to Truth is to label them as mystical and esoteric. Freud's work was among those affected, despite his careful measures to prevent this view; any analyst is well stocked with this unloving as soon as his or her experience grows.

The profound denial of truth flows either to Naïve Idealism, the idea that reality is what the mind says it is; or to Naïve Realism, the idea that reality is what the senses apprehend. Either trend subjects to prohibition and abhorrence any attempts to apprehend the numinous "O". There is a persistent failure to realise that mystic or intuitive fact differs from esoteric mysticism. The former is the apprehension of truth without the "brokerage" of rational thinking, unrestricted to sensuous experience. It is based on personal, disciplined education that allows for experience of real facts—akin both to artistic and to scientific disciplined training. In Goethe's times, it was called *Bildung* and *Biedermeier* (in earlier times, a form of ample education; later, an aped cynicism feigning education). The Enlightened-Romantic achievements were full of their authors' interest in still-unknown oriental cultures. These included the Jewish and Christian Cabala, a knowledge of a kind of "wordy calculus"—the detection and deducing of the *sephiroth*—in order to elicit truths applied to old biblical texts (Scholem, 1941; Yates, 1971). The medical tradition, where the Enlightenment revived interest in the individual and their suffering, furnished the last constituent that gave birth to psychoanalysis through the contributions of Freud.

I think that the analyst's need for a personal analysis is the improved—for it is scientific—heir of all those previously "formative" traditions earlier expressed by the Cabalists and *Bildungskrafters*. The continuing experience resembles a known "formative" training, which has already gained a universal denomination, the "personal trainer". One may ask why the continuing need for physical training is omitted when one deals with mental training, when it is not devoted to the professions or anything related. The analyst already knows that students of psychology justify and find social support for their need for analysis through schooling and rules laid down by professors, which do not resist the test of truth. The analyst needs analysis just like any human being, and like any human being needs continuous physical exercise.

The analyst experiences himself as he is—and this is an empirical fact, albeit an expanded (post-Kant) "participant" empiricism. There is a profound reality, seemingly "occult", made visible, for example, in dreams, which in pre-psychoanalytic times was called "mystic". It *seems* to be occult for it is not apparent in a direct way to our senses. Moreover, our sense apparatus has a limited range of apprehension. The "occult" profoundness of the "infra- and ultra-sensuous" (Bion, 1975) is un-thought, but real. It is amenable to be apprehended if and when one deals with symbolic systems *beyond the sign*—the mind does not present itself in a direct way to our perceptual apparatus. There is a need to formulate an underlying fact that seems to be wholly new.

In fact it was not "new"—it was always there, but it remained hitherto unknown to the conscious apparatus. It makes itself present among a penumbra of circumstances, contingencies and possibilities. That which I call "formulating" has similarities with the detection of a "new fact" sought by the mathematician, according Poincaré. His philosophical work was brought to psychoanalysts by Bion. This fact is a link that "unites elements long since known but till then scattered and seemingly foreign to each other" (Poincaré, quoted in Bion, 1958–1979, p. 14). This "new fact" has properties to the observer, but not intrinsically to the observed facts. Bion developed this concept later, with "new" or "demanding to be discovered" facts that belong to the observed facts: namely, "invariance" (Bion, 1965; Sandler, 2005).

Hampering facts

There are some social and individual problems linked to the starting point of respect for truth, both in the consulting room and in the attempts towards applied psychoanalysis in social (group) settings.

People are taught not to trust in what is said to them; often it is a much praised pre-emptive measure against the naiveté of children and youngsters. The analyst seems to start from a principle that people will have to take seriously someone who vows to tell them the truth. *This* is often regarded as the analyst's naiveté; most people use it accordingly. The many examples of difficulties in financial matters (fees) illustrate it.

How can one insert the psychoanalytic vertex of respect for truth in social organisations founded on political networks engineered by greed, evasion and hallucination? Common hallucinations found in analysis include feelings of superiority of some beings over other beings, immortality and fame, which is "no plant that grows on mortal soil", according Milton.

Cure, short- and long-range effects: what is true of psychoanalysis

Psychoanalysis can function right from the start of the first meeting, but to talk of lasting effects is always a matter of keeping in mind that we are dealing with a kind of "fitness situation", much like the personal trainer analogy. Other analogies can be made with life itself, or the refiner's fire. Nourishment is an everlasting need as far as one assumes that life has to be kept.

Two young patients I met at the beginning of my psychiatric career, John and Jonas, were labelled as schizophrenics with drug addiction. John, diagnosed as a paranoid schizophrenic, had bouts of delusion. He felt that he "ate his father's flesh" in a dinner; one day he came to the hospital after "having committed a murder", with details of the person he "killed", what weapon he used ("my Dad's automatic Walther"), the street in which he did it, and so on.

Jonas used to wander naked in the infirmary and urinate against the walls. One day he unwittingly set his room ablaze and risked death, his lit cigarette having ignited his pillow when he had fallen asleep. Jonas was diagnosed (wrongly, as time proved) as a hebephrenic schizophrenic, with a low IQ. Both remained around seven years in treatment.

After leaving, both used to phone me sporadically to tell how they were doing and about their latest achievements. Theirs was a friendly and mildly grateful tone. Ten years were spent in this way. In time the frequency of phone calls faded out until it seemed to end.

One day, an unknown woman phoned me in the same friendly tone. She was John's aunt, and wanted to inform me that John met his fate some years earlier. "John always referred kindly to you, Dr Sandler, I suppose you had to know but I was not able to tell you that he died a painful death, unable to survive the burns consequent on the explosion of a plastic container of alcohol thrown onto a barbecue". The appearances spoke of a peaceful family barbecue. The truth seemed to emit an underlying hiss, and it spelled "suicide". Until that moment—ten years after our "therapeutic" work was interrupted—both of us thought he was "cured".

It was a surprise that Jonas, the so-called hebephrenic, had chosen me to take care of him. It was just after the owner and manager of the hospital, who was his doctor, became severely ill and died. This patient was the son of one of the most famous and powerful politicians of the time; I was a young nobody, just a consultant in the hospital, one of many others. He was referred and put into forced treatment in order to stop him continuously bothering his family with what they regarded as "his shameful behaviour"—which included addiction to cocaine. The worst complication in an already problematic case was the plethora of flatterers, delinquents and people with vested interests who encircled him to please his father, in exchange for favours that included criminal political corruption.

Jonas had frequented in an aloof way a pilot group with psychotic in-patients which I held; from this experience he chose me as his doctor. From then on he made striking social gains, which were continuously torpedoed by his father's entourage. For example, when we initiated a half-way house regime where he would just sleep in the hospital and spend the whole day outside, he was able to finish his basic high school education. Nevertheless, as soon as he did this the flatterers tried to bribe the school officials to give him the diploma without having to sit examinations. When he looked for a job, they arranged a false post in a government body. Anyway, he carried on with the treatment, avoiding seductions as much as possible. Finally he was discharged from the hospital after being there, hopeless, for five years. Continuously striking social gains carried on evolving, as a consequence of analysis. For example, though he was previously prone to homosexual ideas based on lack of sexual development, he made an attempt at marriage, a moving experience that encircles the emergence of hitherto denied, unknown capacities to respect himself and thus other people too, to take care of himself and others, and so on. Twenty years later, he seems to be taking care of his life: he has not been detained for treatment since, even though occasionally he has sought out another psychiatrist, who prescribed him anti-depressants.

One day, five years later, he came to see me to tell about his terror at crossing a certain bridge leading to his workplace: "I am afraid the car's steering might fail and I might be killed". Anyway, fifteen years later he phoned me, requesting an appointment. He asked for help to convince his family to stop forcing him to get false jobs, falsely arrived at—just as his father's sycophants had done many years before! It seemed that Jonas took many years, long after his real contact with me, to realise his posture and projective identifications into his father's flatterers as well as his family and to make him more responsible for himself. Up to a point, nevertheless, for he wanted me to do the work of halting them.

It was a matter of gradual dawning of the light: I came to realise that the curative factor in psychoanalysis is hate for psychoanalysis. This is the stuff that "cures" in our field: broadly speaking, hate for truth, hate for the more basic and elementary facts of real life, described by Freud, for the first time in Western science, as the Principle of Reality.

A complaining and avid housewife had a profound sense of the maternal function. She rescued her professional activity two years after the beginning of our mutual work, lost in the darkness of irresponsibility, lack of self-care and the all-justifying label of "hysteria". Four years later she discovered that she was able to write poetry. She also was able to face her self-envy[5] with more truth, and stopped using some of her husband's seemingly aggressive and possessive, omnipotent behaviour as a cover for her lack of courage to face the truth. Anyway, that woman, who remained in treatment for six years, had to face the loss of her youngest daughter, who was killed in a road accident.

A medical doctor discovered that he is able to play the cello, which worked through his omnipotence, and re-constituted a family, after leaving the first one. Now he is a father of five, three from his first marriage. Another doctor, two lawyers and two bankers were able to work through their homosexual phantasies. They began their search for a natural matching pair and are now fathers and mothers.

Most of my patients were able to entertain second thoughts with regard to their unconscious goal of destroying their families and jobs.

They were able to keep them to the extent that they improved their capacity to tolerate the pain and uncertainty implied in real life as it is.

All patients who were patient enough to tolerate their treatment with me, which necessarily includes my limitations as a human being and the limitations of the method, experienced improvements in their capacity to work: in some cases small, in some cases strikingly large. Some patients—I cannot say they were few, but not so many as to counsel desisting from a difficult job—could not tolerate truth and frustration, and abandoned analysis. An approximate proportion after thirty-eight years is about thirty per cent who reacted like someone who hates the postman when he delivers letters whose content is not welcome.

They cannot realise, as Shakespeare realised, that "there is nothing either good or bad, but thinking makes it so" (*Hamlet*). A banker allowed his false self to prevail over his true self (in Winnicott's sense); he wanted to be an artist. But he found in analysis that he needed to be himself, so he found the pseudo-artist, rather than the real artist he had no gift or inclination to be. A physics professor who dealt just with heavy bodies, limiting herself to Newtonian physics, finally grew to her longed-for goal, immaterial Einsteinian physics, after having worked through in analysis the difficult-to-face immaterial facts in her mind, linked to her Oedipus.

Many patients who came to me became pregnant; many patients' wives gave birth during analysis; one experienced what it is to be a grandfather despite the fact that he could not be a father. He used the experience to be a unique "delayed" reparation-father, following a kind of inverted path towards fatherhood.

My impression is that analysis did help those patients to be more responsible about what they already had, but did not know they had. This casts some serious doubts on the truth of theoretical statements devoid of the empirical truth contained in clinical facts: namely, the often quoted parameters on "psychic change". To put conscious rather than unconscious thoughts, mechanical and unidirectional "travels" from paranoid-schizoid to depressive positions, "where the id was, ego shall be" seemed to me—in the light of almost forty years trying to perform psychoanalysis—a mix of brainy pitfalls with wishful thinking. *Plus ça change, plus c'est la même chose*; all the underlying rationalisations that "prove" how good analysis is, which had returned at full bore in the state intervention of recent years, display the old positivist rationale in new bottles. As regards Freud's aphorisms, they seem to me misunderstandings. As regards Klein's theory of positions, there is a failure to see that she stresses the "to and fro" tandem movement between the positions. She places no special emphasis on the prevalence of the opposite poles, and even less suggests that one of them (the depressive position) might be the pot of gold at the end of the rainbow or paradise promised or regained. When the positions, and therefore the depressive position, are taken just in a concrete form, failures in the apprehension of the concepts and their application in practice do occur.

Above all, the patients gave unequivocal signs of becoming more responsible about their real states of mind, getting more in touch with their capabilities to hate and love and their negative counterparts.[6] They seemed to become more themselves, and widened the time span in which they tolerated not having what they desired. They seemed to allow that at least some facts and persons—figures from their past, friends, relatives, enemies, acquaintances, including themselves—were as they were, rather than demanding that they must be as they wished them to be. Transference is the continual repetition of older patterns that display what the person thinks people, ideas and so on should be, rather than what they are in reality. The principle of pleasure dictates hopes, expectations and "oughtness", to quote one of Bion's neologisms. A common form is to tell people, "Oh, you should have done this and not that". This is one of the least observed disrespectful conditions. How could the person do something differently that is in the past, when time admits just one vector, the "arrow of time" which is non-reversible? To believe in the reversibility of phenomena runs against physical reality as it is.[7]

Some of them, at the cost of rebellious sadness, developed a capacity to abandon lifelong habits, for increasingly longer times, such as the deep-seated idea that life is pure *acting out*. I observed that they entertain a *Weltanschauung* that establishes the primacy of the principle of pleasure and displeasure; its main manifestation is the enthroning of hallucination and delusion. Thus empowered, they are seen as superior to reality. Much of their analysis was continuously entrapped by forceful tests of strength in which they tried to prove the superiority of the hallucinatory method over the psychoanalytic method (Bion, 1965). Therefore, some patients sustained their belief—and sometimes they had good factual reasons to back it— that hallucination, or lie, was superior to truth and reality.

Craving for fullness, something one may call "greed for satisfaction", fuels violence. Those patients, albeit unintentionally, perhaps "helped" the analytic method and me more than I (or the analytic method) "helped" them, because of the extent to which they were always reminding me of my own huge failures and limitations as well as those of the psychoanalytic method.

A lesser proportion of patients, numerically speaking (three per cent of the total), but no less important in the qualitative sense, were not able to make even a workable hypothesis about what happened to them. The same happened with me. The frameworks of reference that seemed to have been so successful with some people proved to be quite ineffectual with them. The work was interrupted when both of us viewed it as wasteful. One of them seemed to be the most amiable, kind and sympathetic person who ever appeared in my consulting room and perhaps in my life. Other patients who came across him, as well as two colleagues working in the same building, felt compelled to remark how sympathetic he was.

Truth displayed another face. A highly skilled civil engineering technician, he had abruptly left his wife and son two years earlier. After one year of analysis, he was on duty. He drove onto a ferry to cross a channel between the mainland and an island, and having drunk more than he should have, he fell asleep as the ferry got to its destination. He had a companion, who also fell asleep. Suddenly he woke up, as he imagined that the ferry had reached the harbour. In a matter of seconds he started the engine, engaged first gear…and saw himself diving into the sea. He escaped unscathed. His companion came off worse, having to be resuscitated, and was left with a paralysis of the left side of the body due to lack of oxygenation. A few months later my patient was involved in an awful accident at his workplace: there was an explosion and some workers were killed. To my surprise, I became aware of this when watching the local TV news at a week-end: the image of my patient, the responsible engineer on that construction site, voiced explanations about the incident both to TV reporters and to the police. He missed the next three sessions without explanation, then returned as if nothing had happened—which was in a peculiar sense true. He would not say anything about those events. I noticed this, telling him that I had seen TV reports of the accident, which had occupied public opinion for many days. Only then did he mention the first event—again, as if it were almost nothing. He was not callous or blasé; he was nothing.

We left each other, but with no manifestation of his expected (but seemingly absent) chagrin.

Another very sympathetic (socially speaking) patient was a medical doctor. Often I found myself having unnamed bad feelings when I began a session with him. Finally I spotted something, after some weeks of personal uneasiness and a sense of being unsafe. He used to come to the session with a subtly disguised gun over his left foot. I told him about my limitation: I was not able to analyse him if he carried physical weapons. He kindly agreed. A few days later he turned up drunk, dirty and dishevelled, displaying evident signs of having been severely beaten.

Truth and community networks

The replacement of a scientific outlook—true and false—with a moral commandment—right or wrong—precludes the realisation that truth and falsity equals reality and hallucination rather than good and evil. The replacement of the paradox-tolerating "and" with the rational splitting expressed by "or" expresses denial, authoritarianism and pleasure-ridden choices.

Perusing Bion's copy of Popper's main work, one can see his disagreement with parts of this thinker's work. An exception is Popper's warning about the danger of *ad hoc* theorising. One point to ponder, even if Bion never made it explicit, may be Popper's criterion that a theory has to be falsifiable in order to be classified as scientific. In other words, to Popper, science is a time-dated, dischargeable commodity, in a profound denial of timeless transcendences or truths independent of their own time and place (space-time, using the more truthful pattern first discovered by Einstein). To Popper and others such as Kuhn, science is a history of lies and false conclusions. Scientists would be just chroniclers of their own zeitgeist.

Professors Karl Popper and Thomas Kuhn were no scientists. The latter gave up his activities as a physicist. In contrast, Bion remained linked to practical, scientific activity. His scientific interest made him value the function of lies as something that exists and seems to have its function, but is not an end-in-itself. Science would not be *only* a history of falsities and lies as Popper and Kuhn proposed. Lies may be an intermediate step in the march into the unknown that leads to pieces of transient knowledge.

Nor does Bion think that there are any "royal roads to truth", as in Meltzer's eulogy to his own fictional "Sir Gawain", the warrior of truth (Meltzer, 1989; Meltzer & Williams, 1988). In *A Memoir of the Future* Bion would cast doubts on the analyst's superiority in perceiving and apprehending truth vis-à-vis other disciplines and vertices. He depicts his ideas vividly through the use of a quasi-Socratic internal dialogue between the fictitious characters P.A. and Priest. His metaphor of many ancestral "psychoanalysts" before Freud, who are seen as his begetters, dates from this epoch. A thought without a thinker, "psychoanalysis" existed long before a Freud appeared to think it.

The risk taken by the thinker is to become a liar. The act of thinking and, more than this, the action of expressing the thought, endangers the underlying truth it strives to convey. The burial of Freud's fundamental observations, for example, infantile sexuality, is evidence of this (Bion, 1975, p. 5). As is pointed out in previous chapters of this work, a few—exceedingly few—analysts warned about his oblivion, which means hate of knowledge (Green, 1995). One must be able to discern—and Bion tried to help with this many times—that the issue does not confuse itself with that which occupied philosophers. So analysis can contribute to philosophy:

> To the problem of understanding I have said that the psychoanalyst can bring something that is unknown to the philosopher of science because the psychoanalyst has experience of the dynamics of *misunderstanding*; the psychoanalyst is concerned practically with a problem that the philosopher approaches theoretically. [Bion, 1970, p. 97]

Practice allows the psychoanalyst to finely focus on the transitive "becoming", rather than a motionless state. If the analyst lacks this focus, through imprecise perception and the deluded theorising consequent to it, pure motion is transformed into a stagnant, wholly understandable and explainable state. The untruths inoculated into the analytic or previously analytic posture through the advancements of professionals educated in the psychological and philosophical schools, devoid of the practical aspects that can be brought by medical training, still require careful study. There is no untruth in medical facts, just as there is no untruth in life and death (as in Hamlet's elegy to Yorick), but this is subjected to continuous denial in the analytic movement, as happened on the overall social (or social in Western thinking) paths. The group denial of the advantages of truth determines that when one flows more to the social pole and less to the individual pole, one is fated to untruthful appraisals. Bion stated this in terms of socialism and narcissism. So one may say: "the more social, the more untruthful"—as demonstrated by Demagoguery and its effects in social engineering, displayed by Stalinism, Nazism, and all isms. The damage imposed by ideological invasion on Art and Science, which encompasses a range from forbidding or denying the existence of Art and Science (murdering them) to making them banal (a form of co-optation) is well known and cannot be denied—though it usually is by the ideologically prone naïve idealist.

"Practice" here means clinical experience with the liar *par excellence*, that is, the psychotic. "Psychotic" here means the in-patient and the neurotic who shelters a psychotic personality in the analysis: in brief, humankind. There remains a controversy about the necessity to analyse the psychotic nuclei of any person, analysts being no exception. The controversy lingers on when analysts state: "I do not analyse psychotics", meaning: "I refuse to analyse my own psychotic features". Hallucinations and delusions can profitably be seen as lies and falsities (Rosen, 1959). A saying attributed to Abraham Lincoln, a man who had regard for truth, is that you can fool some of the people all the time and all the people some of the time, but you cannot fool all the people all the time. Paraphrasing this to the individual being, one may deceive oneself about a few individual truths for a long time and one may deceive oneself about profound truths for a short time, but one cannot deceive oneself about profound truths for a long time.

Rescuing the psychoanalytic vertex, Bion's approach emphasised two things. Firstly, a *lack of judgmental values*: judgments are seen as an offshoot of a lying perspective, in the sense that the incapacity to assess truth and falsity leads to ideas of right and wrong. In other words, lies belong to the realm of hallucination rather than to the realm of morals. As Shakespeare said through Hamlet: "There is nothing either good or bad, but thinking makes it so." Secondly, *tolerance of a paradox*: instead of focusing on either truth or lie *per se*, Bion focuses on the binomial relationship truth-lie. That is, "and" replaces "or". No verbal or any other formulations on truth are needed.

> Provisionally, we may consider that the difference between a true thought and lie consists in the fact that a thinker is logically necessary for the lie but not for the true thought. Nobody need think the true thought: it awaits the advent of the thinker who achieves significance through the true thought. [Bion, 1970, p. 102]

Oedipus existed quite independently, and before there was a Sophocles or a Freud to think it. $E = mc^2$ existed independently of the existence of an Einstein or a Poincaré to think it.

Lying cannot be regarded as a symptom; this approach is conducive to error. In some liars there is a need to deny that lies "become acute and may usher in attacks on linking to stop stimulation which leads to conflict" (Bion, 1970, p 102). This presupposes an aim and therefore there are different patterns to be observed in different liars.

> Hence it is not possible to rely on picking up a symptom, such as a wish to please the analyst that will betray the pattern. For satisfaction, the liar needs an audience; this makes him vulnerable, since his audience must set a value on his fabrications. [*ibid.*]

This observation was recalled, but not expanded, by Elizabeth Tabak de Bianchedi (2000).

Psychoanalytic "Nietzsche's genealogy" of lie and truth

Some deepening insights already outlined in preceding parts of this work (especially in Transformations and Invariants, Container and Contained, and the Realm of Minus) can be shown in Nietzsche's contributions; they deal with immanence, transcendence, paradox and their living manifestations, the sexual couple and Nietzsche seemingly eternal (as long as he lived, because this was his flame, the Brazilian poet Vinicius de Moraes might say), the hallucination of owning "absolute truth", the homo- hallucinosis:

> "How *could* something originate in its antithesis? Truth in error, for example? Or will to truth in will to deception? Or the unselfish act in self-interest? Or the pure radiant gaze of the sage in covetousness? Such origination is impossible; he who dreams of it is a fool, indeed worse than a fool; the things of the highest value must have another origin *of their own*—they cannot be derivable from this transitory, seductive, deceptive, mean little world, from this confusion of desire and illusion! In the womb of being, rather, in the intransitory, in the hidden god, in the 'thing in itself'—*that* is where their cause must lie and nowhere else!"—This mode of judgment constitutes the typical prejudice by which metaphysicians of all ages can

be recognised; this mode of evaluation stands in the background of all their logical procedures; it is on account of this their "faith" that they concern themselves with their "knowledge", with something that is at last solemnly baptised "the Truth". [Nietzsche, 1886, p. 33–34]

This can be confronted with its later version within the psychoanalytic field:

The assumption underlying loyalty to the K link is that the personality of the analyst and analysand can survive the loss of its protective coat of lies, subterfuge, evasion and hallucination and *may even be fortified and enriched by the loss*. It is an assumption strongly disputed by the psychotic and a fortiori by the group, which relies on psychotic mechanisms for its coherence and sense of well-being. [Bion, 1965, p. 129; my emphasis]

Supported by Bion's achievements, one may append to the psychotic function the psychopathic one. Let us go on with him:

The object represented by the term Platonic Form may also be represented in mystical terms such as "One is one and all alone and ever more shall be so", as those of Canto XXXIII of the *Paradiso*: "Eternal light, that in Thyself alone/Dwelling, alone dost know Thyself, and smile/On Thy self-love, so knowing and so known!" The emphasis is altered by Christian Platonism so that the balance between the elements of the configuration is altered; this may be seen most clearly expressed in the doctrine of the Incarnation. The particular representation which is significant for this discussion has been formulated by Meister Eckhart and the Blessed John Ruysbroeck, who distinguish the Godhead from God; thus in Tractate XI "God in the Godhead is spiritual substance, so elemental that we can say nothing about it".

It is evident that in this view God is regarded as a Person independent of the human mind. The phenomenon of Good or Beauty would not then be that which "reminds" the personality of a Form (pre-conception) but is an incarnation of a part of an independent Person, wholly outside the personality, to whom the phenomena are "given". The phenomenon does not "remind" the individual of the

Form but enables the person to achieve union with an incarnation of the Godhead, or the thing-in-itself (or Person-in-Himself).

For convenience I shall refer to these two configurations as "Forms" and "Incarnation". In both there is a suggestion that there is an ultimate reality with which it is possible to have direct contact although in both it appears that each direct contact is possible only after submission to an exacting discipline of relationships with phenomena, in one configuration, and incarnate Godhead in the other. In neither is there discussion of establishing a direct contact with the reality of absolute evil, though it is possible that some of the "repellant" quality attributed to St John of the Cross may be an unconscious tribute to his identification of absolute real evil with absolute real good.[8]

The object of this digression...is to arrive at a postulate. The postulate is that already designated by O. To qualify O for inclusion amongst the column 1[9] categories by defining its definitory qualities I list the following negatives: Its existence as indwelling has no significance whether it is supposed to dwell in an individual person or in God or Devil; it is not good or evil, it cannot be known, loved or hated. It can be represented by terms such as ultimate reality or truth. The most, and the least that the individual person can do is to be with it. Being identified with it is a measure of distance from it. The beauty of a rose is a phenomenon betraying the ugliness of O just as the ugliness betrays or reveals the existence of O. L, H, K are links and by virtue of that fact are substitutes for the ultimate relationship with O which is not a relationship or an identification or an atonement or a reunion. The qualities attributed to O, the links with O, are all transformations of O and *being* O. The rose *is* itself whatever it may be *said* to be. The human person *is* himself and by "is" I mean in both instances a positive act of being for which L, H, K are only substitutes and approximations...

O, representing the unknowable ultimate reality, can be represented by any formulation of a transformation—such as "unknowable ultimate reality" which I have just formulated. It may therefore seem unnecessary to multiply representations of it; indeed from the psychoanalytic vertex that is true. But I wish to make it clear that my reason for saying that O is unknowable is not that I consider human capacity unequal to the task. [Bion, 1965, pp. 138–140]

Perhaps the final part of this text offers an alternative to those who mistake the impossibility of a verbal formulation of O and its consequent unfathomable and ineffable nature for an alleged or pretended forbidding of its intuition and partial apprehension.

Nietzsche's subtitle to *Ecce Homo* (*How One Becomes What One Is*) corresponds in its entirety to the psychoanalytic pursuit of "truth-O" as observed by Bion; both share the concept of "becoming". In *Zarathustra* and in *Untimely Meditations*, two of his many contributions to truthful research into truth, one may read:

> Or is it this: wading into dirty water when it is the water of truth, and not shrinking away from cold frogs and hot toads? [Nietzsche, 1883]

> Nowadays ... the whole guild of the sciences is occupied in understanding the canvas and the paint but not the picture; one can say, indeed, that only he who has a clear view of the picture of life and existence as a whole can employ the individual sciences without harm to himself, for without such a regulatory total picture they are threads that nowhere come to an end and only render our life more confused and labyrinthine. Schopenhauer is, as I said, great in that he pursues this picture as Hamlet pursues the ghost, without letting himself be led aside, as scholars are, or becoming enmeshed in abstract scholasticism, as is the fate of rabid dialecticians. [Nietzsche, 1874]

In Bion's terms, this happens when the psychoanalytic couple spots at least more precisely that "the erudite can see that a description is by Freud, or Melanie Klein, but remain blind to the thing described" (Bion, 1975, p. 5)?

To discover, that is, to unmask, to go beyond the mere appearances, including those disguised by establishments ("the whole guild of the sciences") and by the intuition about the realm of "O" ("the picture"), as well as transient glimpsed contacts with partial aspects of "O" ("a clear view of the picture of life and existence as a whole")[10] means to tolerate the paradox of transcendent immanence:

> The study of quarter-philosophers is enticing only so as to recognise that they make at once for the places in the edifices of great philosophies where scholarly for and against, where brooding,

> doubting, contradicting are permitted, and that they thereby elude the challenge of every great philosophy, which as a whole always says only: this is the picture of all life, and learn from it the meaning of your own life. And the reverse: only read your own life and comprehend from it the hieroglyphs of universal life…The verdict of the philosophers of ancient Greece on the value of existence says so much more than a modern verdict does because they had life itself before and around them in luxuriant perfection and because, unlike us, their minds were not confused by the discord between the desire for freedom, beauty, abundance of life on the one hand and on the other the drive to truth, which asks only: what is existence worth as such?… Every philosophy which believes that the problem of existence is touched on, not to say solved, by a political event is a joke- and pseudo-philosophy. [Nietzsche, 1874, pp. 143, 145, 148]

Bion would formulate a myth that may be seen as coloured by hues from Nietzsche for analysts in order further to enhance the probable power of his warning:

> The liars showed courage and resolution in their opposition to the scientists who with their pernicious doctrines bid fair to strip every shred of self-deception from their dupes, leaving them without any of the natural protection necessary for the preservation of their mental health against the impact of truth. Some, knowing full well the risks that they ran, nevertheless laid down their lives in affirmations of lies so that the weak and doubtful would be convinced by the ardour of their conviction of the truth of even the most preposterous statements. It is not too much to say that the human race owes its salvation to that small band of gifted liars who were prepared even in the face of indubitable facts to maintain the truth of their falsehoods. Even death was denied and the most ingenious arguments were educed to support obviously ridiculous statements that the dead lived on in bliss. These martyrs to untruth were often of humble origin whose very names have perished. But for them and the witness borne by their obvious sincerity the sanity of the race must have perished under the load placed on it. By laying down their lives they carry the morals of the world on their

shoulders; their lives and the lives of their followers were devoted to the elaboration of systems of great intricacy and beauty in which the logical structure was preserved by the exercise of a powerful intellect and faultless reasoning. By contrast the feeble processes by which the scientists again and again attempted to support their hypotheses made it easy for the liars to show the hollowness of the pretensions of the upstarts and thus to delay, if not to prevent, the spread of doctrines whose effect could only have been to induce a sense of helplessness and unimportance in the liars and their beneficiaries. [Bion, 1970, pp. 100–1]

This may remind us of Socrates and Savonarola, or even Thomas More. Bion's probable inspiration from Nietzsche may be hypothesised not only by the content of his proposals, but also by a quote in only one of his later books (*A Memoir of the Future*, Volume 3; also in Sandler, 2005). The fable keeps a direct relation with Nietzsche's emphasis on the importance of false conceptions—in Bion's parlance, column ψ of the Grid and transformations in hallucinosis—that warranted emotional security over millennia. If a contrast is made with inner truth and a growing awareness of it, a goal of analysis, a whole war ensues—if taken under the vertex of historical developments. "To what extent can truth stand to be incorporated?" wonders Nietzsche (1882). Few people would ask the obverse: when do lies not stand? A method to keep them in constant repair to endure the lie's fitness is well known. A fresh new lie is issued to underscore the earlier one, which is dispensed with as a matter of necessity. Five years later, Bion would state:

> SHERLOCK The simple part of it has been dealt with by Watson. You heard that fellow Bion? Nobody has ever heard of him or of Psychoanalysis. He thinks it is real, but that his colleagues are engaged in an activity which is only a more or less ingenious manipulation of symbols. There is something in what he says. There is a failure to understand that any definition must deny a previous truth as well as carry an unsaturated component. [Bion, 1975, p. 92]

A whole psychoanalytic congress, as always devoted more to social ways (being adept at lies) than to analysis, was dedicated to theoretical schemata that "proved" conditions of mental change.

Truth and mental health

> The man who is mentally healthy is able to gain strength and consolation and the material through which he can achieve mental development through his contact with reality, no matter whether that reality is painful or not...No man can become mentally healthy save by a process of constant search for fact and a determination to eschew any elements, however seductive or pleasurable, that interpose themselves between himself and his environment as it really is...By contrast it may be said that man owes his health, and his capacity for continued health, to his ability to shield himself during his growth as an individual by repeating in his personal life the history of the race's capacity for self-deception against truth that his mind is not fitted to receive without disaster. [Bion, 1958–1979, p. 192]

The deciding factor is the tolerance of pain and frustration. Each person has some kind of ability to cope with disaster, and a corresponding quantity or quality of truth that can be received without disaster.

The latter can be expressed either by its narcissistic variation—homicide—or by its socialistic variation—suicide. Psychoanalytic observation of patients shows that some people, when faced by their internal truth that displays the quantity and quality of their hate which cannot be justified by external facts, make covert or overt attempts to extinguish or kill the analysis—and sometimes the analyst—through accusations or pure acting out in the form of non-payment of fees, and so on. Therefore their reaction may be described as homicidal. Other patients who equally cannot face their internal hate become persecuted by their guilt, which in consequence is denied; some of them display suicidal measures. As we have seen before, Bion's observation is that some people have a kind of "loyalty to the K link" which enables them, up to a point, to "survive the loss of [their] protective coat of lies, subterfuge, evasion and hallucination"(Bion, 1965, p. 129). Thanks to the support of his observations, one may state that the "protective coat" is felt to be as such; but "to feel" must be clearly distinguished from "to be". Due to this, the loss may be fortifying and enriching—despite the herd's disapproval of it. Which echoes through the psychoanalytic experience Nietzsche's "fundamental insight" (his exact definition): "There is no pre-established harmony between the furtherance of truth and the well-being of humanity" (Nietzsche, 1878, p. 182).

This view of mental health would undergo some changes from 1967 onwards. The model of cure would be wholly discarded. It may be stated that up to 1964 Bion did adopt, to some extent, the patterns of mental disease and mental health. In fact one may observe that he nourished doubts about it from his post-World War I days. He observes that some soldiers who refused to fight or were discharged on the basis of being schizophrenic were perhaps not really ill (Bion, 1970, p. 111).

My statements in this chapter come as extensions of his observation, dispensing with criteria of normal health or the development of psychological "oughtism" (Bion, 1977b, p. 276). R.D. Hinshelwood, in his preface to a book about the Northfield experiment, noticed that Bion had an aversion to authoritarianism; psychoanalysis is inimical to establishment-induced authoritarianism. It follows—since Freud—the difficult path of looking for a kind of entropic homeostasis between individuals and groups. Either the individual is engulfed and overwhelmed by the herd, or the herd risks being destroyed by the individual. Truth is the question.

This means some obstacles to psychoanalysis in community systems, namely, applied to in-patient psychiatric treatment and to social psychiatry. In my experience, stemming from the pioneering efforts towards the implantation of mental health centres in São Paulo and also from carrying out the first case controlled epidemiological studies on mental illness in that city, those institutions are based in authoritarian structures and political networks indistinguishable from the trafficking of influence. A study of the prevalence of mental illness using an open questionnaire of symptoms, elaborated under a psychoanalytic vertex, encompassed 4,000 households. Two psychiatrists interested in psychoanalysis evaluated more than 15,000 questionnaires individually. Their finding of a 20% prevalence rate for mental illness outraged the authorities, and for political reasons the study was never published. This fact prefigured the vivid emergence of the authoritarian conduct of clinical directors. They were able to *act out* but were unable to put up with the pain involved in perceiving it, during the multidisciplinary group's meetings conducted using Bion's technique. Hallucinations, lies, dissimulation and subterfuge are supplemented by intuitive, quasi-conscious manipulations of emotions in order to obtain preconceived goals.

They proved to be ridden by greed (phantasies of power, prestige, including financial corruption). They seem to be a condition of survival for many, perhaps all social systems. The insertion of psychoanalysis in any—or at least the vast majority of—social systems and engineering is doomed to turbulence in so far as it unavoidably menaces the *status quo* founded in pleasure-seeking hallucination. The establishment deals with the real psychoanalyst in the same way that the authorities in Athens dealt with Socrates. Perhaps it was a tragic, prophetic paradigm. The same fact repeated itself in the Stalinist and Nazi dictatorships, in the fascist governments of South American countries, who had in common the institutionalised hatred of psychoanalysis. The establishment dictates that the dominant oppressive minority's self-attributed duties and rights (Toynbee, 1934–61) replace personal responsibility and respect for others; morals replace ethics.

The moving paradoxes

Numerically speaking, I have been able to deal with a sizeable number of people over a fairly long period, taking into account the history of the psychoanalytic movement and my own lifetime. When I began, analysis was in its seventieth year (I use the publication of *The Interpretation of Dreams* as a starting point); now it is well past its hundredth anniversary. I would never say that I experienced psychoanalysis before going to see my first analyst. On the other hand, I cannot deny that some facts linked to the local (São Paulo) psychoanalytic movement, whose features became partially and slightly comprehensible to me as time went on, formed part of my early education. My father was one of the first IPA-acknowledged analysts in São Paulo; I had some experiences with the founding mothers and fathers of the local group as a small boy and adolescent. I cannot say that my father was an analyst if my criterion for that description is to undergo an analysis with one;[11] my father was just my father and never tried to analyse his family. He was born a generation after the initiators, who were not spared from analysing their own progeny, material and psychic—later professionals could learn from their omnipotent mistakes.

I feel grateful for my patients' patience. This seems to me an apt name for those who need to perform this function (rather than role, more appertaining to theatre or falsity) in medicine and in psychoanalysis, which came from medical practice as a sib. And it was a dismally small number of people in a time that was more often than not felt to be short. An analyst sees too few people, even if he or she works as many hours as a human being can work—and few workers have as long a working journey as analysts do, sometimes over many decades. The analyst sees much of a small amount, which contributes to the social guilt once described by Freud in other concepts (Freud, 1920). Again, this "much" of what can be seen and scrutinised is paradoxically reduced to too little when one considers what each patient needs and what we need to grasp even transient glimpses of their psychic reality—even today, a hundred years after it all began, when a real analysis can take something around ten years.

A possibility to allow the expansion through training of one's "third ear" (Reik, 1948) elicits something closer to the actual *meaning* of the patient's *utterance*. Thus there is no "absolute" or total truth in what they consciously say, in their manifest discourse. What they say contains a paradox that in my view demands to be tolerated: it *reveals* (to the perceptual abilities that go beyond the senses and "hear", "smell" and "see" "things invisible to mortal sight", that intuit what appertains to the infra- and ultra-sensuous realm) and at the same time *conceals* (to the socially oriented and to the patient's sense apparatus) the Truth. Something that is missing, that is omitted, will always remain. Nevertheless, that something is still there, "floating in the air", waiting for someone to think it. It seems to demand a somewhat delicate approach to apprehend the subtlety involved in the fact that the mind reveals itself through the very same means and at the very same moment that it conceals itself. The mind represses, displaces, condenses, denies, phantasises that it can be expelled and put into another person's mind, outside itself.

It became crystal clear to me, in a striking contrast with my initial psychiatric practice, that I do not have fundamental qualitative differences from my patients. This showed me that analysts need a personal analysis that gives them the possibility to work through their excessive clinging to the paranoid-schizoid position or excess of narcissistic traits. If this working through is not possible, the idea is produced that qualitative differences between different people would imply the superiority or inferiority of some of them *vis-à-vis* others. Bion seems to me to have been able to find a direct formulation of this, namely, the *capacity to compassion* and the *capacity to love*, which are indissoluble from *concern for love and truth* (Bion, 1958–1979, p. 125). Psychoanalysis has been proved useful to people who feel that they lack a capacity to love—something that does not depend on the characteristics of the loved object. In some patients this is not a mere feeling. It is a realistic and truthful perception they have about themselves. Few people can put up with this kind of perception. Psychoanalysis seems to be useful with regard to the *consequences* of such a real fact. There are some seemingly insurmountable obstacles in this case: in order to perceive the lack and to have some inner, instinct-dependent motivation to look for an alternative, the person needs exactly the resource that he or she lacks; the resource that would permit and drive him or her to be genuinely searching for some approximation to reality (sensuous and psychic). Anyway, what seems to determine the outcome of what can be at least an alternative to autism will be the "quanta of delinquency": greed, subservience and slavery to the principle of pleasure/displeasure.

If my view, born from my specific experience, that I do not have any *essential* difference from my patients (in the sense that both they and I and have, for instance, a liver and blood, ability to dream and hallucinate and psychotic nuclei as well) is correct, perhaps this view can be generalised to other practising analysts, so we could have a common sense here. Even if this proves to be true, differences between the patients and me do exist and are fundamental in our respective *functions*. If I follow a scientific tenet and *raison-d'être*, which is just Freud's insistent reminder, namely, the function of the analyst, I can say that one of my functions, broadly speaking, is to tell the truth to my patients, no matter what the cost, *without subterfuge or evasion*.

Does the patient have this function too? In the beginning, Freud believed that it would suffice to exhort patients to tell the truth, but soon he realised that there were many unknown, involuntary, unconscious obstacles to them. His patients did not tell him the truth, he observed. Lack of ability to apprehend and transmit the truth and the ensuing situation of falsehood is not necessarily a delinquent trait. A great number of obstacles are linked to the area of perception.

As Freud, after Kant, noticed, our mind is as frail as our senses. Our sense apparatus is a transducer—like a microphone, which transforms acoustic stimuli into electrical stimuli. In the vast majority of cases, it is not a good enough transducer: it falsifies and distorts the stimuli that come from outside and inside us, or does not apprehend them at all. Humans were able to augment the range of apprehension of their senses through inanimate extensions, such as telescopes. There are exceptions, though rare: Aristarchus knew that the Earth orbits the sun even though he did not have any telescope available to him; Kant perceived the limitations of the range of apprehension of our sensuous apparatus two centuries before the appearance of neurophysiology. He said that the senses do not err, because they do not judge (in Kant's epoch, judgment meant thinking).

Notes

1. See the case of Albert in Chapter Six.
2. A psychoanalytic study, focusing on the movements PS⇔D in the history of ideas in Western civilisation as mirrored by the achievements of some philosophers from Ancient Greece up to Nietzsche, was published elsewhere. It includes the distinction between "philosophical systems" and the idea of "totalisation", as well as the view that psychoanalysis is an heir of the Platonic renaissance that occurred in the Enlightenment-Romantic periods (Sandler, 1997–2003). Some of the philosophical sources used here can be seen in the References and may be recognised by some readers.
3. See Volume 2, Part I.
4. Bion used the same metaphor about coins to defend psychoanalytic early truths which had become untruthful ("paramnesia") due to debasement through continuous use by non-careful, loose users who abhorred their own ignorance (Bion, 1976, 1977, 1979).
5. In the commonplace, social view as well as in psychoanalytic authors who were not nourished by Klein (even though they may advertise themselves as "Kleinians"), Envy is regarded as an outbound, superficial emotion, superficially regarded. Analogically, the commonplace view was that Cain envied Abel and Iago envied Othello. The psychoanalytic common sense observed by Klein tells us that Cain self-envied, denigrated and attacked his "brotherness". In the end, Abel was slain, and thus his suffering (including that due to envy) ended, but Cain and his descendants were cursed and their suffering due to envy lasted *per saecula saeculorum*. Iago had a self-envy of his ability to possess a friend and attacked this ability. In Melanie Klein's description of the prototype of all envy, the baby's envy of the nourishing breast has as its aftermath a non-breast baby who will be left starving, and so on. As far as I could see until now, just a single published author, Rafael Lopez-Corvo, was able to spot this in Klein, far from the commonplace view (Lopez-Corvo, 1995).
6. See Volume 2 Part I.

7. The Arrow of Time was a concept first introduced by the physicist Arthur Eddington, one of the first people who saw truth in Einstein's discoveries. It is based on the fourth law of thermodynamics, which resolved a conundrum and confusion that had lasted since Newton's ideas on the reversal of time. See Sandler, 1997b for an explanation dedicated to analysts of the relationship between modern physics and psychoanalysis.
8. Absolute evil produces that which is dead; it belongs to the realm of no-realm, in other words, that which does not exist any more. Death is unfathomable and un-understandable because it just marks what does not exist.
9. Definitory hypothesis, according Bion's nomenclature. See Volume 1 Part II, and Part I of this volume.
10. Much to the chagrin of the relativist-hailers of post-modernism; they have no scruples in continuing to claim the end of any philosophical system that attempts to grasp the whole, and dismiss many parts of Nietzche's contributions, like this.
11. Dr Deocleciano Bendochi Alves and the late Professor Judith Seixas de Carvalho Andreucci. Both profited from personal analysis with Mr Frank Philips, who was analysed by Mrs Klein and Dr Bion. Professor Andreucci underwent supervisions and seminars with Mrs Klein and her collaborators in the early 1950s. I also had supervisions with Mrs Virginia Bicudo, who introduced Mrs Klein's and Dr Bion's contributions to Brazil. She had intensive contacts with Mrs Klein, Drs Herbert Rosenfeld, Hans Thorner and Hanna Segal, and Miss Betty Joseph.

CHAPTER NINE

Two habits of mind: naïve idealism and naïve realism

> Oh for a muse like the fire of a goldsmith and like the soap of the fullers! She will dare to cleanse the natural use of the senses from the unnatural use of abstractions, by which our concepts of things are just as mutilated as the name of the creator is suppressed and blasphemed.
>
> —J. G. Hamann, quoted in Smith, 1960

There are limitations of perception, which may or may not be intrinsic, *natural*, even though in any case they may be linked to our relative immaturity as a living species. Human beings are one of the most recent entities in the life of the Earth. There is evidence that those perceptual limitations are both genotypic and familial and also phenotypic, as in Freud's complementary series. They are perceptual limitations as well as post-sensuous limitations, in the sense of an intra-psychic distortion in apprehending the invariant of the original stimulus. Not even participating observation (the fact the observer interferes with the observed object) can distort the basic invariance of the observed object. I use the term "invariance" in the same sense that the mathematicians Sylvester and Cayley used it in the mathematical realm, that Paul Dirac used it in the realm of quantum phenomena, that Bion brought it to the realm of human unconscious phenomena, and much later, that Nozick brought it to philosophy (Dirac, 1932; Bion, 1965; Nozick, 2001; Sandler, 2006). Psychically, those distortions which are not linked to normal distortions due to the limited range covered by our human perceptual apparatus, in its known and hypothesised senses. Namely, sight, hearing, taste, smell, touch—which includes heat and pressure sense organs, as well as proprioceptive stimuli stemming from inner organs. After Freud, one may hypothesise that consciousness is the sense organ for the apprehension of psychic qualities. The distortions are factors and functions of hallucinated activity. They may be seen as post-sensuous tendencies to distort perception, as in the post-sensuous perception in the eye's *macula lutea*. For want of better names, I propose to call these distortions:

1. The *"sensuous-concretifying"* (Sandler, 1988) tendency, which turns that which is neither sensuous nor concrete into something concrete and thus amenable to be limited to sensuous perception. In another part of this book, I dwell on this tendency, hypothesising an anti-alpha function. This is manifested by what Immanuel Kant called "Naïve Realism". Its main consequence in the history of science is Auguste Comte's positivistic religion.
2. The *"subjectivist idealisation"*, the idea that the external, real, "out there" universe and world has no truth in itself, and in its most extreme degrees of distortion does not exist at all. Therefore, the universe "is" what human beings think it is, or it is what people see it is. This tendency flows to what has been called "relativism". One may see that all those tendencies are characterised by many "-isms", like any socially backed or sponsored tendency. I proposed elsewhere another broad designation for this posture, inspired by Kant: "Naïve Idealism" (Sandler, 1997b; see the previous chapter on Epistemology).

Alfred North Whitehead examined the dispute between Galileo and the Inquisition from the physicist's viewpoint. His conclusions can be extended to all un-scientific (false) controversies described in the history of science. Galileo showed the ecclesiastical authorities the results of his astronomical research using the telescope. According to this research, the Sun was at the centre of the universe. This ran counter to the Catholic idea that the Earth was the centre of the universe. The priests dispensed with empirical proof and thus took up an authoritarian posture. Whitehead proposed that both were wrong. One maintained that the Sun was the centre of the universe and the other that the Earth was the centre of the universe. Nevertheless, the issue is that the universe has no centre: both were prey to the same wrong (omnipotent) belief that it does.

Another version was contemporaneously proposed by Bertold Brecht, who used pseudo-science to prove his views. He resorted to the historical episode to build a theatrical drama with political propaganda purposes. His idea became very well known: Galileo was a scientist who suffered violence stemming from religion. Whitehead's scholarly observation met with oblivion; it became much less trendy than Brecht's ideological transformation of a historical fact. The latter returned to the same original problem, putting the conflict into an authoritarian mode and creating a political situation of warring "pro" and "anti" groups.

In the same sense, Naïve Idealism and Naïve Realism are identical as regards an underlying feature: both claim that Truth does not exist. To the former, Truth is in things concretely perceived; an immaterial fact has no existence, and as a matter of consequence, as a non-existent thing, it has no importance whatsoever. To the latter, Truth is reduced to personal opinion, which is relative to all opinions and, again, has no importance whatsoever, being an "ideal idea"; its immateriality is again mistaken for non-existence.

Even though both naïves unconsciously decry truth and consciously present themselves as the only truth-holding entities, their postures allow for developing ways. Both belittle the ultimate lack of access to Truth. The Naïve Realist hastily judges that truth is, so to say, in front of his or her nose. He or she claims to have direct and easy dominion over, and authority about, truth. In this sense, he or she "owns" Ultimate Reality, through alleged dominance over its essence—namely, concrete things. The Naïve Idealist also "knows" the ultimate truth, which is that truth does not exist for anyone. To the Naïve Realist, truth exists for everyone (a positive view, like the positive numbers), and to the Naïve Realist, it does not exist for anyone (a negative view); both are in agreement with regard to their "owning" Truth. No approximations or attempts are to be made to approach truth.

The same issue took centuries of philosophers' time. Psychoanalysis seems to illuminate some psychic processes underlying those centuries-old epistemological conundrums, commonly regarded as a war between "realists" and "idealists". Kant waged verbal battles "against" Descartes, Leibniz and Bishop Berkeley. Many times a single author was seen both as "realistic" and as "idealistic"—outstanding among them, Freud, who is criticised as "too positivist" and "physicalist"[1] and too attracted to his "personal ideas".

Both tendencies stem from a common root: hate for the perception of transcendences. Nevertheless, Plato and Kant, among others, intuited their existence. Let us examine these tendencies more minutely. Even though their outward manifestations admit discriminations, both are part of the same continuum, which belongs to psychosis.

Naïve realism

Naïve realism persists in the guise of Comte's positivism, which cannot be mistaken for Schlick's and Carnap's neo-positivism. Positivist denial of transcendent truth was increased by Professor Karl Popper's claim that scientific statements must be amenable to being proved false: therefore, science would be a self-extinguishing activity. For him psychoanalysis—which he confuses with Alfred Adler's now almost forgotten "inferiority complex"—has no way of being proved false and therefore cannot be regarded as a science. Popper's and Kuhn's representatives in the analytic movement claimed to have a unique "experimental" technique, with "experiments" far removed from analytic method, in order to prove the same method they dispense with. They try to "quantify" the events in a so-called analytic session by resorting to inanimate records; some think that they need to count words or terms, or describe a conscious behaviour. They have no qualms in interrupting the sleeping of human beings in the belief that they have "gained" a kind of "dreamscope" which will turn out to be the dream being dreamt. The renewed hope is that machines and statistics would apprehend something that lack of psychoanalytic experience cannot. They believe that the mind is so light a load that it can be carried by the sensuous beast.

Naïve idealism

Bion observed people who are perplexed when they perceive that the laws of natural science do not follow the rules of their thinking (Bion, 1956, 1957). This seems to be the hallucinated nature of the naïve idealist. It legalises and establishes the existence of as many truths as there are individual people. Therefore it denies to truth its reality independent of each person's perception, realisation and approach to it. In colloquial terms, the idea is that the world and people are not what they are, but what one desires them to be.

In psychoanalysis, naïve idealism is increasingly expressed by beliefs that to some eyes subtly underrate Freud's work, shifting the focus from the analyst's analysis and the intrapsychic content. An example of the former is works focusing much more on the analyst's reactions, feelings and emotions than the patient's. They include "confessions of countertransference", as if countertransference could be discovered outside the analyst's analysis. An example of the latter is theories presented as "new" or "revolutionary" which are just a transplant from earlier philosophical trends, such as the intursubjectivist bandwagon. They are taken as truth with no empirical backing (Mello Franco & Sandler, 2005). Diminishing value is attributed to each patient's state of mind, or intrapsychic functioning, to the point of denying its existence. These professionals share the belief of some patients that the most important person in analysis is the analyst (Bion, 1957). A consequence of the diminishing value of the analyst's own analysis is the perusal of his or her own reactions, with a proportionate prevalence of the idea that the analyst can realise them outside his or her personal analysis. The analyst would be limited to issuing personal opinions.[2] Imagination and individual feelings are enthroned as methods of apprehending reality. The "individual" factor forcibly—quite independently of one's desire—makes its presence felt when one occupies different points of view in order to observe anything, or when one permits the existence of different versions of a fact. What remains is that a fact carries on being as it is, whether perceived or not, disregarding the many versions. The same issue was illustrated by the tale of the seven blind men around an elephant—it was an elephant despite their different, conflicting, true or false ideas about it. The "whole" rather than the parts perceived, the elephant itself, should be intuitively realised— and perhaps avoided by those who are next to any of its feet.

Many "replace" the fact with a product of their imagination in an omnipotent way corresponding to philosophical idealism. "Imagination is the basis of knowledge". A great many of today's members of the psychoanalytic movement would happily subscribe to this statement, which was made in the Austrian dialect of the German language ("basis" is a translation for a German term that seems to me to be even stronger: *Grundlage*). We have seen before the historic figure who was fond of uttering this phrase, complementing it with quotations from his favourite novelist, Karl May. According to Hitler, May "knew everything in the world" , referring to May's mélange of imagined entities in which he mixed North American Indians, South American Amazon natives and African people—without ever going there to see them or even bothering to study any anthropological research.

The same hallucination stems from a degeneration of "individuality"—a negative development from the Enlightenment—into "individualism", its decayed form in romanticism. The Enlightenment valued the individual; romanticism overvalued individualism.

Naïve idealism supposes that psychoanalytic interpretation has hermeneutic powers: those of individual imagination. "Creation" is usually regarded as "homo", detached from any links with another person, idea, entity or even media. Hallucination seems to be the underlying factor in naïves, both realist and idealist, although their nature differs.

The persistent difficulty in making the quantum leap necessary to pass from the apprehension of the phenomenal transformations to the numinous invariant illuminates the tendency to naïve idealism. At his or her core, the naïve idealist is equal to the naïve realist: both are distracted by the superficiality of forms devoid of their contents. Invariants may assume various—infinite—guises of immanence.

Musical experience displays the issue of transformations and invariants. Rostropovich or Casals or Fournier or Menezes may play Bach, Beethoven or Dvořák. Theirs are personal interpretations, as diverse as fingerprints. An *avant la lettre* interpretation is a most boring experience, but Bach, Beethoven, Dvořak , or "O-Bach", "O-Beethoven", "O-Dvořak", who in their turn were able to maintain "O-Music", remain as *invariants* (Bion, 1965), recognisably the same, through the times.[3]

A person who was clinging to the paranoid-schizoid position had a first analysis with an analyst from the south of Brazil. She then had to move to Finland, and sought a Finnish analyst. Both Brazilian and Finnish analysts observed this person's attempts to get rid of experiences which she felt as painful through her ability to exercise the phantasy of denying it, projecting it into the outside domain, and "inoculating" it into another person (projective identification). Each analyst's mode of observation differs, just as the patient's modes of expression differ.[4] But the phenomenon whose verbal counterpart is "projective identification" transcends the infinite ways in which it is manifested; that which it effects under multifarious and idiosyncratic transformations, in other words: the real splitting in the thought processes and the phantasy of having to be free from unwanted ideas and feelings, does not vary.

Many professionals in the analytic sphere are seduced by the fashionable naïve idealistic offerings from philosophy. Since the second third of the twentieth century, a distinguished group of French philosophers, starting from the so-called structuralists who became interested in what they thought was psychoanalysis, imported and revamped the old German idealism in its most radical form. Structuralism was fashionable at the end of the third and beginning of the fourth quarter of the twentieth century; like any fashion, it faded away. Their invention denies not only the possibility of apprehending reality but even the very existence of reality and truth themselves. Called "post-modernism", it forces with apostolic ardour the legalisation of desire, indistinguishable from hallucination. Its proponents equate psychoanalysis to satisfaction of desire, throwing the analytic job to the pre-psychoanalytic era.

There is no possibility of a thought without a thinker for those professionals. To start from something which is unknown presupposes that the "something" already exists in reality, quite independent of the observer. The existence of the observer is denied as a matter of consequence. The personal factor, that is, the multifarious interferences of the observer in the reality observed is a bias that can be partially known, and the subject mistakes the knowledge of some limitations of the observer's perceptual apparatus for the creation of reality itself. This seems to me a profound denial of the usefulness of the personal analysis of the analyst as a measure to diminish the observation of the interference of the personal factor with the observed object, crushed by an empire of "subjective-action".

Naïve idealism was tremendously heightened with Fichte's ideas and reached an ambivalent climax with Hegel—but not with Schopenhauer.[5]) It was seen as "unbridled dialectics" (Nietzsche, 1874, p. 72).

Useful indicators on the way to "O"

Common sense: Locke observed that the constant conjunction of one sense with one or more other senses is a way to approach reality. For example: if our sense of sight tells us one thing and our sense of smell another, we conclude that there is some problem of perception (Locke, 1690).

Sense of truth: starting from Hume, Locke, Freud and Klein, Bion formulated the existence of a sense—a verbal term that designates both one of the expressions of the sensuous apparatus and the vector in physics that represents "direction"—of truth. One acquires the sense of truth when one achieves perception and tolerance of the paradox that the loved object and the hated object are one and the same object (Bion, 1961b, p. 119). One may lose the sense of truth, the enabling tool to discern truth from falsehood (or their synonyms made clear by psychiatry and psychoanalysis, reality from hallucination). In this case, like a shipwrecked sailor in turbulent seas, one resorts to *judgmental (moral) values*. The shipwrecked person supposes that these will function as a piece of wood that will save him; but judgments of value are similar to a lump of lead that inevitably sinks into dark and hopeless depths. "Truthful" is confused with "right"; "false" with "wrong". "Reason" passes for "discrimination"; "Mind" for "rationality". This condition is due to primary narcissism and primary envy. The "hallucinatory method" is felt as superior to the psychoanalytic method and to life itself (Bion, 1965, pp. 142–145).

Paradoxes that demand tolerance rather than resolution: these may be called *pairs of opposites* or *contrapuntal pairs*. The ancient practice of Dialectics saw a remarkable development since its inception when its hallmark was a verbal intercourse between rivals which rationalised rhetoric to conquer an opponent. This use remained intact in some offshoots of the revived post-Kantian dialectics. In Schopenhauer, Nietzsche and above all in Freud's work, dialectics evolved and rescued its original sense of "dialect", talk; "dia", through. The pairs of opposites are not "pairs of contras". Rather, they can couple in a combination of productive mutuality. One pole of the pair functions as the negative of the other. It corresponds to the numinous realm as a negative, in the purest Kantian sense. One apprehends and formulates verbally *basic, primitive elements* of the oscillatory and transient, ever-changing mental functioning (Freud, 1916). Bion proposed a quasi-mathematical representation of this tandem transience: the double arrow. I think that the verbal formulations closest to "O" hitherto achieved by human comprehension, due its elemental character, are: the two principles of mental functioning; unconscious and conscious; the paranoid-schizoid and depressive positions; Oedipus, Self and Truthful Self (Bion, 1958–1979, p. 2; 1962, 1975). The psychoanalytic paradoxes always have a third aftermath, the synthesis, which may be seen as inseparable from the paradox;

therefore, a necessary condition for a paradox to be psychoanalytic is the quantum leap from a pair to a creative couple.[6]

An inner epistemological instrument: dream work

Bion's verbal formulation "language of achievement" refers to the realm of action[7] in relation to the action of language, or the most frequent conveyance of human communication—at least in the decisive hour of the interchange between patient and analyst. An earlier formulation of this was Freud's "talking cure". In analysis, Freud warned, there is nothing more or less happening than a conversation between two people. One may expand the verbal formulation "language of achievement" with its implicit consecutive stages which evolve from a previous stage. Bion's earlier formulation was:

… non-saturated statements ⇨ saturated statements ⇨ non-saturated statements …

Later he used the notation drawn from transformations and invariants, relating the final statements from mental processes occurring in the analyst's thinking and emotions ($Ta\beta$) leading to the patient's mental processes as free associations (including pictorial images) formed and propitiated by $Ta\beta$, that is, $Tp\alpha$, which makes a precipitate of $Tp\beta$, which allows for a renewed $Ta\alpha$ (the analyst's mind processes), and then $Ta\beta$ (their final products—interpretation or construction), to be uttered verbally.

In any case, Bion's formulation includes the action of language, but one may have an extension which includes other actions in the analytic hour: the analytic hour itself. Both earlier and later in his work, Bion emphasised the need to cover these actions, which differ from acting out. In his clinical studies from 1950 to 1960, as abridged in *Second Thoughts* (1967) and expanded in *Cogitations* (1958–1979), he warned and awakened small parts of the psychoanalytic movement to pay attention to, rather than ignoring the stares, demeanours and countenances coming from the patient. Later, as reproduced in *Bion in New York and São Paulo* (1980), he observed that many actions (something happening in fact as the analytic session goes on) are not encompassed by existing psychoanalytic theories—quoting specifically projective identification.

One of those actions may not be restricted and conveyed by verbal expressions. I cannot formulate it due to personal limitations without resorting to a clumsily formulated construct: *the achievement of a moment in which the sense of truth can be transiently grasped*. This is a proposed performance, contrary to acting out (a concept of Freud's beautifully reviewed by Fenichel, 1945). The analytic task is the opposite of that of poster-painters—or any propaganda-minded professionals—in the sense that the range analysts cover excludes any attempt to establish lights to the patient's life; or, continuing the range, to furnish, and much less orient the patient to those supposed lights. Conversely, analysts try to elicit and to display the patient's own lights. In order to do this, which includes an interest in truth, analysts can try to achieve a moment in which they can grasp the transient sense of truth—which differs from *getting* the sense of truth. The latter, "getting", conveys a static, final state and sense of ownership of absolute truth in the end. This "achieved glimpse" would have the features of "becoming", sharing the vital nature of life itself. It demands constant maintenance. It may occur through night dream work and day dream work—the analytic session being a privileged space-time to observe it unfolding.

This intuitive glimpse runs on a sword's edge between two opposite realms: dream work and hallucination. The task of the human's ability to apprehend reality, which runs parallel to the capacity to hallucinate, is a constant movement towards and away from the "achieving glimpse of a sense of transient truth". It includes but is not restricted to hallucination. It can be seen as a necessary counterpoint, in the same sense that faeces are the necessary counterpoint to nourishment. Dream work and hallucination appear simultaneously in the process of the apprehension of reality and in the process of "inveigling" food. The appearance of nourishing stuff is simultaneous to, and dependent on, the appearance of faeces; the same applies to the apprehension of reality and the non-apprehension of reality, which gives form either to tolerance of the unknown or to hallucination. We have tried to encircle practically this paradox through most of the earlier chapters of this work; something that Plato, Nietzsche, Freud and Bion, among others, did exceedingly well.

The differentiation between dream work and hallucination does not rely on a formal common feature such as the resorting of both to visual imagery. Hallucination and dream work differ because the former can be individual or collectively shared and the latter is just individual. The former originates from the prevailing of the pleasure/displeasure principle: as Freud observed, a special kind of dream, one which attempts to satisfy desire, has its fulfilment in hallucination. Dreams may mark the inception of the principle of reality. An expression of it is the presence of a mythical element, that it expresses an individual version of something that is human, and thus "generalisable".

Therefore the dream is, in its power to generalise and to encompass individual cases, a scientific tool for the apprehension of psychic reality, which is "a form of existence", as Freud observed. Simultaneously and paradoxically, the dream work both betrays and disguises psychic reality. Hallucination, in its turn, with the help of an analyst, can lead to some hints that secretly betray split parts of reality; at the same time it is destined to disguise this reality.

The dream makes the events of external and internal reality available to the person to the extent that it can act like a transducer, transforming that which is consciously apprehended into an unconscious event. Nothing can be conscious if it has not been unconscious. And if it is not allowed to have an immersion into an unconscious "life", it cannot become available to return to consciousness. Starting from Freud, Bion observed that contact with reality does not depend on dream work, but access to the personality, through the material derived from this contact, depends on dream work.

The post-sensuous perception of reality seems to happen through learning from experience. In other words, the training of sensible intuition is constantly conjoined with dream work. Dream work seems to paradoxically distort and simultaneously allow access to everything that *is*. There is a crucial factor: to be able to distinguish whether the dream is serving the principle of reality or the principle of pleasure/displeasure. A dream, akin to a psychoanalysis, partially presents the person to him- or herself. After all, the person is the one and only being with whom he or she is obliged to live until the end of his or her days. There is evidence of the usefulness of knowing to the fullest possible extent what that person is, as well as what it is not—the false self, according to Winnicott's nomenclature. It furnishes an opportunity for the person to resolve to be him- or herself.

Taking into account the political nature of the human animal, and expanding Niccolò Machiavelli's observations about the action in the political sense to the deeper psychoanalytical sense, analysis augments the probability of intermingling *Fortuna* with *virtú*. Analysis provides increasing *Fortuna* as well as an appreciation and appraisal of each one's *virtú*.

The person will be more able to "marry" or to "adopt" him- or herself, provided he or she is more acquainted with him- or herself. He or she will form an "Internal Couple" according to each one's basic instincts (love, hate and epistemophilic) through each link derived from the three instincts: L, H and K [knowledge]. When Kant's political categorical imperative (to be at one with one's principles) or Freud's superego are known and allowed to be, there are people who can achieve a faithfulness to themselves—that can be heightened by analysis.

Is it possible to have a mental development associated with a capacity to "see the facts as they really are"? Those facts do not present themselves in a direct way to our consciousness, as regards the unconscious (*unbewußt*, not-known). Is it possible to get, internally, "a sense of well-being that has an instantaneous ephemeral effect and a lasting sense of permanently increased mental stability"? (Bion, 1958–1979, p. 6). How can one obtain insight on the numinous realm? If the psychoanalytic movement does not provide a stamping ground for its wild asses, where can one find a zoo to preserve the realm of "O", the unconscious (to paraphrase Bion, 1975, p. 5)?

The failure of dream work: psychosis and psychopathy

From a common psychotic core, there is a social and psychiatric entity subsumed by both the Naïve Idealist and Naïve Realist classification that emerge as the psychopathic personalities. Delinquency can be driven mainly inward, as a destructive tendency—psychosis—or outward towards other people—psychopathic tendencies.

In the latter manifestation, there is a good sense of reality but little regard for truth. Such people's enhanced sense of reality enables them to avoid truth at all costs, including their real life, in a chronic suicide. They may even stumble into it incidentally or by accident. Through evasion and lie they postpone indefinitely—life is so short and they gamble with the probability that it will run out before the moment of a "final judgment"—the possibility of facing the truth. The chronic suicide replaces the acute suicide, which is much more acknowledged due to its sudden violence which impacts on the human sensuous apparatus. The catastrophic change brought about by covert violence subdues its perception; the human sense apparatus is blunted by addiction and repetition of patterns, which are added to the limitations of its range of apprehension.

Idealism is the predominance of paranoid expressions of the paranoid-schizoid position. Greed is the basic nucleus which fuels ideas of superiority, arrogance and delusions of grandeur, creating the election of an ideal, superior to all other ideas, facts, persons and things. In the beginning, the ideas that "sprout" from an individual mind, considered at first as the very person's mind and thereafter, in some times, as a projection or projective identification of the person's mind into others, made for the idea that the universe is a creation of this specific person's mind. Personalities prone to paranoia tend to support idealism and relativism. Taking into account that those people are also skilled in the so-called socialist ideologies, they act violently to impose them, at the cost of their own life and the lives of others.

Starting from Freud, Bion's observation on a "guiding pole", that is, trying to determine the vector or direction of life and death instincts, led him to distinguish between "narcissism" and a "socialism". When the life instincts are inbound, deflected towards the ego, the death instincts are outbound, deflected towards what is social. In the first case Bion talks about narcissistic life instincts and socialistic death instincts. The person nourishes little interest in his or her social environment. A passionate couple is usually "narcissistic". A social reformer displays the obverse case, and so on.

The Naïve Idealist and the Psychopathic Personality have no difference in their paranoid features but differ in their "social bound" origins: the Naïve Idealist thinks he is a social defender but contributes to social extinction. The Psychopathic Personality thinks he is antisocial but ends up putting social forces against his own extinction, or at least contributing to his loneliness. Successful politicians usually complain about loneliness; and perhaps there is nothing as lonely as death. Both have their schizoid phenomena centring on the split of inner feelings; they keep self-destruction at bay, akin to Freud's resistance, in a chronic state. The Psychopathic Personality's paranoid and split behaviour makes him think and act with contempt for all other ideas which do not coincide with his; homo (sexual or not) phantasies prevail. Any concerns for people other than himself are purely incidental. That which is his property is his; that which is not is also his—the Psychopathic Naïve Idealist is a born emperor and a born kidnaper of ideas and property. One of those people, when he decided to "marry" into a famous and well-to-do family, he liked to shout: "I did not marry a woman, I married a name and a family". When both were denuded by his many effective efforts at stealing, he duly abandoned them.

The Psychotic Naïve Idealist—as distinct from the Psychopathic Naïve Idealist—avoids truth because he cannot stand it, and avoids it in a violent, hyperbolic and ever-growing cancer-like tumefaction. It is a paranoid-coloured avoidance, felt as if it were an "overtruth", more than he feels he is able to perceive. He sees the light of truth, but cannot stand what he sees; in a later moment he attacks his perception. To state that one "feels" excludes the perception of that which "is" in reality. Feelings can be inimical to reality or not; if paranoid-coloured, they more often than not are. Psychiatrists talk about a "delusional intuition", always made by unrealistic feelings. Common-sense thought indicates that it is not wise to be guided by feelings: if they really are our internal senses, they err on a scale analogous to or even greater than our sensuous apparatus that apprehends external stimuli. One may differentiate real intuition from deluded intuition: the former is made by experience and emotional experience, which encompasses sensations, feelings, affects and emotions, while the latter is made just by feelings.

The Psychopathic Naïve Idealist displays greed for well-being and greed for satisfaction; his acute sense of reality and acute disregard for truth make him an indefatigable worker in politics, entrepreneurial money-making and robbery. The Psychotic Naïve Idealist displays greed for the avoidance of displeasure. The intra-ego split is a factor in a movement characterised by the prevalence of "running away" from displeasure, with a simultaneous searching for pleasure as a flight into imagination. In this aspect, the Psychotic Naïve Idealist follows the same course as previewed by Freud's formulation on the two principles of mental functioning, when there is a prevalence of the principle of pleasure/displeasure over the principle of reality (flight into pleasurable feelings and flight away from unpleasant feelings). The specific psychotic feature is the flight into imagination, and individual autistic, falsely creative homo and not truly creative, two-body,[8] hetero "'thoughts"; delusions instead of a creative new act between two persons. His ambivalent concern for truth constantly conjoined with abhorrence of reality precludes a socially oriented endeavour or task. "Inner" homo delusions seem to satisfy him.

The Naïve Realists have a prevalence of schizoid phenomena, but it is not in the wake of resistance; it is rather in the "forced splitting" observed by Bion. Corresponding to a centuries-old philosophical problem, the artificial separation (splitting) of matter and mind, the individual person over-values that which is material, at the expense of that which is immaterial or psychic. Milk replaces warmth and solace when the child deals with its breast. Because of this kind of splitting, all Naïve Realists value greatly the concrete, sensuously apprehensible facts, excelling in measuring, material values and so on. Many Physicists today have difficulties in dealing with small bodies in modern physics. Positivists still reign in what is socially considered as science; even Medicine has seen a movement which claims to be "evidence-based", disparaging medical intuition; the evidence is not seen in empirical experiments but in statistical findings in the literature, with no resort to clinical experience. MRI in psychiatry enjoys an undeserved respect under the vertex of reliable findings and clinical results.

The Naïve Realist turns the experience of psychic reality into an act ultimately unavailable to himself. Taking into account that no mental functions exist in a vacuum, a pre-emptive measure that avoids it[9] could be called "psychic unreality", and, in its extreme form, "non-psychic unreality".[10] All those kinds of lie are the casting of hallucination. Out of the hallucinated activity are construed rationalised hallucinations that form palatable, plausible, rational stories—usually called "delusions". They are uttered and swallowed by an adequate receptor of projective identifications. Again, there are the Psychotic and the Psychopathic Naïve Realists. The schizoid Psychotic Naïve Realist can afford to be a positivist scientist, but not a post-positivist expanded scientist; he can be a collector of art, or of any other thing, but cannot be a lover of that which is "some" in "things". The Psychopathic Naïve Realist can act as, but cannot be; he can expropriate and explore things, but cannot enjoy or hate them. Both seem to maintain contact with certain aspects of reality—just enough to avoid the whole inception of truth. The use they make of truth is partial, focused and concentrated. An analogy of this focused concentration may be laser-beam tools. Therefore, the Psychopathic Naïve Realist *learns from the experience of the commonplace* and can perform a fairly good criticism of customs, but cannot respect common sense, which demands regard for truth. Except as regards enjoying love—when he so much as smells this, it will be at once destroyed or neutralised in its effects—the Psychopathic Naïve Realist is able to be that which the German language calls a real *Menschenkenner*, having an intuitive notion of people. In order to equip their greed and lack of regard for truth, for other people and for life, these people have successful non-ideological "political capacity". This consists of manipulating feelings and exploring the weaknesses of individuals and groups in order to try to fill a psychical void (vacuum) consequent to the eternally melting furnace of greed.

As we saw in other chapters of this work, Bion described a situation that he puts as "narcissism versus socialism". After Freud, he scrutinises the vector (direction) of the life and death instincts as the prevailing tendency of an individual mind. They may be group-oriented (called "socialism") or self-oriented ("narcissism"). In our case, there is an exacerbation of the "socialist" deflection of the life instincts, implying that the death instincts are deflected narcissistically.

Truthfulness in untruthful environments?

The Psychopathic Naïve Realist has an acute sense of reality but uses it solely with the intention of never running the risk of stumbling on the truth by mistake. This includes a remarkable splitting of his emotional experiences, avoiding any contact with his hostility and lack of gratitude. Human endeavours and tasks such as medicine and psychoanalysis are subjected to distrust when this mental state prevails. A medically trained psychoanalyst furnished to economically deprived workers socially accepted activities according to their capabilities (masonry). He also looked after, with no money involved, other deprived patients who worked in a weekly street market outside his consulting office; from time to time they asked for medical care, including emergencies. He was known in the neighbourhood, where he had worked over the past thirty years. He lived in a country remarkable for the outrageous inequalities of social opportunity (and financial income) so typical of underdeveloped countries.

One of the manual workers he had helped before decided to commit an act of physical violence. He organised a kidnap and mounted an assault to hold the psychoanalyst to ransom. He imposed his will through threatened (and actual) beating and with the aid of automatic pistols and accomplices (at least three persons seemed to be involved). The analyst was abducted and held captive in a faraway hiding-place for three whole days. He was put into a small windowless room linked to a small toilet; there was a camera in the ceiling and a heavy door which was immediately locked. Over the door there was a written warning, containing grammatical errors, that the analyst should not approach the door: they were watching him 24 hours a day and he would be punished if he did. There was a small horizontal gap in one of the four walls, through which computer-written messages, again remarkable for grammatical errors, and some hot food and water were passed.

The analyst considered that this was his whole life from then on. He seriously contemplated that his past life with his cherished and loved family, patients, colleagues and plans, was over. He decided to offer his services as a physician to the criminals. They promptly dismissed the offer, displaying suspicion of it: they thought it was a trick to enable the kidnapped analyst to see their faces and those of their accomplices in order to denounce them, rather than a genuine offer. Finally he realised that from then on he was no longer either a physician or an analyst—he was just a kidnapped person.[11]

Untruth prevailed; the criminals—like any criminals of this kind, either the successful ones who occupy political functions in underdeveloped countries or the unsuccessful ones who populate the streets of all megalopolises—wanted to "own" some money they had hitherto done nothing to earn.[12] How could one be truthful in an untruthful climate like this? The victim had already decided not to make requests during the kidnap, and avoided by all means calling them criminals. They seemed to be very young; he asked them their names, which they did not give. In a country where informal address like the German Du is a rule among youngsters and the lower classes, he decided to address them formally, as one would a superior. In the final moments of the event, one of the kidnappers said "You could be my father". Under the specific circumstances, as the hours passed and an attempt at dialogue was made, the kidnapped analyst felt that they were treating him humanely by giving him some warm food and plenty of water, as well as drugs that he told them he needed for a heart condition. After all, they needed him alive in order to get the ransom—a fact of which he often reminded them: "I am no use to you dead". He just saw them and told them that according to his thinking, they were people doing their own work, earning money. His personal opinions, moreover, if they belonged to the realm of judging the morals involved in this kind of work, were not voiced at any time. That is, he accepted the truth involved and refrained from having expectations, nourishing hopes and, even less, demanding anything. He thought that all his expectations, hopes and demands were personal, intimate affairs, and that the criminals should have no access to them due to the possible misuse they could make of them. He thought they were not competent to deal with other people's feelings and treated them accordingly.

From the first moments, the kidnap victim openly agreed to pay them; he thought that he could "raise" something in the environs of 25% of the ransom demanded. The kidnappers did not trust him; after some hours, the victim realised that the sum (25% of the total) was seen as too high, rather than too low. The criminals balked and told him: "We will consult our bosses". A message was to be sent to the family, but something happened to prevent the family receiving it: someone noticed the paper and took it before the members of the family could reach the place where the message was deposited.

This forced the victim to continue dealing alone, which was happening in a spontaneous way from the beginning of the kidnap. In fact, he insisted right from the start that he wanted no police go-between.

Transient truthfulness in human relations can be earned through superegoic pressures, codes of conduct such as *omertà*, the code of silence within the Mafia. Among some momentous events during the kidnap, a fearful one occurred after the making of a deal between the kidnappers and their victim. The adjustments regarding money had been made, with many menacing statements, including the criminals claiming: "We know your home address, and wouldn't think twice about harming your family". Nevertheless, after having displayed a rather profound knowledge of the victim's day-to-day habits, they asked him to write his home address down on a piece of paper. The victim said: "I'm not dealing with you from now on. Our deal is suspended. I can't trust you any more. This is a deal where mutual trust is fundamental, but you told me that you knew my address and now you are telling me that you don't know it. Please kill me or do whatever you must do, but I don't want to do business with you any more. Talk to the police, to my family, whatever." Fear invaded the victim, intimately, in the small windowless room. He supposed they could come in and beat him in order to extract the information under duress or heightened torture. But the criminals gave up their demand, even after having used some rationalised verbal attempts to convince the victim to tell them what they wanted, such as "Our bosses want to know", and so on.

This was an unexpected outcome, for under the local customs in this kind of criminal activity, where hiding places are constructed and rented, the average stay in captivity is usually more than two months.

The aftermath was equally unusual. Being left alone to deal with the criminals, the victim began to propose a course of action. He would phone the branch of the bank in which his savings were deposited and ask to have the ransom available immediately. The criminals would arrange access to a mobile phone. In due time the call was made, and this led to another anxious situation. The account manager soon recognised the victim's voice and asked if he was well; the victim became afraid, thinking that the criminals would overhear the brief conversation, perhaps listening to it through a clamping device. Nevertheless, they were as hurried as he was, fearing that the police could track their whereabouts (as was indeed the case), and also wanted the call to finish as soon as possible. Therefore, acting on the victim's own proposal, the criminals took him to the bank in order for him to give them the money they wanted. This took some hours, and was a kind of comic opera situation involving a change of clothes, and taking a cab with an accomplice driving and another following on a motorcycle.

Then things took a weird turn. The criminals decided to let him enter the bank alone. They displayed their feeling: it would be safer for them not to go into the bank together with the victim. They were afraid of being caught. Their intuition—that is, their sense of reality—proved to be right. The bank was full of specialist police officers; ordinary customers had been sent out earlier. The bank staff had been warned by the bank and by the analyst's family.[13] The kidnappers let the victim enter the bank on condition that he would go out and give them the money outside the building.

The Mafia-minded criminals perceived—this is an action of the sensuous apparatus, gained by intuition—truthfulness in their victim and trusted him. In hindsight, even though many people who heard the story were surprised that those criminals behaved "like idiots" or "were idiots", the most knowledgeable and experienced professionals who dealt with the case saw it under another vertex. According to the police,[14] there were some hypotheses as well as certainties. The hypotheses were that the criminals could not be real professionals; or perhaps they really had bosses and had betrayed them in order to keep the money themselves. The police were certain that the criminals were not idiots; in their view the victim had gained their trust. The kidnappers trusted him to make every effort to pay them.

Things did not happen as planned. The police and the bank staff put forward strong arguments to prevent the victim leaving the bank with the money. The victim exhibited some symptoms corresponding to Stockholm syndrome, proposing to go out and deliver the ransom, and if the police wished, they could then arrest the criminals. "Too risky for you" was their argument. In this phase, the victim had some difficulties in apprehending the new reality: he was no longer a kidnap victim; he was free—up to a point. The criminals were outside, and he was protected. With the help of the police officers and some phone calls to his family, he came to understand his new situation, that his external reality had changed for the better. He realised that he was no longer at the mercy of his tormentors, who remained outside the bank. He finally accepted the police advice; his argumentative, heated talk subsided and changed too. This conversation took more than a full hour, and in the end the criminals escaped.

The now "former kidnap victim", just released through the conjoined action of the police and special circumstances partly likened to luck, returned to his work. He felt a mixture of happiness and other feelings, one of which might be called "sadness". There remained an itching awareness furnished by one aspect of the experience of his "negotiations" with the criminals.

This aspect interests us now: the "ex-victim", now a returning psychoanalyst, had found more truth in his dealings with the self-confessed criminals than with some colleagues in his profession, both paychiatric and psychoanalytic. This same issue is examined in more detail under the heading of groups nourishing scientific meritocracy versus groups that favour political meritocracy, in the next part of this work. It was not only in South Africa during Gandhi's times that some people won self-respect at the expense of disrespecting other people; this inhumanity of man to man, part of the human condition, still remains popular and widespread, under the guidance of the Psychopathic Naïve Idealist.

The same problem occurs in terminal patients: younger doctors have doubts about telling them the truth, which is felt as awful. Words like "cancer" are forbidden and usually arouse anger. Some make Oedipus' mistake, that is, to get to the ultimately unknown truth (one's own birth) at any cost. Why tell a patient what he already knows—that he has cancer, for example—when in some cases where hate for truth prevails, truth is put on the level of un-awareness? Again, you cannot be true when immersed in an untruthful environment; truthfulness is present when other doctors refrain from talking about an issue which the patient adamantly makes himself unavailable to talk or think about. Truth used to damage falls into the untruthful realm.

These experiences display truthfulness in an environment inhospitable to truth and the keeping of truth as conditions—circumstances in external reality—eventually change. Truthfulness is never contingent, even though external appearances of reality are and the expressions of truth may be forbidden by contingencies. Perception and awareness of truth can be obliterated but truth-in-itself cannot. Human life is short, and the Psychopath can live a whole life avoiding this awareness, for fear of depression.

The Psychotic Naïve Idealist and Realist avoid *learning from experience* and unconsciously choose in infancy relations to part-objects, without ever achieving a wholly integrated object relation. The adult but undeveloped, immature counterpart also proves to be a part relationship with parts of reality which cannot be integrated.

Morals, ethics and the Psychopathic Naïve Realist

The Psychotic Naïve Idealist abhors frustration to such an extent that an activation of powerful mechanisms of evasion from reality is at work. This personality "develops omnipotence as a substitute for the mating of the preconception, or conception, with the negative realisation" (Bion, 1961b, p. 114), creating a hallucinosis of self-conception, "homo", devoid of the creative couple which would be furnished by the mentioned mating of preconception with realisation. This mental state is composed of hallucinations and ensuing delusions. Instead of negative realisations, which produce real thinking, one seeks positive realisations, ever-fulfilling and intolerant of ideas of frustration.

The Psychopathic and the Psychotic Naïve Realist have sophisticated notions of reality, but contempt for truth, due to their own splitting tendency. The Psychotic is a skilled positivist, looking for "positive" realisations, as stated above. The Psychopath has a constantly conjoined innate imbalance of trust in his or her parents; in later times rigid motion (transference) to other people completes the picture. The split concerns a movement (tropism) towards reality and truth, which in this case are no longer interchangeable because of the split. If one integrates some scattered observations of Bion about the issue, one is able to discern the split tropism that overvalues material reality and undervalues personal ethics, because of a murderous superego opposed to the real superego. Again omniscience wins the day; there is no activity to distinguish between true and false.

> Omniscience substitutes for the discrimination between true and false a dictatorial affirmation that one thing is morally right and the other wrong. The assumption of omniscience that denies reality ensures that the morality thus engendered is a function of psychosis…There is thus potentially a conflict between assertion of truth and assertion of a moral ascendancy. The extremism of the one infects the other. [Bion, 1961b, p. 114]

It is a well-documented fact that priests of any religion manifest self-righteous behaviour; a Mafia-like allegiance is made under rigid moral codes (*omertà*). Usually the Mafia (the origin of the word is Arabic, meaning "hidden") resorts to terrorism, a form of destruction.

A kind of mosaic personality is analogous to the desired part of immature adults whose most fervent desire is to be children, as children fervently desire to be adults. The common idea is that adults are children who have gained the physical strength to satisfy their desires, and children are people who are able to live in a desire-satisfying world, without responsibilities. In any case, lack of intuitive apprehension of oneself leads to no knowledge of one's needs and at least some responsibility for nourishing them. Satisfaction of desire replaces nourishment; everything and a sense of whole replace that which is possible.

This kind of incomplete thought is devoted to clothing or proving one's desire-ridden points of view. If the Psychotic Naïve Realist can reach a positivistic, concrete, causal forerunner of science, the Psychopathic Naïve Realist is fated to be a non-scientific researcher; in fact, today there are many cases of "already proven" pseudo-sciences that go along known roads and prove things which were in the basic assumptions (e.g. pharmaceutical laboratories that hide double-blind research and shovel out the same kind of drugs, say, anti-depressants, with different names).

Clinical experience, as Freud, Klein and Bion had already noticed, shows that the Psychotic Naïve Realist and Idealist can be prone either to schizoid tendencies or to paranoid tendencies; or both are innate and genetically determined and can be seen as endogenous. Bion also observes that feelings of poor regard for truth and feelings of incapacity to love are intertwined, and this is a clinical manifestation of the mutually interacting links between epistemophilic and love instincts, each being a factor and function of the other (Bion, 1960, p, 125). If this feeling is based in real endogenous, innate narcissism—some American schools of psychiatry inspired by psychoanalysis regard it as a "malignant narcissism", under a medical vertex of cure—psychoanalysis can help with some manifestations of it; if it is based in an environment-induced narcissism, psychoanalytic insights can give the person living alternatives to it. Under a medical system of therapeutic indication, psychoanalysis has poor or no success in the former case and better results in the latter.

The Psychopathic Naïve Idealist and Realist always have an endogenous endowment of narcissism and primary envy or greed. Their behaviour is smashed by the unavoidable hopelessness of those who feel that their precocious personal annihilation is a fact. They are trapped in a Catch-22 situation: either they face their inner hostility and risk resorting to self- or hetero-annihilation, or they will suspect that hallucination and acting out will not do as living methods.

It was stated that the Naïve types, Idealist and Realist, in both manifestations, Psychotic and Psychopathic, belong to the same realm, psychosis, and compose a continuum. The fringes between them are not borders; in twilight, the Psychotic Naïve Realist can be slipping into Psychopathic Naïve Realism, especially when the innate psychopathic situation makes its inception. For example, a false scientist who collects data in order to "prove" the ideas they had from the beginning.

> P.A. Are we, even today, prepared to tell our children, or our children's children, what price they would have to pay if they served their fellows? Are we to tell them not to do it, that it might cost them too much? What would it cost them if they did *not* serve their fellow men? [Bion, 1979, p. 508]

The necessary and the possible

Slave-like subservience to the principle of pleasure/displeasure produces a prevalence of mindlessness, religiosity, omnipotence, greed and envy. Originating from an intrapsychic Hope, a link with a breast which nourishes self-development and superego, the development through projective identification creates an external Hope, extrapsychic in the sense that it is directed to the environment. Necessary until the advent of the depressive position, it becomes like a pleasurable habit thereafter, fuelling idealisation. In family life it carries on being normal, but directed outwards, it begets Expectation. It constitutes a disgrace; parents expect so much from their children and cannot adopt them; the children do the same. In more extreme form, widening the social spectrum, Expectation begets Exigency, which turns a social disgrace into social horror, full of disrespect and inhumanity of man to man.

One confuses and uncouples a conjoined couple, Necessity and Possibility. In this case, one mistakes Necessity for Pleasure and Possibility for Certainty. Uncoupling the necessary from the possible results in a lack of perception of one of them.

One could hypothesise a Marco Polo instinct, an expression of the epistemophilic instinct, or an anti-autistic attitude: the "desire to know" referred to by Aristotle and much later by Kant. Born travellers and discoverers intuit that they must go outside, abroad, into the unknown. The same occurs with the curiosity of the tomb-robbers (Bion, 1977): forebears of science, challenging established authority and taboos. Is living (facing an ocean of difficulties, in Hamlet's musings) a need? From the medical point of view, is it possible for the human being to smoke? There is a remarkable confusion between what we need, what we can do, and what we in fact cannot do but obtain factual proofs that we could do.

This confusion may be linked to a natural human endowment: namely, the plying capacity of human hands, determined by two opposing muscle groups (thenar and hypothenar). Our built-in pliers equipped our already long tradition of self-deception. There are things and deeds we think we can do but in reality cannot. An example is turning unreal ideas into factual things: in other words, acting out our fantasies. We develop this practice and make more tools in order to keep the acting out going on and on. Bion noticed that our tool-making ability, seemingly unique in the zoological spectrum (some birds and primates seem to make rudimentary tools even though they do not have opposing thumbs, but they are never tools that make tools), enables us to construe unreal thoughts, or delusions and hallucinations, into concrete forms.

Expansions on hallucination, after Bion

In my opinion (and I have made some efforts in this regard, even though they may be regarded as feeble on some scales of measure[15]), a psychoanalyst must define precisely the terms he or she uses, whether communicating with colleagues or with patients. As I advanced elsewhere, the terms hallucination, hallucinosis, illusion and delusion have in analysis the same meaning they had in classical psychiatry and academic psychology, even though their use by psychoanalysis is more extensive.

Hallucinations are objectless perceptions, or perceptions with no real external realisation. Hallucinosis is the presence of hallucinations in an otherwise preserved personality. In psychiatry, those manifestations are indicative of pathology. In psychoanalysis, they form part of the psychotic personality (Bion, 1956) and can be seen in dreaming activity, asleep or awake. In this sense, analysis is an expanded psychiatry, in that it dispenses with the illusory character of "pathology". This furnishes a hint to define illusion. In some very specific areas of physical medicine, the term pathology is no illusion—e.g. in surgery for cancer—but in other areas, including psychoanalysis, which encompass immaterial perceptions, superficial concrete and sensuously apprehensible appearances induce one to make errors of illusion. In other words, illusion is a defect of perception when an object is available. For example, a patient saw what was a tree blowing in the wind but thought its shadow was a snake-moving robber. Therefore, illusions have their form aroused by external and/or real objects. Delusions are plausible ideas and statements construed out of rationalisations (as in the prototypical case displayed in Schreber's diary as analysed by Freud) assembled with the aid of objectless and/or objective perceptions (illusions and/or hallucinations).

Taking into account that there is no organ or event in nature without a function (in this case, mind abhors a vacuum), even though we hardly or never know what that function is, hallucination and its often ensuing delusions must have a function.

Bion made explicit and defined Freud's earlier analogical model of the mind based on the digestive apparatus. Its advantages are its natural feature, both embryological (brain and digestive tract) and instinctual, at the service of life, death and epistemophilic drives. Taking it as a model, one observes that the digestive apparatus takes a meal—which potentially brings with it food—from outside. Carefully the digestive tract selects and separates nourishment from non-nourishment. In its final forms, the former—nourishment, or food-in-itself—follows on in the sanguine flow, blood, and then to the Krebs cycle, resulting in glycogen which is stored in some organs, remarkably the hepatic system, and then transformed by the mitochondria into adenosine tri-phosphate (ATP). As far as we know today, this is the most elementary, basic compound of nourishment, furnishing energy to all living cells in human and non-human bodies. ATP is the closest human research has been able to come to "numinous-food". In this sense, ATP presents—more than represents—truth (or the truth of nourishment). Bion was able to emphasise that truth is the food of the mind (Bion, 1967; Sandler, 2005).

At the same time, the digestive tract, through a whole, rather large and complex form (still wholly unknown, but at the same time known to the extent that the knowledge is useful) "extracts" from the same "meal" that which is known as faeces. This is digested matter that demands to be separated carefully from contact with the blood and other systems of the body (respiratory, reproductive, hormonal, brain, etc). Usually faeces is known as "waste", which it is not. From the vertex of the internal body, it demands to be isolated, split and ejected outside, being contaminated by bacteria and other noxious material (noxious to continuing life). To regard it as waste is equivalent to owning its "absolute truth", for as soon as it is ejected, through contact with sunlight, dehydration and other pressures and physical stimuli it will undergo transformations which may return it to living bodies: for example, it may be classified as manure, which is not waste-in-itself.

The movement in which excreta are formed corresponds to Klein's discovery of projective identification, which is made by denial, splitting and phantasies of ejection into other beings. It is empirically verifiable in infants and in analysis. This furnishes a view on the role of hallucination. The formation of hallucination (as well as of illusions and delusions associated with and developed from it) is the counterpart in psychical reality of the formation of faeces in material reality. Both, as Freud pointed out, are one and the same reality (or existence, in Freud's parlance in Chapter VII of *The Interpretation of Dreams*). This would be the function of hallucination—again, a more approximate form to see its truth. Hallucination is not truth—it is the opposite of truth. That is, hallucination is lie. But the process of hallucinating is truthful to the extent that it has a function. Processes of dreaming and hallucinating go on all the time, day and night, in the human mind. In addition, a "digestive" and "reproductive" process around them, with striking counterparts in material reality, goes on all the time, as long as life goes on. Dreaming, contact with truth and simultaneously with lie, are psychic functions, a movement, illuminated by many paradoxes described by psychoanalysis, such as the tandem movement between Klein's Positions, the paradox of the two principles of mental functioning, and so on.[16]

One may hastily see this way of looking at hallucinations as new; it would be imprecise, for newness is an error of perception about oblivion. But it can be seen as a development, in the form of making explicit some discoveries made by Freud, Klein and Bion.

Delusion, its raw material (hallucination) and its medium (rationalisation) may be regarded as everything unnatural, and therefore not needed inside (intrapsychically), demanding to be expelled as soon as it is formed and detected. Lies are a conjoined condition of truth that must be disposable, but not morally dispensed with, or subject to contempt. They are the "It is not": Falsehood, Lies. They are the stuff of make-believe.

Critical analysis, in the sense proposed by Kant of analysing the methods used to obtain truth, is a kind of detection of lies in order to obtain truth. Psychoanalysis can be seen as a register of the names of our lies. Conversely, free associations are the invariants of one's mind.[17]

One's rational capacities, constantly conjoined with one's capacities to hallucinate and to make tools, are well ahead of one's capacity to perceive what is needed and what is possible. Having acquired concrete and factual forms, they seem to be real, but they still appertain to what is not possible and what is not needed. This fuels greed. One gradually loses one's ability to distinguish the possible and the necessary.

Intra-session operative use

> P.A. The price of freedom is constant vigilance. This is true of psychoanalysis; the individual is not analysed, "cured", so that he can then go to sleep for the rest of his life. If that were all that occurred one could regard it as an exercise in "good resolutions".
>
> ALICE Psychoanalysts I know have wonderful intentions and make "good resolutions" to put them into practice, but I cannot say I am impressed with the lives they lead as a good examples of a fine philosophy finely practised.
>
> P.A. I cannot say anything about other analysts; I do not even know if the analysts of whom you talk are people who have been analysed. I know something of myself and can see how I conform to civilised behaviour. I hope that the failures I see will in time lead to something less sterile than "remorse" and good resolutions.

ALICE I know I certainly have it frequently bought home to me that I do not conform to the behaviour I regard as desirable or even decent.

P.A. The hope is that psychoanalysis brings into view thoughts and actions and feelings of which the individual may not be aware and so cannot control. If he can be aware of them he may, or may not, decide—albeit unconsciously—to change them. [Bion, 1979, pp. 509–510]

I try to differentiate a *sense of truth* from hyperbolic feelings (Bion, 1965, p. 142). The latter are an immobilisation in PS. They produce feelings both of *existence* and of *ownership* of "Absolute Truth". One feels identified with the thing-in-itself. Words, themes and issues from the patient exhibit features of "possibilities", and the unknown emerges from them, depending on intuition, attention and detection of invariants and selected facts. Both analyst and patient must do it, on the way to *insight*.

Facts are not good or bad, rational or irrational. They simply *are*. Facts cannot be in agreement with human theories that strive to depict them, without ever succeeding—be they *a priori* or *ad hoc*. For the analyst there is a discipline that preserves a sense of truth, given by an empirically verifiable (by participant observation) factual background of which the analyst is part. This background may have a counterpart in verbal, theoretical formulations—good, transcendent and durable "theories".

The analyst cannot know what happened outside the analytic session, but he or she can observe *how* the analysand reports them. The analyst can hear the "music" if he or she respects that which the analysand's words and issues indicate and hide—which they do simultaneously. The analyst may try not to manipulate or fit them in some idea he or she already has, ingeniously or formalistically. He or she may exercise his or her capacity to be precise, pay attention and be rigorous, here understood as a disciplined concentration on the clinical experience, the here and now of *what is really occurring* (Bion, 1962, p. 39). The analyst may formulate those facts in such a way that they can attain the *status* of models or myths. They can be seen as shadows in a sculpture, or pauses and rhythms in a musical score: they entrap the light, or reveal the music, which is seen by the analytic couple. The patient, too, is able to do this, and often does, disguised as both "normal" and "abnormal" statements. The individual myths are embedded in the "abnormal" statements, often made *en passant*, as if they were not important. There is a distortion of this posture, in the way the analytic contact becomes superficial and turns towards a psychology of consciousness, far from the analytic posture, in taking the variegated issues and their corresponding verbal statements as if they were things-in-themselves. In other words: the analyst does not have the opportunity to verify empirically the reported, alleged events. The analyst did not experience them. It is not a case of whether or not to trust the patient's report; it is a case of admitting the lack of direct experience. Some analysts are prone, due to the force of the report, to understanding them as if they really had occurred, rather than as representations. The patient's models of what he or she feels has occurred are lost from sight.

A patient dreamt that he was lying on a stretcher at a hospital emergency unit and that his neck was bleeding. During the session he actually puts his hand on his "bleeding" neck, then carries on reporting the dream, that he is paraplegic, looks at his hand and concludes: "No blood there". If I say that he feels pierced by the analysis, or he feels confused as to whether he is a potent man or a weak menstruating woman, the words "paraplegic" and "blood on the neck" are the patient's theories and models depicting to himself a given emotional experience in the here and now. My models are intended for immediate use, are not universal, and are disposable even though they include some human universals as they are presented in the patient's way. Those models are a coupling of something learnt from the psychoanalytic experience with something apprehended in the experience of the session, and there seem to be hints of the existence of homosexual phantasies and of an undifferentiated sexual condition. The scientific validation—the "truth-value"—of my statements will depend on the evolution, the patient's reaction, the exercising of his intuitive free associations. The analyst must talk with no ambiguity, as far as possible. Nevertheless, the diminution of ambiguity will always depend on the patient's capacity to hear. When the patient hears, he or she has unrestricted freedom to choose *how* he or she will hear. At this moment it seems to me that we have a unique opportunity in analysis, beyond rational thinking. The reaction to an interpretation may seem anomalous if measured against our rational codes. It *seems* to be anomalous; when it is not and it fits smoothly, the conversation becomes a collusion in agreement or disagreement, providing no chance to evolve into the unknown. I think that the "anomaly" felt indicates that we are facing some instinctive manifestation, a free association. The impact of that which is new is that of a living seed of life itself, pulsating. Conversely, agreement and disagreement do not seem to propitiate real conversation. They serve well for religious, authoritarian and rival links between people. I am proposing to consider the existence of modes of talk and verbal intercourse that yield space for tolerating paradoxes and the emotional experience that emerges when one faces the different and the difference, always felt as an unknown. This mode of conversation starts from mutual respect and demands neither concordance nor discordance, but rather observation (Bion 1965, p. 145).

Truth can be differentiated from hallucination. This is not a moral issue. That which *is*, *is* in its own way. Also, it *is not* in any other way, despite the fact that it can—and must—be regarded from infinite individual points of view, in a continuous differentiation from that which *is not*. The *is not* is hallucination or lie, using the common psychiatric and colloquial terms; it is an essential contrapuntal "parameter" if one is bound to make approximations to reality *as it is*. I consider "transference" in the way Freud defined it, namely, the hallucinated repetition of infantile patterns of feelings linked to significant figures from past times of one's life, attributed to other persons with whom one becomes acquainted or simply meets in later times (Freud, 1912). If one cannot experience and work through—be transiently mobile from unconscious to conscious and back—the "transference", one perhaps will not gradually get a more realistic or truthful perception of people (including oneself).

> I assume that the permanently therapeutic effect of a psychoanalysis, if any, depends on the extent to which the analysand has been able to use the experience to see one aspect of his life, namely himself as he is...It follows that a psychoanalysis is a joint activity of analysand and analyst to determine the truth; that being so, the two are engaged—no matter how imperfectly—on what is in intention, a scientific activity. [Bion, 1958–1979, p. 114]

Notes

1. Including fashionable internal (i.e. within the psychoanalytic movement) "Freud-bashing" accusations from many authors and their respective scholastic followers; one may see it in Meltzer, Kohut and intersubjectivsts, to quote a few, but broad examples.

2. Alas, some analysts regard Bion's contributions as allowing and recommending this tendency. A split and partial reading of some chapters of *Transformations* with reference to the self-sincerity demanded by a real psychoanalytic posture, excising the part from the whole of the text, seems to be linked to this conclusion. It is outside the scope of this chapter to discuss this misunderstanding, which was dwelt on elsewhere (Sandler, 2005).
3. "O" is Bion's notational sign for the numinous realm.
4. Obviously a given person—in the same session or in different sessions—offers, again and again, different modes of expressing projective identification, or any psychoanalytically apprehended fact, such as transference, allegiance to the pleasure-displeasure principle, and so on.
5. This hypothesis and the facts cited as evidence for it can be seen in Sandler, 2001–2003.
6. Please see Volume 2, Chapters Five and Eight.
7. Corresponding to the last phase of ego functions after Freud (1911a) and Bion's assignments of facts corresponding to column category 6, rows A to H.
8. See Rickman, 1950.
9. Please refer to the Versus realm, Volume 2 Part I.
10. This concept is suggested in *A Apreensão da Realidade Psíquica*, vol. I (Sandler, 1997b).
11. If Bion's generalised scientific formulations that encompass this particular case could not be understood before, perhaps this statement may help one's grasp of it. The new contingency demanded not to be loved or hated; discipline of memory (past life) and desire (expectations, demands, future planning), and understanding (of violence) was demanded; life was at stake.
12. Criminals believe that earning money is an easy task; they often collect huge quantities in a short time. Easy come, easy go: according the police, they waste it as soon as they grab it, usually on drugs. The idealistic phantasy of "ease", or the belief that there are easy things, marks the psychotic and psychopathic way.
13. In a country where kidnapping was common, a system had been set up for swift communication between banks and the police in such cases.
14. One of the detectives had in ten years of experience assisted with 600 kidnaps, successful or not. His superior, curiously younger, had faced 200 cases. The anti-kidnapping police special forces have sophisticated training compared to other police squads.
15. *The Language of Bion: A Dictionary of Concepts* (Karnac, 2005) may be regarded as evidence of my efforts to define precisely the terms used by analysts. This is the acknowledged way in scientific communication

and in real artistic manifestations. Alas, it has not been followed in the psychoanalytic movement, where different senses and meanings are attributed to the same phenomena, as well as constantly unwarranted (for the lack of empirical evidence) changes in established definitions. Bion asked, in *A Memoir of the Future*, how one may state today (in 1975) what Freud understood by "paranoid", or "transference". Bion dwells on transference in the same work, with amendments made in 1977, and one may see that he meant the same thing that Freud meant (a repetition of one's infantile patterns of ideas, feelings and affects, justified or not, in later times of one's life). In my view, a few thousand copies of *The Language of Bion* sold to a hundred universities and psychoanalytic libraries, as well as a few thousand copies sold to individuals, cannot be regarded as more than feeble. Though from another vertex, say, that of the publisher, fortunately, it may be "not-feeble". It may even approximate to an appreciative, profitable business.
16. Please see Volume 2 Part 3 (Binocular Vision), Volume 2 Part I (Versus) and Volume 1 Part I (Dreams).
17. I owe this observation to Dr Miguel Marques, in a course about the apprehension of psychic reality given at the SBPSP.

PART IV

GROUPS

CHAPTER TEN

A sixth basic assumption?

"Passionate love" is the nearest I can get to a verbal transformation which "represents" the thing-in-itself, the ultimate reality, the "O" as I have called it, approximating to it.

—Bion, 1975, p. 197

P.A. Poor as it is and poorly though we use it, verbal communication is one of the latest and most astonishing discoveries ... It is a great improvement on physical violence.
ROLAND I am not sure that I agree. "Faire entrer la sagesse par le cul" still has its advocates.
ROBIN So it has, as we have good reasons to know. Witness Nazi Germany.
ALICE There is a danger that our concentration on Nazi Germany will distract us from observing its development elsewhere.
P.A. Bigotry and ignorance are two well-developed and ancient characteristics of the human being. In psychoanalysis, and in those who practise it, it shows up with startling freshness and

vigour. I trust that our ability to detect it will not become jaded, our taste for it not so surfeited, that we cease to be aware of it.

—Bion, 1979, p. 89

Bion abandoned his therapeutic practice with small groups, focusing his attention on pure psychoanalysis, a two-body psychology according to Rickman, his first analyst and then close friend, which continues to be a group activity. The two-body psychology known as the mother-baby relationship and mass psychology phenomena were an integral part of *Transformations, Attention and Interpretation* and *A Memoir of the Future*.

Clinical experiences form the empirical basis that seems to back the following hypothesis. It belongs to the realm of psychoanalysis proper and of applied psychoanalysis. It is dedicated to those colleagues who are interested in dealing psychoanalytically with the so-called "crises" of the psychoanalytic movement, studying intra-group tensions, investigating possible factors involved in the allegedly diminishing numbers of gifted younger professionals seeking analytic training, a trend which has spread through many parts of the world and was first noticed by Wallerstein (1984) and Kernberg (1984), and investigating possible factors implied in the feeling that there are diminishing numbers of people seeking analysis.

This study was written before a kind of "Hitler's bestiality reborn" obtruded in the form of a kind of bin, laden with invitations to the basest drives of man.[1] It appeared as a sudden act; it proved to be chronic in its effects.

Bion observed that groups are forged in shared hallucination. Therefore, they are a fertile soil for wars against reality (Bion, 1961a, 1965). My experience shows that groups provide social loci to shelter a psychotic feature, described by Bion (1965, pp. 132–133) as a factor in hallucinosis: the phantasy of superiority, a function of primary narcissism (Freud, 1914c) or primary envy (Klein, 1957). Those theories express, in the phenomenal realm, a freezing in the paranoid-schizoid position, the outcome of which is contempt for truth and life.[2]

The sixth basic assumption: the hallucinosis of exclusion/appertaining

After Bion (1961), the analytically trained intuition, exercised through psychoanalytic "participating observation"[3] in group settings,[4] allows for the detection of three underlying modes of organisation/

disorganisation of groups, the "basic assumptions": (i) *fight/flight*, where the group splits itself in a mutual destruction of its members; (ii) *pairing*, a fragmentation whereby the members form pairs that would bring forth a saviour;[5] and (iii) *messianic or dependence*, where the group agglutinates itself around a leader felt as superior. The psychotic nature of the three basic assumptions was clear in Bion's original writings in the 1940s. Thanks to his later advancements in grasping those facts about the herd, especially after the publication of his later books, *Transformations*, *Attention and Interpretation* and *A Memoir of the Future*, we can now see that those three underlying modes of functioning are the stuff of shared hallucinosis in masses. They hamper or preclude the formation of "work groups", whose existence is dependent on regard for truth:

> The assumption underlying loyalty to the K link is that the personality of analyst and analysand can survive the loss of the protective coat of lies, subterfuge, evasion and hallucination and may even be fortified and enriched by the loss. It is an assumption strongly disputed by the psychotic and *a fortiori* by the group, which relies on psychotic mechanisms for its coherence and sense of wellbeing. [Bion, 1965, p. 129]

Under the psychoanalytic vertex of observation which apprehends the underlying, infra- and ultra-sensuously apprehensible appearances, I observed the existence of another basic assumption, which I propose to name "Hallucinosis of Appertaining and Exclusion". A quasi-mathematical notation may be Groups {A, A̶}, where A represents those who are "included" and A with strikethrough those who are "excluded".

Observation allows one to suppose that people hallucinate that they have a functional part in a naturally (biologically) non-existent reality and unquestioning (in this sense, absolute) socially shared position. For this reason I use the word "appertain", which has a different semantic field from "belonging". Therefore one hallucinates that one appertains to a given group (or subgroup within the group) and/or hallucinates that one is excluded from the given group that one aspires to be positioned with or to be a functional part of. The very group (or socially shared role) is a product of the mind and has no counterpart in reality, its "materiality" notwithstanding.[6] I will leave to a forthcoming study the discussion of the possibility of "natural groups" that *may* qualify to be endowed with realness. I will only hint now that those groups were adumbrated by Durkheim. He observed two kinds of solidarity that cohere people in groups: "mechanical" and "organic". The latter can foster a real "appertaining centrifugal tropism" towards and between its members. It is a matter of interest (Sanders, 1986).

This work is indebted to the contributions of another harbinger in the treatment of "diseased groups", S. H. Foulkes, who noticed, at the same time as Bion and Rickman, and working in the very same place, difficulties in developing "the most precious" (Foulkes, 1948, p. 165) output of human beings—during the era of the most compressed and successful inhumanity of people towards other people and towards themselves.

The difference between sociological ideas and scientific hypotheses

A preliminary terminological remark: why sixth basic assumption rather than fourth? During the span of time that this work was developed, I was ignorant of earlier attempts to establish basic assumptions other than Bion's original three. Therefore the title of my original Brazilian paper is "The Fourth Basic Assumption". After its presentation I was kindly informed by a knowledgeable colleague, Dr Victor Bazzo Jr, about the existence of ideas on a fourth and a fifth basic assumption. Scientific patterns (respect for truth, or truthfulness) demand recognition of their historical precedence. In 1974, Pierre Turquet stated that there is a fourth basic assumption, which he called *Oneness*:

> ... a mental activity in which members seek to join in a powerful union with an omnipotent force, unobtainably high, to surrender self for passive participation, and thereby feel existence, well-being, and wholeness ... the group member is there to be lost in oceanic feelings of unity or, if the oneness is personified, to be a part of a salvationist inclusion. [Turquet, 1974, pp. 357, 360]

This corresponds to Max Weber's "charismatic leader" (Weber, 1947). Starting from him, W. Gordon Lawrence, Alastair Bain and Laurence Gould named a fifth basic assumption: *Me-ness*. According to them, this fifth basic assumption is the opposite of Turquet's *Oneness*. It consists of an anti-group group mentality. The authors "do not want to explain away baM [basic assumption Me-ness] in terms of individual narcissism, as can be found in analysands and patients, because [they] are focusing on baM as a cultural phenomenon". They hypothesise that this basic assumption is becoming "more salient in our industrialised cultures": an individualist tendency that they detect in different ages of Western civilisation (Lawrence, Bain & Gould, 1996).

There are some differences between my hypothesis and the ideas of those authors. I deal with it as a hypothesis based on empirical findings, to be discussed and eventually verified or refuted by other researchers, hopefully equipped with new empirical findings that may either ratify or rectify it (including expansions). In contrast, those authors make a socio-philosophical exercise based on logical, conscious thinking drawn from intelligible and rationally plausible comparisons of some socio-economic and political dated or fashionable facts of a specific moment. Their experience is drawn primarily from their "roles as consultants to and directors of ... working conferences" about group relations and education in addition to their "practices as social scientists, organisational consultants, psychoanalyst, and university teachers" (all quotations from the authors). It contrasts with my experience, drawn from the psychoanalytic clinic, group dynamics (small and medium, according to Patrick de Maré: Bion, 1961; Pisani, 2000) in various settings, community psychiatry and actions within psychoanalytic institutions.

It was not clear, at least from my scrutiny of their paper and chapter in a book, whether the phenomenal expressions depicted by those authors are just variations (or transformations) around the same basic invariant, that is, Bion's "messianic leader" and "dependence" assumptions. If this is the case, there would be no scientific or psychoanalytic justification for attributing to it the status of a different basic assumption. In describing a myriad of external manifestations it falls into a psychology of consciousness, which is halted before reaching the unconscious numinous invariant or basic generalising scientific definition that encompasses particular cases (transformations). Describing individual manifestations (or low empirical data) has a function in the building up of scientific and psychoanalytic "laws".

This condition seems to fulfil the main "rules" of transformations in hallucinosis (Bion, 1965, pp. 130–140). Hallucinosis is a psychiatric description which corresponds to a precise definition: the presence of hallucinations and delusions in an otherwise conserved personality (Campbell, 1940; Sandler, 2005). Its everyday occurrence and manifestations in the consulting room were emphasised by Bion. The condition here described fulfils Bion's criteria of hallucinosis: an object or an idea is considered to be "the top"; a group or a person is considered to be self-fulfilling at the expense of anyone or anything else. Moreover, groups are especially liable to function under hallucinosis, as we have seen before.

Some phenomenal expressions that originated the hypothesis

This study will be mainly about experiences in the "two-body psychology" (Rickman, 1950) group, that is, psychoanalysis proper, formed by the basic group: two people in a room, trying to converse. The formidable caesura provided by groups composed of more than two people clouds the formidable continuities between two-body groups and larger groups, even though Bion's contributions on groups emphasise those continuities. Some, like Winnicott, who warned that "there is no such thing as a baby", were aware of this. In order to avoid a lengthy description of cases, I will try to display the issue in a generalised form. This is the pattern of a scientific appreciation: generalised descriptions that are able—and the reader will judge for him- or herself whether or not they are—to encompass the particular. By particular I mean classical descriptions of lower-level data material, the analytic sessions.[7] Both generalisation and the truthful description of empirical data, with its attendant vertex that allows observation, qualify them to be considered scientific and so they can serve as evidence (counterparts in reality).

An initial warning must be made: "to feel" as used in this work has nothing to do with "to experience (or suffer) emotional experiences" or "to be affected by real emotions". Rather, "to feel" must be linked to "sensations", so that an excessive preoccupation with "feelings" would mean a tendency to nourish and enshrine illusion, hallucination, hallucinosis and delusion as the preferred functioning of the psychotic mind. In this state the individual is intoxicated with a constant search for pleasure, enslaved by desire. He or she cannot make the quantum leap performed by alpha function, which may be seen as the "de-sensified" function of the mind.

The psychoanalytic couple: a basic group

I suppose that the experiences I will try to depict are familiar to any practising analyst. The presence of the hypothesised sixth assumption in private practice is so pervasive that it borders on obviousness.

It perhaps demands mention due to the fact that the obvious is difficult to observe. There is a seemingly unavoidable blunting of the senses that habit, the noxious companion of the obvious, brings with it.

Our issue can be approached by the layman's bewildered question often posed to psychoanalysts: "How can you work *alone* all day, every day, in *that* same small space?" This statement has the evocative ethos of any commonplace affirmation, seen in at least two features: (i) It is a statement travestied into a question, while affirming a certainty from the one who states it; (ii) it is based on outside, external, conscious appearances, which furnishes its judgemental commonplace (as distinct from common sense) nature.

There is no verbal explanation that could replace the living experience of an analysis. This question may sound familiar to most readers, and could possibly even have been asked by them, at least in initial situations at the beginning of their analytic training, or later in seemingly difficult situations too tainted with projective identifications, for example. Sometimes, when I intuited that I was talking with perceptive individuals, either in the analytic establishment or outside it, I tried to convey that it is not the case. For I—meaning the psychoanalyst—am never alone. I am accompanied enough. The patient is my companion, allowing the analysis to show him or her who he or she is in reality, up to a point and transiently. Moreover, in my solitude I am accompanied by myself.[8]

The sense of exclusion is just a product of the layman's imagination with no counterpart in either form of reality, material or psychic. In material terms, which are easier to grasp because of their sensuously apprehensible appeal, psychoanalysis is a two-body group. If one uses one's imagination under a psychotic vertex (with no bearing on reality as it is), one "excludes" the other person in hallucination; the other person will remain present whether or not he or she feels excluded. Therefore, under this hallucination, there are people who feel entitled to think that they can perform the impossible task of "excluding" their real self.

"Exclusion" of the real self

A sizeable number of patients come to us due to the fact that they have excluded themselves (or important aspects of themselves) from themselves. Analysis can be quite useful to create an alternative to this crippling outcome of avoidance and evasion from pain, to the extent that psychoanalysis is the most powerful technique hitherto devised to present the person to who he or she is in reality.

This means that many feel, from early infancy, that pain and frustration of desire are to be excluded. A heightened tolerance of frustration demands a lessening of paranoid traits. Nevertheless, it seems to be an innate endowment. The variable degree to which it can appear may or may not condemn the person to try to be someone he or she is not in reality. The resulting vacuum is occupied by a false self (in Winnicott's sense). This involves being responsible. Projective identification would be an attempt to exclude one's own mind.

"Exclusion" of psychic reality

Analysis seems to be a last resort for some people who feel entitled to exclude real life from their lives. In other terms, they imagine that they are able to exclude from their life the form of existence that Freud called "psychic reality" (Freud, 1900). Psychic reality is manifested by a moving homeostatic equilibrium between the three basic unconscious instincts described through their phenomenal manifestations by Freud: death, life, and its specialised form, the epistemophilic instinct. Psychic reality is regulated by another homeostatic pair, the principles of mental functioning: pleasure/displeasure and reality. Both are fundamental in one's inhabiting another pair which functions as a tandem: the paranoid-schizoid and depressive positions. Imbalance between them can be analytically visible through dream life and deeds manifested by behaviour, such as sexual, usually under the sway of features of the paranoid-schizoid and depressive positions. A detailed model of their interrelationships can be seen in Volume 2 of this series (pp. 131–188). It leads to one type of the hallucinated "fact" of appertaining/exclusion which seems to me basic and universal in the analytic setting. It is linked to the hate that the human being seems to nourish against psychic reality and truth in particular, or the homeostatic balance of the two realities—a partially unconscious awareness of the arrow of time[9] in life which brings unending surprises, most of them not pleasurable, and the unavoidability of death.

This assumes multifarious forms. Experience may vary among analysts. To quote one example: men who hallucinate that they are able to exclude their femininity, and women, their masculinity.[10] The phenomena are multifarious but the invariant is the same: there is a hypertrophy of infantile stereotypes of pseudo-masculinity: authoritarian violence, physical superiority, "don-juanism", or the prevalence of homosexual phantasies. The female counterparts are a stereotyped hypertrophy of subjection, pseudo-passivity and pseudo-delicateness that usually serve as a cover for irresponsibility as well as homosexual phantasies. In both cases, there is an envious attack against the breast.

There are patients who express in the session their phantasy of being able to exclude their mental life when they swear: "I do not dream", "I have nothing to say", "I think nothing", "My mind is black" or "My mind is blank" or "has a hole". The exclusion of dream life is often coupled with a sense of appertaining of hallucinosis, both awake and in sleep. It is one of the manifestations of one's false self. This kind of patient is talkative but keeps saying nothing. Emptiness prevails in acoustic noise that mimics real talk. There are exhaustive reports of seemingly concrete facts, also seemingly poor in free associations which challenge the analyst's ability to see them. It is not the case that free associations do not exist. The patient feels they do not exist and attempts to convince the analyst about the truth of his false feelings, with all kinds of manoeuvres to get the analyst's associations instead. It indicates the prevalence of a hallucinated state: the person feels capable of excluding the principle of reality. It differs from the classical paranoid psychoses due to the skilful mimicry of reality. It is a perverse use of reality, which furnishes a socially accepted intelligible shell. The ability of the analyst to spot real free associations underlying the material depends on his experience, which enables him to divest the colluded codes and habits of thinking which ape those of the patient. For example, when an analyst feels: "This is an intelligent (or wealthy, or professionally successful, or physically beautiful, or married, and so on) patient", there is a high probability of this kind of plausible, intelligible, socially shared collusion. Bion illuminated this fact in differentiating the psychotic from the non-psychotic personality (1957), which allowed him to further the issue of functioning under hallucinosis (1965).

If habit imposes, the consequence for the individual who proves to be comparatively successful in excluding contact with dream activity is a *real* exclusion of psychic reality. It corresponds to the "real effect" that splitting exerts on thinking processes.[11] Myths such as the Apocalypse, Armageddon, the Day of Judgement, the practice of the last rites[12] depict the unavoidable eruption of the perception that a given unwelcome truth, manifested by a false self or chronic state of hallucinosis, cannot be kept hidden forever. "Falstaff, a known artefact, is more real than countless millions of people … whose births, deaths—alas even marriages—we are called upon to believe in, though certification of their existence is vouched for by the so-called official certification" (Bion, 1975, p. 4). In my experience, that which is called "panic syndrome" is an attempt to escape from the perception of a cultivated, tendered nothingness.

"Exclusion" of material reality

Psychopathic personalities, moved by the exercise of cruelty and inhumanity on humans and other beings, perform serial and massive projective identifications of their own feeling of appertaining and exclusion, creating environmental conditions of a mafia-type gang inclusion and physical exclusion where death is not precluded. The typically mafia system of kidnapping seems to be the climax of this projective identification. The kidnapped person is forced to feel excluded; as soon as he is not obliged to be excluded from himself (in the sense briefly depicted above) he can keep at least a minimal survival link with his own human psychic reality (meaning life and death instincts and a restricted sense of epistemophilic instincts where possible). Kidnapping offers a blind-optioned situation: one is kept between four walls with no windows.[13]

The same kind of psychopathic criminality in excluding material reality occurs with what could be named *homo excludens*. Children are used, but never accustomed, to the cruel game of not hearing, not seeing and not conversing with some other children, usually those marked by an external difference. It seems that these practices continue in adulthood; geniuses and discoverers, as well as benevolent people and groups, are subjected to this. In the limited field of medicine and psychotherapy, treating or not treating patients may imply less than adequate conditions for survival.

The enforced exclusion of minorities, of those who are different in terms of skin colour, religion or ideology is, again, a specialised type of group kidnapping and the massive projective identifications of self-attributed elites. The deterioration of the Ancient Greek practice of *polis* into today's politics (oppressive elites run by greed and contempt) exemplifies it.

Enforcing inclusion

Patients often resort to the phantastic state of hallucinosis to become entitled to feel excluded from the analytic situation due to what Bion called reversion of perspective (Bion, 1963; a review of the concept appears in Sandler, 2005). Phenomenally they perform the role, but not the function, of being patients. The patient may state subtly and implicitly (in free associations) or sometimes explicitly that he or she is a poor ignoramus, and the person there with them is a "skilled technician" or "professor", wise in who-knows-what arts and powers. Transference phenomena as described by Freud are dominant. The analyst is "invited" and then obliged to perform the role of a figure from the patient's past.

A variation of this can be seen in a sizeable number of people who submit themselves to analysis and then develop an interest in becoming analysts. They abandon their profession, training, inclination or skill to pursue an analytic "career". In some of them, the possibility of a genuine "inner call"—which is undeniably true in many persons—and the sense of exclusion lingers on. Exclusion of what? Of that which is seen as pleasurable. How many are able to face the fact that "an analyst is not doing his job if he investigates something because it is pleasurable or profitable"?[14] This occurrence later in life resembles little children who choose to be medical doctors at an early age, linked to some painful infantile experience of illness coupled with the aid of a good enough physician, or an unsuccessful treatment under the prevalence of the principle of pleasure. Both events are variations of a still earlier tendency: one of the things children desire most is to become adults—because in their eyes, adults are empowered with cunning strength to get all their desires fulfilled. At a later age, the same would-be-adult mostly desires to be a child again—seeing children as being entitled to enjoy an easy-going, fulfilled life. Hope has no memory; as in the case described by Freud, children are pictured as angels—again, a desire-fulfilled existence.

The continued presence of infantile emotions prompts an eagerness to "appertain". I suppose that many "successful" analyses could benefit from a close scrutiny of this point; it relates to the "endogamy" that seems to plague our activity.[15]

Another manifestation was described by Bion in 1957, in a paper entitled "On Arrogance", which could well be called "On Arrogance,

Stupidity and Curiosity".[16] It deals with some forbidden attempts at projective identification; in this state, patients become interested in the analyst, in the analyst's personal life and tastes, in the analytic movement and establishment, in the works of the great authors. It seems that the analyst has become the most important person in the room; in hallucinating the enforced inclusion of the analyst, they unconsciously put themselves off and are being excluded in hallucination. Rivalry, envy, emulation, imitation can be singled out as factors in this posture. But as far as my experience goes, the problem persists even after analysing all of this. Oedipus under the sixth basic assumption may be at work. Further acting out displays a desire to include themselves in the analyst's life,[17] to know where the analyst lives and what he does in his private life. Humdrum realities assume an important shape: the kind of car he drives or does not drive; where he spends his holidays. Nevertheless, as soon they obtain analysis, they refrain from suffering it (hallucinated exclusion). The same problem remains with those who, as soon as they glimpse the couch, resolutely go and lie down (hallucinated appertaining).

Projective identification of exclusion

Some develop a reaction formation, and through projective identification they phantasise that they may exclude the analyst. They try to force him to feel excluded. Often they are of the talkative kind, in reality mimicking talkative characters and people they know (or knew) outside the analytic room. They hope that the analyst will feel what it is like to be excluded, through being "excluded" from many beautiful parties, meetings, businesses, properties, travels and friends enjoyed by the patients.

How many people can listen to what is said to them? At the beginning of the majority of analyses, it still amazes me how rarely I come across people who can listen to me, the analyst. I am not concerned with the sensuous apprehension that the patient's auditory apparatus can perform. Repeating the analyst's words will not do: an inanimate tape recorder or a mindless bird would suffice for that. I believe that another kind of attention is needed to be worthy of the description *listening*. It is an act that expresses an emotional experience that "cannot be conceived of in isolation from a relationship" (Bion, 1962, p. 42).

Some patients *seem* to try to make efforts to include us analysts. The very effort, implying consciousness, hints (in terms of resistance) at the underlying exclusion. There would be no point trying to include someone who is already there. Conscious effort equates to convincing and contriving, which spells falsity. The inclusion is hallucinated. The initial manifestation of the hallucinated "inclusion" is the patient taking us for their parents or any other past figure in their life, in the sense described by Freud as transference. To identify with us or to project something into us is not real inclusion but phagocytosis. If Freud was correct when he stated that analysis begins when the transference neurosis is resolved, then in my experience many of my patients interrupted their analysis just when it was about to begin, excluding analysis from themselves as a step to excluding themselves. For as soon as they feel a little bit free from their transference phantasies, they also feel free from their symptoms and think they are "cured". The idea of cure displays an appearance of appertaining—what more can be asked of a treatment than a cure?—but it is the incarnation of "exclusion-in-itself". The cured patient avoids analysis, a fact described by Freud as the "negative therapeutic reaction".

The sense that something "appertains" to analytic sessions may be a warning that the analytic vertex has been lost. Common manifestations are collusive links, with plenty of rational explanations, pseudo-agreements, rational talking with the aid of theories already known, choosing "issues to be worked through". "My analyst said this and that", "I am dealing with this and that in my analysis" are paradigmatic statements that in my experience spell danger. The sixth assumption would be at its height when a pair "understands"—mutual inclusion—but in reality may be marching unabated to collusion. Winnicott recommended that analysts should write about cases that were not successful (Winnicott, 1969). Bion presented to us painful evidence of a seemingly successful analysis that ended in suicide. Later he warned explicitly about analyses that were felt to be "profitable": "Anyone who is not afraid when he is engaged in psychoanalysis is either not doing his job or is unfitted for it" (1979, p. 83).

The sixth basic assumption in larger groups: wars among psychoanalysts

PAUL (soliloquising) Anyone would think psychoanalysts never quarrel. When the Wars of Psychoanalysis start we shall see something—and no holds barred. Santayana feared the day when the scientific blackguards would get the hold of the world. [Bion, 1977, p. 51]

The psychoanalytic movement, as distinct from psychoanalysis proper, is full of perverse, painful examples: Freud's exclusion from the Viennese academic and medical milieu, or the exclusion of psychoanalysis itself from the various intellectual establishments due to contradictory rational argumentation. It was simultaneously Victorian, bourgeois, non-Aryan, Jewish, anti-religious, too German, avant-garde, pornographic, too innocent, too judgemental, excessively libertarian. In its turn, the authoritarian use of the three-pillared system of training for analysts—personal analysis, supervision and courses—was an attempt to include that promoted exclusion. In the 1930s there was a violent reaction by the self-styled "Freudians" and "Annafreudians" against Melanie Klein. This would soon repeat itself in the 1950s: a violent reaction against Winnicott by those who became self-styled "Kleinians". Across the pond, there was the exclusion of Lagache and soon after of Lacan on the rationalised basis of politics: too rightist, too leftist, and so on. The 1960s witnessed the exclusion of Bion, against whom it was stated that his work was not neo-Kleinian enough, due to his revision of countertransference usage. He returned to Freud's original concept and left aside Heimann's modifications, which he never fully endorsed. This was followed by hostile comments such as his work being "not psychoanalysis any more"[18] and "the frolics of a senile man"; the roots of these comments probably being manifestations of envy and rivalry (Meltzer, 1981; Segal, 1981; Joseph, 2003). The exclusion did not spare Freud's work. In an attempt to out-Freud Freud, many excluded the word "displeasure"—*Unlust*—from Freud's original concept of 1910, the principle of pleasure/displeasure (*Lust/Unlust*).

What was born as a scientific criterion and precise definition turned into a value judgment exercise and playing at cruelty. The swift adoption of Kuhnist peer review teams implanted ideology over analysis.[19]

The examples are legion; if one cares to perform a statistical study[20] using papers published worldwide, one will find that the vast majority display as their underlying rationale Freud's *pre-psychoanalytic* theory of trauma. This is equivalent to excluding proper psychoanalysis from the psychoanalytic movement. The efforts towards exclusion are blatantly explicit as regards Freud's post-1920 modifications.

Attempts to out-Klein Klein appeared first with some of her so-called "followers" joining Heimann's and Racker's bandwagon of "using countertransference"—which in the end simply equates to stating that the unconscious realm is a kind of dubious "privilege" of patients that the analyst is able to master to the point of "using" it.[21] More recently they denied the existence of envy. Turning "neo-Kleinism" into a political movement devoted to exclusion and inclusion—against which Winnicott warned—may have had good political rewards but had noxious effects on psychoanalytic knowledge.

The so-called splitting and dissidences in "psychoanalytic" societies seem to me to be chronic states of hallucinosis of appertaining and exclusion, or in our proposed notation, {A, A̶}. Some analysts resorted to the law courts, creating a legal public conundrum, much to the liking of the scurrilous press, which praises, enjoys and is fulfilled by hyperbole and lies. It proved to be an expression of distrust—once more in ourselves, the analysts, with regard to our competence to do our job. It contributed to the poor opinion of our movement and its representatives held by knowledgeable and intelligent people from the outer social milieu. No wonder that after some turbulent and highly publicised cases, the number of people looking for analysis diminished. Some members of the psychoanalytic establishment imagine that law courts, barristers, administrators, laws and rules could provide a way to deal with the emotional turbulence that characterises the paradoxical pair of human conviviality and frostiness. Is it a manifestation of our inner hate and distrust towards analysis and truth and life? Many were not able to perceive and much less to apprehend and have the alternative to put up with the projective identifications, and readily assumed the group function of "evicted". This depends on one's own analysis and proves to be a durable event in groups. In some of them, it furnishes the *raison d'être* of the group. Some tried to form other groups free from rivalry, but there is no chance that Group A will tolerate it. How could it live without those it excluded? Some alternative groups were created without resentment and under the aegis of life instincts, something that could provide a peaceful, mutually fruitful coexistence between the many centres of training. The feeling of being part of a "superior alternative", "dissent", is a manifestation of rivalry (as distinct from a division that could be regarded as a natural growth, such as the progeny that leave their parents' home) and in my view destructive to the psychoanalytic movement. Usually the professionals who look for those alternative centres are biased by phantasies of superiority.

{A, ⇌} shelters mania, envy and rivalry; it is a social place for those who seem to replace analysis or re-analysis with acting out in the establishment. The former analytic societies become places for organised groups involved in fratricidal wars. One of the best known cases was the legal action taken in the US courts by psychologists against the International Psychoanalytical Association at the dawn of the last century; there must be no scarcity of examples in any environment.

The members of the ⇌ sub-group collude in a shared hallucinosis: they feel excluded. They feel or are concretely subjected to some actions intended (albeit unconsciously) to make them feel that their wishes or even need to grow in the institution are blocked. They turn to actively promoting some movements in order to transform the A sub-group, those who currently hallucinate that they "appertain", into a new ⇌ sub-group. At a certain point, the hallucinosis prevails and succeeds—the former A, now ⇌, feel themselves victorious in their pushes. They do not observe that they are mere unconscious and unwitting characters in an unobserved unfolding human tragedy. The "new" ⇌, the former A, assume their new functions with remarkable disposition.

This situation is overly complicated when hate towards truth—or unconcern for truth and life (Bion, 1958–1979, p. 125)—which characterises the authoritarian psychopathic personality dominates the scene. The banalisation of cruelty, which profits from the other part idea of being excluded, forms what Toynbee called "oppressive minorities" that exacerbate, rather than resolve, emotional problems in groups. This is the very condition of survival of the authoritarian and idealistic psychopathic personality. If the definition of idealism (and relativism) in the psychoanalytic research and movement sounds imprecise to any readers, other details can be found elsewhere.[22]

Social scientists or professional politicians would say, with their customary denial of emotions, that "each government *must* have its opposition". But {A, ⇌} is not a dialectical opposition under the aegis of the life instincts, in the sense of a complementary pair that produces synthesis. A more inclusive discussion of primitive forms that featured warring, pre-dialectical pairs which never develop into antithetical and pregnant couples, as well as the possibilities opened by the German Romantics (mainly Hamann, Kant, Goethe, Hegel and Freud) may be found elsewhere (Sandler, 2000, 2001; abridged in Volume 2 Part I and Part III of this volume).

{A, ≠} is a warring, friend-foe primitive mentality under the aegis of the death instincts. Real people in those situations act in a more unreal way than characters that were known artefacts, as Shelley and Bion noticed (Bion, 1975, p. 8). They act out (for multifarious individual reasons) factual manifestations and put forth the everlasting cycle of the sixth basic assumption.

A worrying new cloud hovers as an offshoot of the sixth basic assumption. There is a growing hope, sometimes explicitly stated, that political manipulation is a good replacement for science and personal analysis. People hallucinate "enemies" and "allies" in the guise of "-ists" and "-ans". Political debate replaces scientific debate. The issuing of rules, laws, byelaws and codes of conduct is seen as a solution to emotional problems in human relationships. The psychotic phenomena include the erection and subsequent enshrining of mythical figures who are conveniently dead; they cannot say whether or not they would agree with their new status in the group.[23] The contempt for truth inflicts injustice and wasteful suffering on all individuals involved. Members of A feel happy and hallucinate blissfully that they are "victorious", at least for the time being. But they will suffer to the extent that they will be forced to occupy functions that they cannot exercise.

Those who are excluded (≠) suffer to the extent that they unwittingly function as "adequate" containers for projective identification. The non-analysed superficial appearances are personal issues, rivalry, political pretensions, co-optation, and opportunistic "friendships". I think that those are mere media of the Sixth Basic Assumption that lingers on unacknowledged non-analysed psychotic traits. There are no reports of analysts using firearms to solve their differences with other analysts,[24] but the violence, number of victims and destruction consequent to "dissensions" in the psychoanalytic movement and institutions cannot be dismissed without analytic scrutiny. I suppose that those "wars" are implicated in the growing discredit of many analytic institutions, expressed by dwindling numbers of patients looking for analysis, and the fact that promising young professionals choose other careers—a fact already noticed over the past thirty years by outstanding authors (Wallerstein, 1984; Kernberg, 1984; Wallerstein, 1998–2001; Green, 2001). Parthenope Bion Talamo, who never involved herself in this kind of thing, even when it culminated in a violent splitting of the psychoanalytic society of her chosen environment (Italy), once remarked, with her characteristic humour, that she did not know how analysts manage to keep any backs at all after so many years of back-stabbing.

Those facts are commonplace to anyone who has experienced the hardships of surviving joint ownership of whatever it may be: sporting bodies, foundations or academies. We may consider this imaginary conversation between a common-sense ordinary man, an intuitive analyst and a scientific priest:

> ROLAND Institutions wear out; like things, they are inanimate and obey the laws of all inanimate objects; they are *not* alive. *Members* of "institutions" are people; they may not subordinate their developmental qualities to the framework, the structure.
> P.A. An idea, it seems, has to submit to the structure if it is to be communicated ... Erasmus had to break through a cultural prison wall are least as limiting as a wheat germ cell, or a pharaoh's tomb. Tutankhamen's ideas were enclosed within the preservative shells of Thebes.
> PRIEST But before we blame the shell for the death of the idea we should acknowledge the "preservative" function. [Bion, 1979, p. 68]

Is one too naïvely optimistic if one expects that analysts could form different kinds of gatherings? Or is there an intrinsic inefficiency in our own training, reminding us of medical doctors who have real perception of their patients' unhealthy aspects while displaying a remarkable lack of care about their own? There is a pervading unconscious reproduction, in the scientific micro-cosmos, of some fashionable features of the encircling macro-cosmos; it expresses itself as the interference of politics in art and science, which *always* extinguishes the latter.[25]

Psychiatrists and psychoanalysts: a Brazilian experience

As distinct from what happened in the US in the 1930s and 1940s, and echoing the European environment, during the 1940s, some psychiatrists linked to the local public University of São Paulo (the most prestigious one in the whole country) formed a Group A (hallucinosis of appertaining), excluding the psychoanalysts, who were "chosen" to be A̶ (hallucinosis of exclusion). In the following decade, due to a "reversed perspective", an expression of projective identification (Bion, 1963, pp. 55, 60, 66), the analysts, who until that time had formed the A̶ group, became a new A group (hallucinosis of appertaining): they founded their own institution. That institution was widely acknowledged by the encircling social milieu due to the results it obtained, compared to the results of the non-analytically oriented psychiatrists. The psychiatrists linked to the University now saw themselves as the A̶ group (hallucinosis of exclusion). Duly performing their new function of being "excluded", they split into two groups: one of these renewed the attacks against psychoanalysis, while the other expressed a wish to be admitted to the previous A̶ group, now shining in its A functions in a brand new institution. In this specific environment, I observe alternating cycles that last approximately twenty years. There is a destructive outcome of this state of affairs. It ranges from the loss of scientific advancements previously achieved (with the attendant backwardness) to the clinical mishandling of patients, who are deprived of past knowledge that has fallen into oblivion. Also, there is a loss to the personal life of the professionals involved. The acted out hallucination of exclusion engenders concrete losses.

Attempts to insert the psychoanalytic approach in community mental health centres and other community agencies

I will briefly list experiences over the thirty years between 1971 and 2001:

1. The implantation of psychoanalytically oriented services in two Community Mental Health units;[26]
2. Voluntary work in a military setting[27] in a pilot programme of preventive psychiatry (Caplan, 1966) linked to delinquency and drug abuse;
3. An attempt to propitiate a "therapeutic community" environment (after Maxwell-Jones) in a traditional mental hospital;[28] and
4. The observation of wars between members of three psychoanalytic societies in Brazil and two abroad, which resulted in a concrete schism in all but one of them.[29]

The empirical data corresponding to those experiences are available to any readers who are interested.[30]

Some factors in the sixth basic assumption

Subservience to desire: the desire to be "the top". It is identified with an idea, or an idol, linked to delusions of fame and immortality. It corresponds exactly to the "acting out of rivalry" described by Bion (1965,

p. 136), and the group acts according the "rules of transformation in hallucinosis", especially rule A (Bion, 1965, p. 132). "The top" is the sub-group A, hallucination of appertaining. It is seen as the "superior" group, both by its members and by the members of the ⇌ group. The A group is self-envious and self-destructive, due to its oppression of and contempt for the ⇌ group. Greed and envy in A falls short of attempts at material fulfilment; it demands that the other group, chosen to feel inferior, should have nothing: this is the projective identification of "exclusion". Consumerism, *nomenklatura*, elites, oppressive ruling minorities (Bion, 1947; Toynbee, 1972) are its macro-social expressions. The "inferior" group, in its turn, is equally envious and greedy: it attacks enviously its own position—which may be quite comfortable in terms of being spared arduous and unrewarding institutional duties. The social fact, the existence of "haves" and "have nots" throughout human history can be seen as a macro-manifestation of the sixth basic assumption. Subservience to desire is a determinant in the next factor.

Lack of concern for life: Lack of compassion means contempt for that which is alive and animate. Under the aegis of the sixth basic assumption, people feel at home with other people who display this feature of the personality—the unending search for material comfort. It is an expression of greed, forced splitting as described by Bion in the fifth chapter of *Learning from Experience* (1962). Real interest as described by Sanders (1986) turns into commercial interest, profits. The use of an object is replaced by the exploitation of it (Winnicott, 1969). In the members of both warring groups the life instincts are deflected in the direction of the socialistic tendency (Bion, 1958–1979). They will favour the establishment, and promote the erection of idols and concrete buildings to shelter the institution. Idolisation is more successful when the elected idol is physically deceased. Politics is implanted according to the model of mafia-type knots between people rather than in the sense of the Greek *polis*. The deflection of death instincts in the direction of narcissism means that destruction will prevail; the efforts are all at the expense of humanity, fraternity, life, art and science. Under the aegis of the sixth basic assumption, the group wages wars against Nature, Mother, Breast, Woman, against the supremely creative parental couple (Klein, 1932). There are so many expressions in everyday life that it is difficult to pick a few for illustration: the abandonment of one's own progeny, the mask of sanity,[31] the ferocity of the coward, the lack of gratitude of the pseudo-friend, the empowerment of the thug, of the political meritocracy at the expense of the technical or scientific meritocracy. The intelligentsia erects academies and universities under the aegis of the sixth basic assumption.

Contempt or lack of regard for life culminates in the use of a tool that enables a "sensuous-concretising" tendency of the mind. It can be seen as the reversal of alpha function or, if one accepts the model, as anti-alpha function—the tendency to transform mental stuff into material-sensuous data and pseudo-facts (Bion, 1962, p. 101, n. 10.2.1; for anti-alpha function, see Sandler, 1990, 1997a and Volume 2, Chapter Ten of this work). The myth of Midas already described the fact. Under the aegis of the sixth basic assumption, the person may lose his very real self. Bion described it as the co-optation of the mystic by the group. As I understand it, in terms of the individual, there is a co-optation of the "inner mystic" in the common man by commonplaces, habits, socialism. "If the development of the Herd is incompatible with that of the individual either the individual will perish, or the Herd will be destroyed by the individual who is not allowed to fulfil himself" (Bion, 1979, p. 31; see also Bion, 1979, p. 62). In 1989, the conductor Kurt Masur was pressed to occupy a "prestigious" post in the then still East German government. It was after his courageous and opportune action to counteract his friend Honecker's ruthlessness. "Am I so bad at music that now I will have to transform myself into a politician?" he asked, embedded in bewildered realism. Political and honorific posts; theories and temples: two-edged weapons that can both protect and bury under a hard, cold tombstone the truth that they strove to express. When and how we will finally obtain a dynamic equilibrium between the establishment's protecting/integrating function and its debasing action? Perhaps on the day that the human being will finally be able to develop its femininity.[32]

Lack of concern for truth (reality) implies taking the products of the mind (that can be hallucinated) as a replacement for facts (that the idealist cannot grasp or is afraid to grasp, due to arrogance, delinquency or naïveté). It enshrines relativism that derives its forceful effect from its use of rationalism as a way to just impose one's ideas of ownership of absolute truth. The A group tries to fulfil its members' phantasies of power and superiority through the action of maintaining their dignity at the cost of the dignity of others, something that made a lasting impact on Gandhi when he studied law in South Africa. Foulkes was aware of the need for leadership in some groups, as well as of the need for medical indication in many therapeutic activities. The initial difference between Foulkes and Bion as regards leaderless groups (Pisani, 2000, p. 20) was later subdued under the impact of reality (Bion, 1979, on the cruelty that can exist when a group's natural leader refuses to lead it).

Value judgement: A and ⱥ (appertaining and exclusion) are always critical of each other in the sense that they are guided by feelings of knowing what is "right" and what is "wrong". Under the aegis of the death instinct, hallucinosis of being the top turns *differences* into a fuel for prejudice. Mutual collaboration in the complementary interplay between people would be an alternative if a balance between life and death instincts could prevail, for interplay between people is something that only differences can furnish. T. S. Eliot once observed that self-criticism produces poetry whereas hetero-criticism produces rhetoric. Psychoanalytically, self-criticism expresses itself through dreams and hetero-criticism through acting out. Under the aegis of the sixth basic assumption, the phenomenal manifestations include defamation, gossip and traps. Among many gifted historians, one may quote Professors Alan Bullock and Ian Kershaw, who furnished the many political moves of Stalin and Hitler. Theirs may be fair examples, in later times, of the functioning of the sixth basic assumption at the macro-social level and its destructive consequences. New versions appear in oppressive, authoritarian ideas on "Islam" and "non-Islam". The self-attributed superiority of the many "chosen peoples" throughout history (ancient Egyptians, Hebrews, Romans, and, in later times, French, British, Serbs, etc) are versions of the same idea.

Value judgement expresses a belief in the existence of an Absolute Truth, added to which is the idea that someone or some group owns it.[33] After Klein, Bion formulated the "Sense of Truth" (Bion, 1961b, p. 119; Part III of this volume). It arises when the person realises that the loved object and the hated object are—is—one and the same object. There is no possibility to pursue "truth-O" (Bion, 1970, p. 29); the person or the group feels that Right or Wrong can replace True and False. *Truth seems to be a load too heavy for the desirous beast to carry*. I am paraphrasing Bion: the mind is "too heavy a load for the sensuous beast to carry" (Bion, 1975, p. 38).

In *War Memoirs*, Bion brings out in a living way, through some literary descriptions of characters, what Melanie Klein called projective identification: the omnipotent phantasy that one is able to split, deny and expel unwanted aspects of one's mind, of mind itself, and of the whole personality (Klein, 1946). Perhaps some will feel the second thoughts concerning Major de Freine (acquired through the use of a sense of truth) as poignant (1997). This character was first presented as lazy, cowardly and corrupt. An anachronistic cavalry officer of the old times, he avoided battle, staying sheltered in bunkers. He had a distinct preference for occupying the German bunkers, which were better built and deeper, thus providing more protection under heavy artillery fire. De Freine also maintained physical amenities: a comfortable chair, port wine served in crystal glasses; he arranged to have as his adjutant the same servant he had in more peaceful times. Also, one may compare the young Captain Bion's opinions about his fellow officers Aitches, Clifford, Homfray and Bargate, in three passages of the 1919 diary, with the second thoughts from 1958 and 1972. This writer thinks that the description of "poor Aitches" (p. 190) is especially serious. This man would die of influenza three days after arriving in London, having finally succeeded in his strenuous efforts, "moving heaven and earth", to get a promotion that would warrant a legal flight from the front. He is described as dedicated to politicking; having obtained a commanding position only to abandon his men in the hour of battle, he came to be hated for his exhibitionism and cowardice. Looking back as an old man, Bion realises that he was making projective identifications of what he saw as his own cowardice and fear. As in Oscar Wilde's description in *Dorian Gray* of the changing opinions of the progeny about their parents, first hating them and later forgiving them, Bion seems to be trying to forgive himself through these writings. He indicates that he attributes to his fellows some features he hates in himself:

> B Company was left with Bargate in command and Cook second in command—he was formerly company reconnaissance officer and was a bit later in hospital. Clifford, Bagshaw, Homfray, and Harrison were our session commanders. They were all, except Harrison, regarded with contempt and deserved it all. [1997, p. 65]

Perhaps those people behaved badly and displayed cowardice, perhaps they avoided facing action, but the issue is not that. The issue is that the young Bion used their behaviour as an adequate container. As time goes by, the young Captain, now a seasoned officer who has seen action many times, begins to emulate Major de Freine, who up to now has been the object of criticism, concerning the damage caused by propaganda, triumph and self-eulogy.

How many of us analysts, especially those who involve themselves in "wars" against colleagues, are able to perceive that projective identification is a phantasy? How are we to deal with other people's limitations without attempting to use those limitations to destroy them?

Bion recommended that researchers look for the possible existence of links other than L, H and K; functions other than alpha function; and transformations other than those in rigid motion, projective, hallucinosis, in K and in O. The hypothesis of appertaining/exclusion is illustrated by the attempt to use Bion's recommendation in groups contemporary to the authors of the attempts. The researcher risks exclusion: the group resists, sometimes violently, getting out of the basic assumption of dependency. Therefore, right from the start, the "included group", composed of people who attribute to themselves some qualities like those of authorities, ministers and owners of the great author's writings, accuses the researcher of iconoclastic arrogance, inadequacy and wrongdoing. Melanie Klein was accused of this very early on, when she extended Freud's observations on the death instincts, despite the fact that Freud himself never left written documents disapproving of her extensions. A well-known personality in the psychoanalytic milieu, from the height of his then powerful political position, once stated in an interview to a Brazilian periodical that Dr Bion's extensions of Freud were unwarranted, for "Bion did not understand enough of Freud so he was free to fantasise". His own status as an authority on Freud, vouched for by himself, seemed to him to authorise such a statement. Those ideas would justify contempt for the researcher who tries to further the study of a given author's contribution away from the beaten track of religious repetitive adoration that maintains the blindness to the thing described. Some authors have already tasted this kind of contemptuous exclusion from their groups when they proposed hypotheses that extended Bion's studies. They began with studies on cognitive processes (Money-Kyrle, 1968), the proposal of a "dual-track" perspective and the numinous realm (Grotstein, 1981, 1995, 1996), clinical applications of the minus realm (Green, 1973, 1975, 2000; in this case there was a belated acceptance of the ideas in parts of the psychoanalytic movement not exactly known for their interest in Bion's work), applications of the theory of transformations (Britton, 1997), narrative derivatives of alpha function (Ferro, 2011), a proposal of an anti-alpha function and of a tri-dimension Grid as well as extensions of the theory of thinking (Sandler, 1987a,b, 1997a,b, 2000). The present study offers a paradoxical comparison. As soon as it was presented, it was regarded in the customary way; but something happened, probably linked to some very specific instant features of the establishment that for a while ceased to privilege politics and came to make a free, scientific appreciation of the text, and the work was awarded a coveted and prestigious prize. If, as Bion once stated, an unpublished work is not a scientific work, this generous distinction makes this effort a scientific one, through giving it the opportunity of public action.

There is another manifestation of the sixth basic assumption, "appertaining/exclusion", that demands scrutiny. If scientific attempts to expand and extend the great authors' contributions are invariably unwelcome, explicit or veiled destructive criticism that attempts to invalidate, make obsolete or dismiss those great authors is usually applauded. There is no doubt that, for example, Jung strove for and gained unprecedented popularity due to his hostile and critical posture; it would suffice to compare his popularity, initiating the now long lineage of "dissidence", with the unpopularity of many authors who left useful and important contributions, such as Abraham, Federn, Fairbairn, Ferenczi and Jones. After Jung, flickering stars strove on this posture: Binswanger, Rogers, Szondi and Moreno; other "better" ways sought to replace real psychoanalysis: transactional analysis, neuro-psychoanalysis, and others, too many to mention. Most of them disappeared leaving no trace, or, in terms of popularity, became shadows of their former selves. Truth is robust and will prevail, but the apprehension of truth may be obliterated for long periods. In the analytic movement proper, one may see that the popularity of Kohut over some years was also construed on the basis that his approach was "superior" and should replace the "classical" one. See, for example, his "Two Analyses of Mr Z" (1979): Kohut went as far as stating that "his" psychology was phasing out "Freud's" in the same way that Einstein's physics phased out Newton's. I think he was wrong on both counts, for Einstein was the first to acknowledge his debt to Newton and never stated that he was phasing out the great British physicist's work. It is doubtful to state that some theory is the property of a given author—being scientific, it is universal, a thought without a thinker. Truth has no owners and knows no copyright. But Kohut gained instant popularity of a kind that authors such as Searles, Menninger, Reik, Money-Kyrle and Bowlby never knew. And I have quoted just two examples, for their popularity and scholastic followers, in the first and second half of the 20th century. The same happens with Mrs Klein's legacy: political use of her work had as one of its results the fact that a whole course about "her" work delivered at a large psychoanalytic institute does not demand that students even read her papers, but replaces it with readings of her papers written by "authorities"! It is no wonder that there is a movement to exclude the study of envy, and statements that "envy is something that does not exist", among self-styled "neo-Kleinians". Finally, many have the habit of aping Jung and Kohut in setting the works of Klein, Winnicott and Bion against those of Freud, claiming that they are superior. They disrespect the express disapproval of those authors concerning this kind of attitude. I think that it is just this hallucinated idea of superiority, rivalry and so on that attracts "followers".

The issue may be put in terms of transforming pride into self-respect rather than into arrogance. Perhaps in the future, if psychoanalysis is bound to develop, further analysis of analysts will help all to see that when we talk about colleagues, we are in fact talking about ourselves—about unwanted and denied aspects of ourselves. It is not easy to see clearly what those aspects are. But they are there: gossip informs us more about the one who speaks than about the one he or she is talking about. In his *War Memoirs*, Bion creates a dialogue:

> MYSELF I thought your comment that they had gone into Tanks to avoid fighting was quite breathtaking in its disparaging insolence. Do you still mean it?
> BION Let it stand, like my lack of lack of culture, as a monument to my effrontery. I am ashamed and would like to cross it out
> MYSELF As long as it serves as a reminder of what we are really like and not a slur on "them".
> BION I fear that much of the diary will appear, on this reading, to be an exercise in sheltering my complacency from the chilling blast of truth ...
> MYSELF Your description of Méaulte, which was admittedly a horrible camp, a horrible Christmas and a period of low morale in the troops, is certainly evocative, but I am disagreeably impressed by your sanctimonious priggishness—not only in the army, but at Oxford where you wrote your account. I cannot believe that your army friends were as bad. If so, it was not surprising that Cook, Homfray, and Clifford disliked you as much as you did them.

BION I think the "diary" is a fair enough reflection of me. [1997, pp. 201, 208]

Socially speaking, under the aegis of the death instincts, there is a delinquent use of projective identification.

> The trouble about these damned Christians is, of course, that although they're so full of high ideals, and so packed with enthusiasm, and so determined that the right will triumph, they fail to appreciate some of the more seamy sides of this business. Then when at last it does get through to them, they have a nasty way of cracking up—in my opinion. I remember a poor devil. We used to think the world of him, but he just went west when he discovered his colonel was trying to do a bit of graft on him and had thwarted his possibilities of promotion simply because the colonel himself was afraid that if he promoted such a promising officer, his own job would be jeopardised. He became unstuck, and the next thing he did was to have a kind of breakdown. This had the effect of proving that the Colonel was quite right, when in fact he was quite wrong. [*ibid*, p. 232]

Or as I was once told by a colleague who was climbing in the institution and involved himself in a political dispute against another colleague: "It will suffice to give him the rope and he will hang himself". The phrase came originally from Lenin.

Narcissism, socialism and delinquency: When death instincts prevail and are deflected against the self, life instincts are deflected towards the group. Bion called this "socialism". A cunning, often intuitive use of projective identification is linked to delinquency; the leader forms mafias and is welcomed by parts of the group that he is keen to divide in order to govern, through seduction, manipulation and co-optation. The Sixth Basic Assumption appears at a high pitch. People are "admitted" and "evicted". The delinquent being has an acute sense of reality, in order to avoid stumbling into it; he or she has a sense of beauty, in order to be able to destroy it. Suicide surfaces only after the homicidal attempts against the group were destructive enough. The socialist is a cross-dresser, disguised as a protector of the group.

The 20th century produced examples: Stalin and Hitler. But all of us shelter an "internal Hitler". This fact was observed in a highly psychoanalytic speech uttered by a person who officially was not a psychoanalyst,

Klaus von Dohnanyi, the Mayor of Hamburg, in the opening ceremony of the 1986 IPA Congress. He was schooled by Baldur von Schirach's "Hitler's Jugend" (Hitler's Youth); he was one of the sons of a civil servant in the Nazi Justice Ministry. The Mayor's father collaborated with the attempt to kill Hitler on 20 July 1944; he was executed a matter of weeks before the Soviets occupied the Reich Chancellery, in a cruel act of bloody vengeance. The Mayor, who became an orphan very early and had full contact with the paradoxes of life, said in his speech that if the German people were allowed to say: "Our Bach, our Freud, our Marx", they had to add: "Our Hitler".

"And it is not only the vehemence of the subject's uncontrollable hatred but that of his love too which imperils the object" (Klein, 1934, p. 286). Can we analysts put a stop to the unconscious repetition of the encircling society's most primitive traits in our own micro-cosmos, "societies of psychoanalysts"?

Splitting, denial and projective identification: discussion

Appertaining and exclusion, {A, A̶}, seems to encompass both primitive and developed levels of mental functioning. The former would be expressed, in the sixth basic assumption, as a "factualisation" of a splitting, as paranoid ideas of superiority. The latter level can be seen as the group manifestation of a sadistic "sense of exclusion" that seems to accompany us from the caesura of birth. It is re-ignited with Oedipus, with the appearance of siblings, and can be disastrously stimulated when it couples with emotionally unavailable mothers and fathers. There is a point of no return when the person has a paranoid intolerance of pain and frustration.

i. *Neurosis and psychosis*

A scientifically minded researcher may deal with "null hypotheses". An objection that I personally raised to myself when I was working through the hypothesis of the possible existence of phenomena that could be described as constantly conjoined under the heading of a sixth basic assumption was: do the theories already available encompass those phenomena? The choice of Bion's psychoanalytic vertex on groups rather than, for example, Foulkes on one pole and Stuart Mill or Durkheim on another pole, is linked to the fact that as far as my research goes, no other author illuminated the psychotic nature of those phenomena. Foulkes was aware of them, as a psychoanalyst, but his approach was different and would not go on to psychosis. This made it easier to restrict my critical scrutiny of my hypothesis to verify whether Bion's three basic assumptions already encompassed the phenomena. I think that I was able to distinguish some reasons to maintain the hypothesis.

Bion's original three basic assumptions express psychotic functioning specifically linked to more purely paranoid-schizoid manifestations, as he made explicit in *Experiences in Groups*. The sixth basic assumption, adding to its psychotic nature, also depends on Oedipal constellations linked to the neurotic part of the personality (or non-psychotic personality).

It seems to me that the emphasis I am trying to give to the hallucinatory nature permeating many mental configurations is not often made explicit or even noticed. I suppose that the sixth basic assumption, if it exists at all, is a medium that encompasses the three basic assumptions, through which they occur. Fight-Flight, Dependence (messianic leader) and Pairing always express themselves when something or someone is excluded, attacked, isolated as a leader or evicted from the pair (the excluded third in Freud's description of Oedipus). In mathematics, one can see it in the Euclidean logical law of the excluded middle. In 1965, Bion had a clearer idea that the medium of the two outstanding psychoanalytic theories, transference and projective identification, was the transformation in hallucinosis.[34] The whole idea of a sixth basic assumption tries to profit from this remarkable unearthing of Freud's and Klein's contributions: the fact that psychic reality may shelter the psychic non-reality, or even a non-psychic non-reality (the feeling of ownership of the thing-in-itself). The insight on the hallucinated (Freud's term, 1912) nature of transference and the phantastic nature (Klein's term, 1946) of projective identification revived by Bion avoided once and for all (in my view) a kind of sorcerer's apprenticeship that still plagues the psychoanalytic movement. This makes many professionals prey to collusion and shared hallucination, becoming bearers of the placenta rather than of the baby that could be psychoanalysis proper, seduced by naïve idealism.

ii. A worrying future?

The Sixth Basic Assumption may be useful to illuminate more than intra-group issues (the group being the psychoanalytic establishment). Analysts often say that the encircling milieu hates, isolates and excludes analysts and analysis. Is this true? Would an attempt to seek out the culprits from among ourselves reflect an analytic posture? Is the distrust towards psychoanalysis something originating from ourselves or from outside us? Is the problem with analysis, as many who are prone to importing models to save analysis insist? Or is it with analysts? I propose to examine the thing that is repeating itself in our movement: a resilient tendency to transplant extraneous, non-psychoanalytic models to psychoanalysis. They usually prove to be heterologous transplants. The exclusion is of knowledge in first instance: those who are ignorant of their history are fated to repeat it.[35] The seriousness of the problem can be seen if one considers that it may be true that history occurs first as a tragedy and repeats itself as farce.[36]

The cycles seem to me to occur every 20–25 years. They first surfaced in the form of Jung's attempts. I suppose that they were emotionally flawed: full of rivalry and mysticism, stating that Freud was wrong in this and that. This resulted in a serious difficulty in appreciating his eventual contributions. Let us examine this under the vertex of the sixth basic assumption. Jung had an excluding posture: "Freud's psychoanalysis" had to be excluded.[37] Very soon other authors tried to bury the discovery that infants have a sexual life, a fact pointed out by Bion in 1975. Later, sexuality itself and even free associations were excluded, a fact noticed by Green, who issued worried and generous warnings intuiting the dawn of oblivion for psychoanalysis itself (Bion, 1975, p. 9; Green, 1995, 2001).[38] One may notice the increasing exclusion of seminal psychoanalytic issues, adding to the exclusion of research into sexuality and the Id—in other words, the exclusion of metapsychology, psychic reality and interpretation of dreams in favour of explanations about the Ego (Kohut, 1971, Modell, 1981, Arlow, 1996).

The exclusion is inseparable from the appertaining; the vacuum of ignorance is felt as demanding to be filled. It took the form of an enthusiastic adhesion to behaviourist models in the 1940s; hasty and superficial attempts to amalgamate highly doubtful neurophysiological models with psychoanalysis[39] during the 1950s; the seduction exerted by existentialism that lasted from the late 1930s to the early 1960s; oversimplified distortions of Hans Selye's theory of stress during the late 1960s; enthusiasm for the biochemistry of mental illness in the 1960s and 1970s; and the transplantation of structuralism and other anthropological and sociological models during the 1970s. The 1980s and 1990s witnessed those attempts at a higher pitch.

Few people ask whether the "psychoanalysis" that is under attack is psychoanalysis proper. Rare exceptions were Menninger, who tried a theory of technique; or Bion, who suggested the possibility of a "real analysis" (Menninger, 1958; Bion, 1977).

Old wine in new bottles: there is a fascination for textualist post-modernism which argues that psychoanalysis is a form of literature, without realising that it simply proposes the institution of naïve idealism and boundless blind relativism that Freud avoided. We hear the bandwagon of so-called neuroscience and other sense-based systems such as the positivistic alternative of returning to "psychoanalytic research" enshrined as unique, with non-psychoanalytic methods. It inherited the positivistic claim to be the one and only science, excluding others— which resulted in its limited anachronism since the advent of modern physics and psychoanalysis. We cannot know what idea Newton or Euclid would entertain about Einstein and Riemann, but we know that no real physicists or mathematicians deprecate Newton's or Euclid's achievements—discoveries which allowed later developments—in their own vertices. Many of the ideas attributed to "neuroscience" were not scrutinised in their wild, fashionable, unproven hypotheses that are taken as theses. The basic invariant that underlies all these different forms (transformations) seems to me to be the hallucination of appertaining/exclusion. It is linked to fashion and attraction to what seems to be technologically sophisticated. These attempts throw us back to positivism through excluding what Freud provided, even before Planck and Einstein: an alternative to positivism. We also witnessed the exclusion of truth itself in the hasty transplant of Popper's, Kuhn's and others' denials of science and truth. Their names are legion; I mention them briefly to illustrate the analyst's tendency to self-exclusion. To further complicate the issue, there lingers on in our times a recycling of the demand for openness to an ill-defined "social approach". It is striking to see the dismissal and sheer ignorance of the experience gained with the worldwide failures of the movement for social and community psychiatry heavily influenced by psychoanalysis. Many of the difficulties were linked to the fundamentally different nature of hallucination-oriented social demands and political interests *vis-à-vis* the truth-oriented scientific/humanistic approach of psychoanalysis.

All these transplants may be seen as manifestations of Mackay's "extraordinary popular delusions" whose psychic base is a revival of infantile helplessness.[40] This also includes the efforts at a "regulated" social insertion of a profession that many understand to be "the psychoanalyst". There is a failure to realise that analysts will be excluded from their social contexts to the extent that they try to have contact with mind itself; to the extent that they try to be themselves and help people to become themselves. This provoked, provokes and will provoke a reaction from the herd. Our "inclusion" and "appertaining" are, respectively, paradoxically exclusive and abstinent, due to our scientific/artistic/humanistic nature. Gratitude depends on the inception of the depressive position, but this is not a universal occurrence in the human being in our present stage of development. So trying to force "inclusion" will perhaps deliver the final "exclusion" of analysts. Who, having abandoned the investigation of their own minds, will become socially certified psychoanalysts, but in fact theorists, healers, social workers, naïve realists, naïve idealists, relativist philosophers—without any training, experience or function for that. Conversely,

> We are involved in a philosophical prejudice in favour of a person, in favour of the uniqueness of the human individual. There will be an emotional pressure against every single one of us who dares to attach importance to an individual and who dares to be an individual himself ... Analogically one can say that psychoanalysis itself is at its birth, so we don't know much about it or this peculiar, unpredictable development—growing up. That can be unpleasant; even the analyst can feel, "I don't like being aware of this universe in which I live". After World War I everybody decided that the Western Powers had won and that now we were in for a very good time—all would be well. Santayana wrote that the Great War was not an aberration from which we had now got back to normal happiness and good health, but that it was an *hors d'oeuvre* which ushered in a return to the normal state of affairs—fighting, destruction, rivalry and hatred. [Bion, 1980, p. 42][41]

Notes

1. A perverse use of a human discovery, the aircraft: transforming two of them into battering rams to suddenly destroy the lives of something in the environs of 3,000 working people of all ethnic origins, and more slowly and chronically destroy the lives of at least 12,000 people (4 per household) related to them, as well as two gigantic buildings.

2. Bion's "autobiographic cycle" is dwelt on elsewhere (Sandler, 1987, 1988, 1997, 2001; see also Volume 2 Part II). I think it has striking formal similarities with Goethe's *Dichtung und Wahrheit* (Poetry and Truth). Max Planck's *Scientific Autobiography* seems to have inspired Bion, judging from the quotations in *Transformations*, *A Memoir of the Future*, *The Long Week End* and that which I regard as its "laboratory": humanistic testimonies fully embedded with the ethos of the Enlightenment and Romantic movements. It is a scientific, mythical-universal, non-individualistic but nevertheless personal writing. One may contrast this autobiography with the one written by another British citizen, Field Marshal Bernard Montgomery, and the widely publicised memoirs of the Corporal/Führer Adolf Hitler. All of them were decorated soldiers who wandered in the same soil of death in the battle of the Somme—in the very same days. What use did each make of his experiences? Bion's use brings him close to poets like Siegfried Sassoon, Robert Graves and Rupert Brooke, who experienced war. Literary production about World War I is remarkably scarce. It seems that the vast majority of those who survived preferred not to recall or tell their experiences. Bion knew well the war poetry that exuded painful perplexity and perplexing pain. Sassoon was perhaps the most gifted among them and Brooke the best known; both died in action. Bion also seemed to appreciate Rudyard Kipling's work. Those poets speak about non-human humanity, groups, and violence—and in Bion's case, psychoanalysis too. Is he writing a war report? Or is his autobiography a sincere description of real life as it is, as well as some effects of psychoanalysis? Of Hamlet's "sea of difficulties"? Where and how does any real human being differ from the young tank captain's memoirs? "You felt you were being pushed into the unknown" (Bion, 1917–19, p. 79). The reader can infer that analysis helped Bion to transmute the young man's hetero-criticism into the mature man's self-criticism. The manifestations of hetero-criticism included pride in uniforms, decorations and ranks. This translates in the psychoanalytic establishment into the ranks of members, training analysts and "official posts", and criticism of colleagues ("controversial discussions").
3. I tried to develop elsewhere the concept of "participating observation", as distinct from the positivistic fallacy of a neutral observer. It was discovered simultaneously by Freud in psychoanalysis and Planck and Einstein in quantum/relativistic physics (Sandler, 1997, 1999, 2000). Albeit not known to me, the same concept also exists in anthropology. Eric Hobsbawm also used it.
4. Analysis, a "two-body psychology" in the term coined by Rickman, is also a group setting. There is no humanity possible in isolation or in abstraction, which corresponds at best to autism, depression or masturbation.

The sense of solitude (Alves, 1989) differs from loneliness: the person is with him- or herself, and even one person, when he or she realises the existence of his or her mental life, can be regarded as something endowed with a "two-ness" (Bion, 1977). Aristotle perceived this and wrote about the *nous*—the mind thinking about itself.

5. I would add: "homo" pairs, where members cling to each other due to features felt (invariably in a hallucinatory way) to be similar or identical.
6. See Volume 2, Chapter Ten on anti-alpha function.
7. Lower-level empirical data in psychoanalysis are attempts to describe clinical experiences. One can see those definitions in the work of Hempel (1962), Bradley, Braithwaite (both quoted by Bion, 1958–1979, p. 2) and Schlick (1936).
8. This differs sharply from loneliness. Bion, starting from Klein, displayed this in the many personae of *A Memoir of the Future*, which does not lack one named Myself, or "Bion himself as he is" as far as he could see him. Alves (1989) made a specific display of the difference between loneliness and solitude.
9. A term borrowed from Sir Arthur Eddington, who used it in Physics (Eddington, 1928; Sandler, 1997).
10. See Volume 1, Part IV.
11. Melanie Klein's observation that splitting has real effects in the realm of thinking despite the fact that it is a phantasy was—unfortunately in my view—distorted in a sensuous-concretised way by some of her followers after her death, in the sense that projective identification could have concrete, material effects, turning it into a kind of telepathy.
12. Wonderfully depicted in the death of Sebastian's father in Evelyn Waugh's *Brideshead Revisited* (adapted as a TV serial with Sir Lawrence Olivier in this role).
13. The introduction of this book mentioned that no part of it was exempted from experience. The author was subjected to a real-life kidnapping by criminals, a fairly common situation in culturally underdeveloped, albeit wealthy countries—in itself, a hallucinated exclusion: greed and forced splitting (after Bion, 1962) does not mean real development.
14. Bion, 1979; or in Freud's terms, an analysis must be conducted in abstinence.
15. The fact that more and more "psy" people, professionals in this area, seek analysis but ordinary people refrain from it. This has many causes, but I think that the one I try to encircle merits attention.
16. I never met Dr Wilfred Bion personally and therefore could not offer him this title, which could be justified to the extent that it does justice to what is made explicit under the other two headings in his seminal

paper. Bion observed that the trio appears when a person feels impeded in using projective identification. It can be seen in the light of the sixth basic assumption. If a falsely mature, pseudo-Oedipus exists, projective identification as a means of communication often cannot obtrude. I cannot dwell on this now, but only hint at the fact.

17. Again, this sixth assumption does not mean that known phenomena, such as (say) a "peeping Tom" attitude as described by Winnicott and others, do not exist; it is an added fact to scrutinise.
18. Virginia Bicudo described an event at the panel on Thinking at the Edinburgh Congress on Psychoanalysis, 1961. The panel's chairman is reported to have thrown the original manuscript from the table, angrily remarking: "This is not psychoanalysis any more" (Bicudo, 1995).
19. See Chapter Seven, Epistemology.
20. Unpublished data, covering studies from 1978–1998 published in three leading journals.
21. One may see the unambiguous change in Bion's statements on the matter, whose definitive form appears in *Transformations* and *A Memoir of the Future*, where he fully endorses Freud's original view that countertransference, being unconscious, is a matter to be dealt with in the personal analysis of the analyst. This is also made visible in his rewriting of a now classical paper on schizophrenia that was first published in *New Directions in Psychoanalysis* and in modified form in *Second Thoughts*.
22. Part III of this volume.
23. In a lineage that seems to have a remarkably influential moment in the establishment of so-called apostolic selection from the memoirs of a deceased Christ, in order to perpetuate a political system: namely, a thinly disguised typically Roman system of power. The same experience was repeated many times, as for example, in Stalin's use of selected memoirs of a conveniently ill and then deceased Lenin to fit his authoritarian-murderous goals. Idol-erection is a time-proven group tendency with individual factors studied by some analysts, such as Thorner (1973).
24. Even though Jung's attacks against a "Jewish psychoanalysis" in the Nazi movement imperilled Freud's physical survival.
25. Authors such as Althusser, Latour, Kuhn and Feyerabend consider that any science is ideological per se; their posture differs from Nietzsche, Adorno and Habermas, to quote a few. The former seem to give basis to those who preach relativism just to defend a naïve idealism (the idea that the world is a creation of our minds), who hate truth to such an extent that there is an absolute denial of the possibility of scientific activity at all (Callinicos, 1997, Norris, 1997, Sandler, 1997, 2000, 2001a, b). The murderous influence of politics on science is demonstrated even when

it is welcome, like Hitler's ultimate inability to get nuclear weapons. How can we compare this with his and Stalin's successful abolition of much of German and Russian creativity for a whole century?
26. One in a general hospital and another in a community health care centre, both linked to a government-sponsored programme of mental health care (1974–1983).
27. FAB: Força Aerea Brasileira (Brazilian Air Force), 1999–2001.
28. Instituto Aché, São Paulo (1971–1979).
29. 1983–2001, 1995–2001, 1989–2001, 1992–2001, 1997.
30. The original description was awarded the 2001 Durval Marcondes Prize for training analysts in the Brazilian Congress of Psychoanalysis. Usually people submit papers for the Prize, but in this year, the organizers of the Congress decided to choose an eventual winner from the pool of all papers. It was published by Revista Brasileira de Psicanálise, 2002.
31. Cleckley's term for delinquents; the basic process was described by Bion in the use the psychotic personality makes of the non-psychotic personality (Cleckley, 1941; Bion, 1957).
32. *Femininity*: Is war a male issue? This is the idea since Athens. It seems to me that the capacities to intuit and to care are functions of femininity. They characterise the analytic situation. They offer an alternative to greedy search for material comfort and fulfilment of phantasies of superiority. For example, after many months of unthinkably cruel battles, Captain Wilfred Bion, DSO, improvised small tin water reservoirs and had them inserted into the exhaust tubes of the tanks. He used the high temperatures generated by the gasoline-powered motor to provide a welcome luxury for his crew: hot tea before and after the battle. Well, hot tea for the two out of three fighters who returned alive. It was a unique experience to get a hot meal in the European winter, in the mud of Flanders. The crew endured at least ten hours of tedious maintenance services such as lubricating gears and checking the calibre of the ammunition during an epoch of primitive metallurgical technology, in order to obtain the minimum conditions for functioning. For any failure meant certain death in the interior of those bestial steel-made traps, the tanks. Then the crew had to endure a 20 mile route, averaging 6 miles per hour, in order to reach the point from which an attack would be launched. At this point, they had to cope with the terror of facing imminent battle as well as clearing the marks from the road. The gigantic and heavy tanks, equipped with tracks, left marks that had to disappear as soon as possible. Highly visible, they were easily detected by the low-flying aircraft of that time as well as by reconnaissance balloons. Captain Bion invented a way to avoid this insane

overload of work: he improvised a gigantic brushwood broom that he tied to the tail of the tank. It performed the task automatically and mechanically.

> MYSELF As you had not realised?
> BION Your success, I think. I hesitate to say it, because it sounds ungrateful. I cannot imagine what was wrong, but I never recovered from the survival of the Battle of Amiens. Most of what I do not like about you seemed to start then …
> BION I remember. Asser was about to die—refusing to surrender. He could have been fighting for something of which I could not be aware. But his death killed me. At least, it made me feel I could never be a man with such intensity that I would knowingly embrace certain death.
> MYSELF Years later, many years after, I learned that I could hardly claim to love a woman because the woman's love included her love of the father of her children. I do not know. I can only aspire to such love and suffer the uncertainty that it is only an aspiration of which I fall short.
> BION I had no doubt—do not ask me why, but I repeat, no doubt—that Asser, nearly a year younger than me, was such a man. I do not feel that about you, who I have survived to become.
> MYSELF I certainly do not claim it. I am still "becoming", though. It depends if death forestalls my growth. I can hardly claim more time as for a right. [Bion, 1997, pp. 209–210]

"Passionate love" and its complementary partner, "bestial hate": that is the question.

33. In 1914, over a period of one week, in the main cities of the old continent, two million people, the vast majority of them adolescents, enlisted to fight against "evil". In 1917, the "evil" became the bourgeoisie. In 1933, it was the Jews. In 1950, it was the communists and their opponents. In the psychoanalytic milieu, in 1950, it was the "Kleinians". The list is long and each reader will identify his or her own listing.
34. Bion proposes to call transference a transformation in rigid motion and projective identification a projective transformation (Bion, 1965; Sandler, 2005; see also Volume 1).
35. Paraphrase of George Santayana, *Reason in Common Sense*, 1905.
36. Marx, *The Eighteenth Brumaire of Louis Napoleon*, 1852.
37. It is no wonder that he endorsed the advent of the new *Homo excludens*; the hallucinated "SS Aryan race" almost provided him with the tools to exclude Freud physically.

266   A CLINICAL APPLICATION OF BION'S CONCEPTS

38. Bion quotes Green twice in *The Dawn of Oblivion* (pp. 101 and 102); he is one of the five analysts Bion quotes in his Trilogy, among hundreds of non-analytic thinkers. The others are Freud, Klein, Money-Kyrle and Strachey, who is acknowledged for his contribution as a translator (Bion, 1979, p. 105).
39. The mix of Freud's so-called structural theory with Broca/Penfield models: the ego would reside in the cortex and the id in the limbic system, as if both existed in fact! I have referred elsewhere to mistaking the model for the reality it purports to describe, in an animistic and anthropomorphic concretised way (Sandler, 1997b, 2000).
40. I am grateful to Mrs Francesca Bion, who informed me of the existence of this book by kindly sending me a copy of it. An amusing and at the same time worrying observation marks its timeless value. It would be a useful companion for analysts, and even more so for those seduced by politics.
41. The same happened in 1989 with the fall of the Berlin Wall, in 1992 with the end of the Soviet Empire, with the formation of the European Union, with the idea of unrestricted economic growth based on leverages and securitisations promising the good life for all for ever. The surge of neo-Nazism, nationalistic wars within the former Soviet countries, the return of authoritarian rule and state-owned enterprises run by kleptocrats in South America and Asia, continue to be unavoidable facts, but denied to awareness.

REFERENCES

Adorno, T. et al (1969). *The Positivist Dispute in German Sociology*. London: Heinemann, 1976.
Allison, D. (1977). *The New Nietzsche: Contemporary Styles of Interpretation*. Cambridge, MA: MIT Press, 1999.
Althusser, L. (1967). *Philosophy and the Spontaneous Philosophy of the Scientists and Other Essays*. London: Verso, 2012.
Alves, D. B. (1989). Sobre o Sentimento de Soledade: Paidéa II. *Rev. Bras. Psicanal.* 23: 209.
Aristotle. *Metaphysics*. London: Penguin, 1998.
Arlow, J. A. (1996). The Concept of Psychic Reality—How Useful? *Int. J. Psychoanal.* 77: 659.
Bachelard, G. (1938). *The Formation of the Scientific Mind*. Manchester: Clinamen, 2002.
Bacon, F. (1620). *The New Organon*. Cambridge: University Press, 2000.
Bacon, F. (1625). Of Unity in Religion. In: *The Essays*, ed. J. Pitcher (p. 67). London: Penguin, 1985.
Bacon, F. (1625). *The Essays*. London: Penguin, 1985.
Bianchedi, E. T. et al (2000). The Various Faces of Lies. In: P. B. Talamo et al, *W. R. Bion: Between Past and Future* (p. 220). London: Karnac.
Bicudo, V. (1995). Personal communication.

Bion, W. R. (1947). Psychiatry at a Time of Crisis. In: *Cogitations* (pp. 337–352). London: Karnac, 1992.
Bion, W. R. (1953). Notes on the Theory of Schizophrenia. In: *Second Thoughts* (p. 23). London: Karnac, 1984.
Bion, W. R. (1956). Development of Schizophrenic Thought. In: *Second Thoughts* (p. 36). London: Karnac, 1984.
Bion, W. R. (1957a). Differentiation of the Psychotic from the Non-Psychotic Personalities. In: *Second Thoughts* (p. 43). London: Karnac, 1984.
Bion, W. R. (1957b). On Arrogance. In: *Second Thoughts* (p. 86). London: Karnac, 1984.
Bion, W. R. (1958–1979). *Cogitations*. London: Karnac, 1992.
Bion, W. R. (1961a). *Experiences in Groups*. London: Tavistock.
Bion, W. R. (1961b). A Theory of Thinking. In: *Second Thoughts* (p. 110). London: Karnac, 1984.
Bion, W. R. (1962). *Learning from Experience*. London: Heinemann Medical.
Bion, W. R. (1963). *Elements of Psychoanalysis*. London: Heinemann Medical.
Bion, W. R. (1965). *Transformations*. London: Heinemann Medical.
Bion, W. R. (1967a). Commentary. In *Second Thoughts* (p. 120). London: Karnac, 1984.
Bion, W. R. (1967b). Reverence and Awe. In: *Cogitations* (p. 284). London: Karnac, 1992.
Bion, W. R. (1967c). Notes on Memory and Desire. In: *Cogitations* (p. 380). London: Karnac, 1992.
Bion, W. R. (1970). *Attention and Interpretation*. London: Tavistock.
Bion, W. R. (1975). The Dream. *A Memoir of the Future, Volume 1*. London: Karnac, 1990.
Bion, W. R. (1976). Evidence. In: *Clinical Seminars and Four Papers*. Abingdon: Fleetwood, 1987.
Bion, W. R. (1977a). *Two Papers: The Grid and Caesura*. London: Karnac, 1989.
Bion, W. R. (1977b). The Past Presented. *A Memoir of the Future, Volume 2*. London: Karnac, 1990.
Bion, W. R. (1977c). Emotional Turbulence; On a Quotation from Freud. In: *Clinical Seminars and Other Works*. London: Karnac, 1994.
Bion, W. R. (1979). The Dawn of Oblivion. *A Memoir of the Future, Volume 3*. London: Karnac, 1990.
Bion, W. R. (1980). *Bion in New York and São Paulo*. London: Karnac.
Bion, W. R. (1982). *The Long Week-End 1897–1919: Part of a Life*. London: Karnac.
Bion, W. R. (1985). *All My Sins Remembered: Another Part of a Life*. London: Karnac, 1991.
Bion, W. R. (1997). *War Memoirs 1917–1919*. London: Karnac.

Borgogno, F. (1999). *Psychoanalysis as a Journey*. London: Karnac, 2007.
Boswell, J. (1791). *The Life of Samuel Johnson*. London: Penguin, 2008.
Bracher, K. (1969). *The German Dictatorship: Origins, Structure and Effects of National Socialism*. London: Penguin, 1991.
Britton, R. (1997). Psychic Reality and Unconscious Belief: A Reply to Harold B. Gerard. *Int. J. Psychoanal. 78*: 335.
Brown, D. G. (1985). The Psychosoma and the Group. *Group Analysis 18*: 93–101.
Brown, D. G. (1989). A Contribution to Understanding of Psychosomatic Processes in Groups. *British Journal of Psychotherapy 6*: 5–9.
Brown, D. G. (1997). The Royal Road to the Mysterious Leap: The Psychosoma and the Analytic Process. *Australian Journal of Psychotherapy 16*: 11–26.
Bullock, A. (1991). *Hitler and Stalin: Parallel Lives*. London: Fontana, 1998.
Callinicos, A. (1997). Postmodernism: A Critical Diagnosis. In: J. van Doren (Ed), *The Great Ideas of Today 1997* (p. 206). Chicago: Encyclopaedia Britannica.
Campbell, R. J. (1940). *Campbell's Psychiatric Dictionary*. Ninth edition. Oxford: University Press, 2009.
Celibidache, S. I. (2001). *Sergiu Celibidache's Garden*. Chicago: Facets Video.
Cleckley, H. (1941). *The Mask of Sanity*. Literary Licensing, 2011.
Cohen, P. (1989). *The Architecture of Doom*. Documentary film. New York: First Run Features.
Coveney, P. & Highfield, R. (1990). *The Arrow of Time*. London: W. H. Allen.
Derrida, J. (1966). Structure, Sign and Play in the Discourse of the Human Sciences. In: *Writing and Difference*. London: Routledge, 2001.
D'Arcy, M. C. (1930). *Thomas Aquinas*. London: Benn.
Descartes, R. (1637). Discourse on the Method for Guiding One's Reason and Searching for Truth in the Sciences. In: *Discourse on Method and Related Writings*. London: Penguin, 1999.
Dirac, P. A. M. (1932). *The Principles of Quantum Mechanics*. Oxford: University Press, 1999.
Domhoff, G. W. (2005). Refocusing the Neurocognitive Approach to Dreams: A Critique of the Hobson versus Solms Debate. *Dreaming 15*: 3–20.
Eddington, A. (1928). *The Nature of the Physical World*. London: Macmillan.
Eddington, A. (1933). *The Expanding Universe*. Cambridge: University Press, 1988.
Einstein, A. (1916). *Relativity: The Special and the General Theory*. London: Routledge, 2001.
Fairbairn, W. R. D. (1952). *Psychoanalytic Studies of the Personality*. London: Routledge, 1994.
Fenichel, O. (1945). Neurotic Acting Out. In: *The Collected Papers of Otto Fenichel*. New York: Norton, 1954.

Ferenczi, S. (1920). Mathematics. In: *Final Contributions to the Problems and Methods of Psychoanalysis*. London: Karnac, 1994.

Ferenczi, S. (1926). The Problem of Acceptance of Unpleasant Ideas: Advances in Knowledge of the Sense of Reality. In: *Further Contributions to the Theory and Technique of Psychoanalysis*. London: Karnac, 1994.

Ferenczi, S. (1928). The Elasticity of Psychoanalytic Technique. In: *Final Contributions to the Problems and Methods of Psychoanalysis*. London: Karnac, 1994.

Ferro, A. (2001). Le Rêve à l'Etat de Veille et les Narrations. In: A. Green (Ed.), *Courants de la Psychoanalyse Contemporaine, Revue Française de Psychanalyse, numéro hors-serie*. Paris: PUF.

Ferro, A. (2011). *Avoiding Emotions, Living Emotions*. London: Routledge.

Feyerabend, P. (1975). *Against Method: Outline of an Anarchistic Theory of Knowledge*. London: Verso, 1993.

Feyerabend, P. (1978). *Science in a Free Society*. London: Verso, 1982.

Fonagy, P. (2001). Saisir les Orties à Pleines Mains, ou Pourquoi la Recherche Psychanalytique est Tellement Irritante. In: A. Green (Ed.), *Courants de la Psychoanalyse Contemporaine, Revue Française de Psychanalyse, numéro hors-serie*. Paris: PUF.

Foucault, M. (1963). *The Birth of the Clinic: An Archaeology of Medical Perception*. London: Routledge, 2003.

Foulkes, S. H. (1948). *Introduction to Group Analytic Psychotherapy*. London: Karnac, 1983.

Foulkes, S. H. & Anthony, E. J. (1965). *Group Psychotherapy: The Psychoanalytic Approach*. London: Karnac, 1984.

Freud, S. (1895). Studies on Hysteria. *SE 2*.

Freud, S. (1900). The Interpretation of Dreams. *SE 4–5*.

Freud, S. (1901). Determinism, Belief in Chance and Superstition—Some Points of View. Chapter XII of The Psychopathology of Everyday Life. *SE 6*.

Freud, S. (1905). Three Essays on the Theory of Sexuality. *SE 7*.

Freud, S. (1906). Psychoanalysis and the Establishment of the Facts in Legal Proceedings. *SE 9*.

Freud, S. (1909). Notes on a Case of Obsessional Neurosis. *SE 10*.

Freud, S. (1910a). Five Lectures on Psychoanalysis. *SE 11*.

Freud, S. (1910b). Leonardo da Vinci and a Memory of his Childhood. *SE 11*.

Freud, S. (1911a). Formulations on the Two Principles of Mental Functioning. *SE 12*.

Freud, S. (1911b). Psychoanalytic Notes on an Autobiographical Account of a Case of Paranoia. *SE12*.

Freud, S. (1912). The Dynamics of Transference. *SE 12*.

Freud, S. (1913). Totem and Taboo. *SE 13*.
Freud, S. (1914a). Remembering, Repeating and Working Through. *SE 12*.
Freud, S. (1914b). On the History of the Psychoanalytic Movement. *SE 14*.
Freud, S. (1914c). On Narcissism. *SE 14*.
Freud, S. (1915a). Instincts and their Vicissitudes. *SE 14*.
Freud, S. (1915b). Repression. *SE 14*.
Freud, S. (1915c). The Unconscious. *SE 14*.
Freud, S. (1916). On Transience. *SE 14*.
Freud, S. (1916–17). Introductory Lectures on Psychoanalysis. *SE 15–16*.
Freud, S. (1920). Beyond the Pleasure Principle. *SE 18*.
Freud, S. (1924). The Dissolution of the Oedipus Complex. *SE 19*.
Freud, S. (1925). Negation. *SE 19*.
Freud, S. (1926). The Question of Lay Analysis. *SE 20*.
Freud, S. (1933). New Introductory Lectures on Psychoanalysis. *SE 22*.
Freud, S. (1937a). Analysis Terminable and Interminable. *SE 23*.
Freud, S. (1937b). Constructions in Analysis. *SE 23*.
Freud, S. (1939). Moses and Monotheism. *SE 23*.
Freud, S. (1940). An Outline of Psychoanalysis. *SE 23*.
Fulgencio, L. (2000). Convocação para a Fundação de uma Sociedade para a Filosofia Postivista. *Natureza Humana 2*: 429.
Gardner, M. (1989). Foreword. In: R. Penrose, *The Emperor's New Mind: Concerning Computers, Minds and the Laws of Physics*. Oxford: University Press, 1999.
Gombrich, E. H. (1960). *Art and Illusion: A Study in the Psychology of Pictorial Representation*. London: Phaidon, 2002.
Green, A. (1973). On Negative Capability—A Critical Review of W. R. Bion's *Attention and Interpretation*. *Int. J. Psychoanal. 54*: 115.
Green, A. (1975). The Analyst, Symbolization and Absence in the Analytic Setting. *Int. J. Psychoanal. 56*: 1.
Green, A. (1986). *The Work of the Negative*. London: Free Association Books, 1999.
Green, A. (1995). Has Sexuality Anything to do with Psychoanalysis? *Int. J. Psychoanal. 76*: 871.
Green, A. (1997a). The Intuition of the Negative in Playing and Reality. *Int. J. Psychoanal. 78*: 1071–1084.
Green, A. (1997b). The Primordial Mind and the Work of the Negative. In: P. B. Talamo, F. Borgogno & S. A. Merciai (Eds.), *W. R. Bion: Between Past and Future*. London: Karnac, 2000.
Green, A. (2000). The Central Phobic Position. *Int. J. Psychoanal. 81*: 429–51.
Green, A. (2001). La Crise de l'Entendement Psychanalytique. *Revue Française de Psychanalyse, numéro hors-serie*: 401.

Green, A. (2002). *Key Ideas for a Contemporary Psychoanalysis: Misrecognition and Recognition of the Unconscious.* London: Routledge, 2005.

Grotstein, J. S. (1981). Wilfred R. Bion: the Man, the Psychoanalyst, the Mystic. A Perspective on his Life and Work. In: *Do I Dare Disturb the Universe?* London: Karnac, 1983.

Grotstein, J. S. (1995). Bion's Transformations in O, the "Thing-in-Itself" and the "Real": Toward the Concept of the "Transcendent Position". San Francisco: IPA International Congress.

Grotstein, J. S. (1996). Bion's Transformations in "O", Lacan's "Thing-in-Itself" and Kant's "Real": Towards the Concept of the Transcendent Position. *Journal of Melanie Klein and Object Relations 14*: 109.

Grotstein, J. S. (2000). *Who is the Dreamer who Dreams the Dream?* Hilldale: Analytic Press.

Grotstein, J. S. (2004). The Seventh Servant: The Implications of a Truth Drive in Bion's Theory of "O". *Int. J. Psychoanal. 85*: 1081.

Grotstein, J. S. (2007). *A Beam of Intense Darkness: Wilfred Bion's Legacy to Psychoanalysis.* London: Karnac.

Grubrich-Simitis, I. (1993). Back to Freud's Texts: *Making Silent Documents Speak* (trans. P. Slotkin). New Haven, CT: Yale University Press, 1996.

Grunwald, H. (1992). The Year 2000: Is it the End or Just the Beginning? *Time 139*: 45–48.

Heisenberg, W. (1958). *Physics and Philosophy: The Revolution in Modern Science.* London: Penguin, 2000.

Hempel, C. G. (1962). Explanation in Science and in History. In: D. Ruben (Ed.), *Explanation.* Oxford: University Press, 1993.

Hume, D. (1748). *An Enquiry Concerning Human Understanding.* Cambridge: University Press, 2007.

Isaacs, S. (1948). The Nature and Function of Phantasy. In: M. Klein, P. Heimann, S. Isaacs, & J. Riviere (Eds.), *Developments in Psychoanalysis.* London: Karnac, 1989.

Jaques, E. (1960). Disturbances in the Capacity to Work. *Int. J. Psychoanal. 41*: 357.

Jaynes, J. (1976). *The Origin of Consciousness in the Breakdown of the Bicameral Mind.* Boston: Houghton Mifflin, 2000.

Jones, E. (1953). *Sigmund Freud: Life and Work.* Vol. I. The Young Freud. London: Hogarth.

Jones, E. (1955). *Sigmund Freud: Life and Work.* Vol. II. Years of Maturity. London: Hogarth.

Jones, E. (1956). *Sigmund Freud: Life and Work.* Vol. III. The Last Phase. London: Hogarth.

Joseph, B. (2003). Recorded public supervision of Paulo Cesar Sandler's clinical case given at a scientific meeting in the Sociedade Brasileira de Psicanálise.

Kant, I. (1781). *Critique of Pure Reason*. Cambridge: University Press, 1998.
Kant, I. (1783). *Prolegomena to Any Future Metaphysics*. Cambridge: University Press, 2004.
Kernberg, O. (1984). Changes in the Nature of Psychoanalytic Training. In: R. S. Wallerstein (Ed.), *Changes in Analysts and their Training* (pp. 55–61). IPA Monograph 4. London: IPA.
Kershaw, I. (1999). *Hitler 1889–1936: Hubris*. London: Penguin.
Kershaw, I. (2000). *Hitler 1936–1945: Nemesis*. London: Penguin.
Klein, M. (1932). *The Psychoanalysis of Children*. London: Hogarth, 1959.
Klein, M. (1934). A Contribution to the Psychogenesis of the Manic-Depressive States. In: *Contributions to Psychoanalysis*. London: Hogarth, 1950.
Klein, M. (1940). Mourning and its Relation to Manic Depressive States. In: *Contributions to Psychoanalysis*. London: Hogarth, 1950.
Klein, M. (1946). Notes on Some Schizoid Mechanisms. In: *The Writings of Melanie Klein, Volume 3*. London: Hogarth, 1975.
Klein, M. (1957). Envy and Gratitude. In: *The Writings of Melanie Klein*, vol. 3. London: Hogarth, 1975.
Kohut, H. (1971). *The Analysis of the Self*. Chicago: University of Chicago Press, 2009.
Kohut, H. (1979). The Two Analyses of Mr Z. *Int. J. Psychoanal.* 60: 3.
Kohut, H. (1984). *How Does Analysis Cure?* Chicago: University of Chicago Press.
Krause, E. (1999). *The Death of the Guilds*. New Haven: Yale University Press.
Kuhn, T. (1970). *The Structure of Scientific Revolutions*. Chicago: University of Chicago Press, 1996.
Kulish, N. (2001). The Psychoanalytic Method from an Epistemological Viewpoint. *Int J Psychoanal.* 83: 491.
Lakatos, I. (1963–4). *Proofs and Refutations*. Cambridge: University Press, 1976.
Lakatos, I. & Musgrave, A. (1970). *Criticism and the Growth of Knowledge*. Cambridge: University Press.
Lawrence, W. G., Bain, A. & Gould, L. (1996). The Fifth Basic Assumption. *Free Associations* 6: 2855.
Lévi-Strauss, C. (1950). *Introduction to the Work of Marcel Mauss*. London: Routledge, 1987.
Lévi-Strauss, C. (1962). *The Savage Mind [La Pensée Sauvage]*. Oxford: University Press, 2004.
Locke, J. (1690). *An Essay Concerning Human Understanding*. London: Penguin, 2004.
Lopez-Corvo, R. (1995). *Self-Envy: Therapy and the Divided Inner World*. New York: Aronson.
Lüdecke, G. (1938). *I Knew Hitler*. London: Jarrolds.

Lyotard, J. F. (1979). *The Postmodern Condition: A Report on Knowledge*. Manchester: University Press, 1984.

Mackay, C. (1841). *Extraordinary Popular Delusions and the Madness of Crowds*. Ware, Herts: Wordsworth Editions, 1995.

Mawson, C. (2002). Pseudo-Free Association: The Sophisticated Analytic Patient and "As-If" Relating. *British Journal of Psychotherapy 18*: 509–522.

Mello Franco Fo., O. M. & Sandler, P. C. (2005). Intersubjetividade: Progresso em Psicanálise? [Intersubjectivity: progress in psychoanalysis?] *Rev. Bras. Psicanal. 39*: 89–112.

Meltzer, D. (1981). Memorial Meeting for Dr W. R. Bion. *Int. J. Psychoanal. 8*: 3–14.

Meltzer, D. (1989). Foreword. In M. H. Williams & M. Weddell, *The Chamber of Maiden Thought*. London: Routledge, 1991. Also (entitled "Psychoanalysis Acknowledges its Poetic Forebears and Joins the Artistic Family") in M. H. Williams, *The Vale of Soulmaking*. London: Karnac, 2005.

Meltzer, D. (1998). Public seminar. Sociedade Brasileira de Psicanalise de São Paulo (10 August 1998), recorded. Biblioteca da SBPSP.

Meltzer, D. & Williams, M. H. (1988). *The Apprehension of Beauty*. London: Karnac, 2008.

Menninger, K. (1958). *Theory of Psychoanalytical Technique*. New York: Basic Books.

Merendino, R. (2003). Alcune Riflessioni sull'Esperienza Psicoanalitica con Pazienti Affetti da Tumore. In: R. Pisani, *Seminari di Neuropsichiatria e Psicoterapia* (pp. 177–184). Rome: Edizioni Universitarie Romane.

Modell, A. (1981). Does Metapsychology Still Exist? *Int. J. Psychoanal. 62*: 391.

Money-Kyrle, R. (1968). Cognitive Development. In: *Collected Papers of Roger Money-Kyrle*. Strathtay: Clunie Press, 1979.

Nietzsche, F. (1873). *On Truth and Lies in a Non-Moral Sense*. http://filepedia.org/on-truth-and-lies-in-a-nonmoral-sense

Nietzsche, F. (1874). Schopenhauer as Educator. In: *Untimely Meditations*. Cambridge: University Press, 1997.

Nietzsche, F. (1878). *Human, All Too Human*. Cambridge: University Press, 1996.

Nietzsche, F. (1882). *The Gay Science*. Cambridge: University Press, 2001.

Nietzsche, F. (1883). *Thus Spoke Zarathustra*. Cambridge: University Press, 2006.

Nietzsche, F. (1886). *Beyond Good and Evil*. London: Penguin, 2003.

Nietzsche, F. (1887). *On the Genealogy of Morality*. Cambridge: University Press, 2007.

Nietzsche, F. (1888). *Twilight of the Idols* and *The Antichrist*. London: Penguin, 1991.
Nietzsche, F. (1888). *Ecce Homo: How One Becomes What One Is*. London: Penguin, 1992.
Nietzsche, F. (1901). *The Will to Power*. New York: Random House, 1968.
Norris, C. (1997). *Against Relativism: Philosophy of Science, Deconstruction and Critical Theory*. Oxford: Blackwell.
Nozick, R. (2001). *Invariances. The Strucutre of the Objective World*. Cambridge, MA: Harvard University Press.
Nupen, C. (1974). *Pinchas Zukerman: Here to Make Music*. London: Allegro Films.
Penrose, R. (1989). *The Emperor's New Mind: Concerning Computers, Minds and the Laws of Physics*. Oxford: University Press, 1999.
Penrose, R. (1994). *Shadows of the Mind: A Search for the Missing Science of Consciousness*. Oxford: University Press, 1996.
Penrose, R. (2004). *The Road to Reality: A Complete Guide to the Laws of the Universe*. London: Cape.
Pisani, R. (2000). *Elementi di Gruppoanalisi*. Rome: Edizioni Universitarie Romane.
Pisani, R. A. (2005). Disturbi Psicosomatici e Gruppoanalisi. *Atti della Accademia Lancisiana XLIX*, n.1.
Planck, M. (1949). *Scientific Autobiography and Other Papers*. New York: Philosophical Library, 1968.
Popper, K. R. (1959). *The Logic of Scientific Discovery*. London: Routledge, 2002.
Popper, K. R. (1963). *Conjectures and Refutations*. London: Routledge.
Reik, T. (1948). *Listening with the Third Ear*. New York: Farrar, Straus & Giroux, 1983.
Rickman, J. (1950). The Factor of Number in Individual and Group Dynamics. In: *Selected Contributions to Psychoanalysis*. London: Karnac, 2003.
Ricoeur, P. (1977). The Question of Proof in Freud's Psychoanalytic Writings. In: *Hermeneutics and the Human Sciences: Essays on Language, Action and Interpretation*. Cambridge: University Press, 1981.
Rorty, R. (1982). *The Consequences of Pragmatism*. Minneapolis: University of Minnesota Press.
Roth, A. & Fonagy, P. (2005). *What Works for Whom? A Critical Review of Psychotherapy Research*. New York: Guilford.
Ruskin, J. (1865). *Sesame and Lilies*. New Haven, CT: Yale University Press, 2002.
Sanders, K. (1986). *A Matter of Interest*. Strathclyde: Clunie.
Sandler, E. H. (2001). O Nome do Medo. *Psicanálise e Universidade 14*: 95.
Sandler, J. (1970). Personal communication.

Sandler, P. C. (1986). Grade? *Rev. Bras. Psicanal. 21*: 203.
Sandler, P. C. (1987). The Long Week-End ... (review). *Int. Rev. Psychoanal.14*: 273.
Sandler, P. C. (1988). *Introdução a "Uma Memória do Futuro" de W. R. Bion*. Rio de Janeiro: Imago Editora.
Sandler, P. C. (1990). *Fatos (A Tragédia do Conhecimento em Psicanálise)* Rio de Janeiro: Imago Editora.
Sandler, P. C. (1997a). The Apprehension of Psychic Reality: Extensions of Bion's Theory of Alpha Function. *Int. J. Psychoanal. 78*: 43.
Sandler, P. C. (1997b). *A Apreensão da Realidade Psíquica* Vol. I. Rio de Janeiro: Imago Editora.
Sandler, P. C. (1997c). What is Thinking? An Attempt at an Integrated Study of W. R. Bion's Contributions to the Processes of Knowing. In: P. B. Talamo, F. Borgogno, S. A. Merciai (Eds.), *W. R. Bion: Between Past and Future*. London: Karnac, 2000.
Sandler, P. C. (1999). Um Desenvolvimento e Aplicacao Clinica do Instrumento de Bion, o Grid. *Rev. Bras. Psicanal. 33*: 13.
Sandler, P. C. (2000a). *As Origens da Psicanálise na Obra de Kant*. Vol. III of *A Apreensão da Realidade Psíquica*. Rio de Janeiro: Imago Editora.
Sandler, P. C. (2000b) *Turbulência e Urgência*. Vol. IV of *A Apreensão da Realidade Psíquica*. Rio de Janeiro: Imago Editora.
Sandler, P. C. (2001a) *Goethe e a Psicanálise*. Vol. V of *A Apreensão da Realidade Psíquica*. Rio de Janeiro: Imago Editora.
Sandler, P. C. (2001b) Le Projet Scientifique de Freud en Danger un Siècle Plus Tard? *Rev. Franç. Psychanal*. Número hors-série, 181–202.
Sandler, P. C. (2001c). *Psychoanalysis, Epistemology: Friends, Parents or Strangers?* Presented at the Congress of IPA, Nice, July 2001, Official Panel on Epistemology.
Sandler, P. C. (2002a). *O Belo é Eterno*. Vol. VI of *A Apreensão da Realidade Psíquica*. Rio de Janeiro: Imago Editora.
Sandler, P. C. (2002b). *Os Primórdios do Movimento Romantico e a Psicanalise*. Vol. II of *A Apreensão da Realidade Psíquica*. Rio de Janeiro: Imago Editora.
Sandler, P. C. (2003). *Hegel e Klein: A Tolerância de Paradoxos*. Vol. VII of *A Apreensão da Realidade Psíquica*. Rio de Janeiro: Imago Editora.
Sandler, P. C. (2005). *The Language of Bion: A Dictionary of Concepts*. London: Karnac.
Sandler, P. C. (2005b). Psicosomatico o Somatopsicotico? *Atti della Accademia Lancisiana XLIX*, n.1.
Schiller, F. (1795). On Naïve and Sentimental Poetry. In: *Essays*. New York: Contiinuum International, 2005.
Schlick, M. (1936). Meaning and Verification. In: *Philosophical Papers: Volume II (1925–1936)*. Dordrecht: Reidel, 1979.

Scholem, G. (1941). *Major Trends in Jewish Mysticism*. New York: Schocken, 1995.
Schrödinger, E. (1944). *What is Life?* Cambridge: University Press, 2003.
Searles, H. (1960). *The Nonhuman Environment: In Normal Development and Schizophrenia*. New York: International Universities Press.
Segal, H. (1981). Personal communication.
Sharpe, E. F. (1937). *Dream Analysis: A Practical Handbook of Psychoanalysis*. London: Karnac, 1988.
Smith, R. G. (1960). *J. G. Hamann, 1730–1788. A Study in Christian Existence. With Selections from his Writings*. London: Collins.
Sokal, A. & Bricmont, J. (1998). *Intellectual Impostures*. London: Profile Books. Published in the US as *Fashionable Nonsense: Postmodern Intellectuals' Abuse of Science* (Picador).
Solms, M. (1995. New Findings on the Neurological Organization of Dreaming: Implications for Psychoanalysis. *Psychoanal. Q. 64*: 43–67.
Solms, M. (2002). Dreaming: Cholinergic and Dopaminergic Hypotheses. In E. Perry, H. Ashton & A. Young (Eds.), *Neurochemistry of Consciousness* (pp. 123–131). Philadelphia: Benjamins.
Strachey, J. (1955). Editor's Introduction. *SE 18*.
Strachey, J. (1960). Editor's Introduction. *SE 6*.
Thorner, H. A. (1973). Das Idol. *Psyche 27*: 356–370.
Thorner, H. A. (1981). Notes on the Desire of Knowledge. *Int. J. Psychoanal. 62*: 73.
Toynbee, A. (1934–1961). *A Study of History*. Two volumes. Oxford: University Press, 1988.
Trevor-Roper, H. (1953). *Hitler's Table Talk 1941–1944*. London: Weidenfeld & Nicolson, 2000.
Turquet, P. M. (1974). Leadership, the Individual and the Group. In: G. S. Gabbard et al (Eds.), *Analysis of Groups: Contributions to Theory, Research and Practice*. San Francisco: Jossey-Bass.
Wallerstein, R. S. (1984). *Changes in Analysts and their Training*. IPA Monograph 4. London: IPA.
Wallerstein, R. S. (1998–2001). Personal communication.
Weber, M. (1947). *Theory of Social and Economic Organization*. New York: Free Press, 1964.
Whitehead, A. N. (1911). An Introduction to Mathematics. In: *Great Books of the Western World*. Chicago: Encyclopaedia Britannica.
Williams, B. (2002). *Truth and Truthfulness*. Princeton: University Press.
Winnicott, D. W. (1958). *Collected Papers: Through Paediatrics to Psychoanalysis*. London: Karnac, 1984.
Winnicott, D. W. (1965). The Price of Disregarding Psychoanalytic Research. In: C. Winnicott, R. Shepherd & M.. Davis (Eds.), *Home is Where We Start From*. London: Penguin, 1986.

Winnicott, D. W. (1966). The Absence of a Sense of Guilt. In: *Deprivation and Delinquency*. London: Tavistock, 1984.

Winnicott, D. W. (1969). The Use of an Object. In: *Playing and Reality*. London: Routledge, 1991.

Yahn, M. (1971). Personal communication.

Yates, F. A. (1979). *The Occult Philosophy in the Elizabethan Age*. London: Routledge, 2001.

INDEX

absolute truth xxii, 9, 12, 17, 25–26, 30–31, 35, 38, 49, 71, 122, 146, 148, 157, 164, 182, 204, 220, 222, 249–250
adenosine tri-phosphate (ATP) 220
Adler, Alfred 198
aetiological equation 98
aggression 21–22, 26, 28, 32, 38, 40
analysts
    individuality 131–132
    neutrality 132
    propitiator-propitiatory posture 108
    psychic reality 69
    thinking and emotions 203
analytic couple 26, 31, 33, 35, 40, 61, 69, 74, 84, 105, 109, 112–113, 119, 127–128, 185, 222, 234
analytic posture xx, 61, 107, 120, 129, 180, 223, 225, 257

anti-alpha function xxi, 114, 249, 252, 262
anti-enlightenment and anti-romantic posture 124
anti-platonic philosophy 107
Apostolic fanaticism 72
atomic bomb dream 39, 61, 68
authoritarianism 121, 131, 170, 179
    establishment-induced 189
    posture 197
    psychopathic personality 244
    violence 237
autonomic nervous system 64–66

Bachelard, Gaston 138, 159
Bacon, Francis 28, 71, 140, 142, 144, 149–150, 163
Bain, Alastair 232–233
beauty-truth 121
Berlin, Isaiah 136–137, 266
    sense of reality 157

bi-dimensional "demeanour" 63
biological-instincual function 73
Bion, W. R. xx, 5, 138
    achievements 183
    acting out of rivalry 247
    aegis of rivalry 50
    A Memoir of the Future 141, 226, 230–231, 262
    atomic bomb and dreamt 29–31
    Attention and Interpretation 230–231
    autobiographic cycle 261
    bi-dimension Grid 7, 46
    case 261
    Cogitations 20, 71, 203
    concept of saturation 63
    construction 17
    contribution to analysis 136
    discipline of memory 107
    dynamic grid 11
    Elements of Psychoanalysis 20, 46
    epistemology of psychoanalysis 147
    evidence 23
    fact-finding tool 67, 148
    formation of α-elements 14
    good-enough intra-session interpretation 23
    grid 11, 19, 23
    grid in time 20
    guiding pole 207
    hallucinosis 233
    Imre Lakatos's attempts 18
    intuition 230
    judgment obstructs observation 9
    language of achievement 203
    Learning from Experience 248
    messianic leader and dependence 233
    multidisciplinary group's meetings 189
    neo-positivism 10
    nomenclature 60
    non-hyphenated preconception 15
    non-psychotic personality 237
    notation for numinous realm 34
    notion of Nietzsche 167
    original first Grid 84
    original Grid 6, 16, 20, 69
    original two-dimension grid 25
    other realms of interpretation 46
    parlance 187
    practical applications 67
    primitive models for mental growth 75
    psychoanalysis 49, 75
    psychoanalytical exercise xxi
    psychoanalytic controversy 81–82
    psychoanalytic vertex 168, 181
    psychotic functioning 257
    quasi-mathematical notation 15
    quasi-mathematical parlance 27
    real psychoanalysis xxii, 9–10, 31
    reverie 108
    Saturations and Non-saturations 4
    Second Thoughts 203
    socialism and narcissism 181
    The Gay Science 169
    The Grid xx, 17, 20
    The Language of Bion 226
    theory of alpha function 14
    theory of instincts 4
    theory of observation 4
    theory of thinking 16
    theory of transformations and invariants 95
    three-dimension grid 29
    Transformations 12, 20, 79, 111, 225, 230–231, 263
    tri-dimension grid 20, 32
    War Memoirs 250, 254
Blanco, Matte 6

Bleuler, Eugen 95, 103, 168
blind idealism 148
blind relativism 122
Brecht, Bertold 197
Bruno, Giordano 159, 171
Bullock, Alan 250

Cantor, Georg 6, 47
  set theory 63
Carnap, Rudolf 5, 10, 114
  neo-positivism 198
Cartesian
  model 154
  plane xx
Cartesian space 51
causality theories 65
cause-and-effect reasoning 13
cause-effect traumatic theory 155
central nervous system 64–66
Christian Platonism 183
clinical-anatomical meetings 72
common sense 15–17, 58, 75, 119, 131, 148, 153, 162, 192–193, 201, 209, 235, 246, 265
  thought 208
Communism 70, 77
community mental health units 247
computer aided design (CAD) 25
Comte, Auguste 10, 108, 139, 149, 196
  positivism 198
concern for life ⇔ death xxii, 74
conscious and unconscious mental processes 46
conscious rationalism 142, 154
consumerism 77, 149–150, 248
conundrum 132, 136, 194, 197, 243
countertransference 9, 104, 131, 242–243, 263
  bandwagon 117
  confessions of 126, 199
  personal factor 120

Darwin xxi, 9, 15, 18, 100
  evolution of species 105
  modern genetics 109
  moving process 105
  psychoanalytic vertex 105
  survival of fittest 105
death instincts 15, 50, 78, 109, 124, 207, 210, 238, 245, 248, 250, 252, 255
Deleuze, Gilles 118, 159, 165
delinquency 130, 150, 156, 192, 206, 247, 249, 255
delusion 12, 51, 58, 99, 104, 141, 152, 173, 177, 181, 207–209, 215, 218–221, 233–234, 247, 259
denial and projective identification 256–260
depressive emotional experience 23, 25
Derrida, J. 118, 170
  textualism 159
de-sensifying process 31
destructive tendency 206
differential calculus 54–55
Dimension of the Senses xx, 64, 66
Dirac, Paul 196
  quantum mechanics 53
  quantum phenomena 196
doggishness 90
Donne, John 76, 143
dream-memories 37
dual-track method 93
dynamic unconscious 118

ecosystem 48
Eddington, Arthur 58, 194
ego functions xx, 6, 13, 15, 17, 20, 25, 32, 42, 63, 225
ego-oriented psychotherapies 129
ego's defence mechanisms 98
Egyptian painting, bi-dimensional 43

282 INDEX

Einstein, Albert 37, 39, 52, 57–58, 62, 70, 119, 140, 145, 149, 159, 163, 171, 259, 261
   abilities and gifts 65
   discoveries 194
   epochal moment 50
   expansions of Newton 155
   free associations xxi
   in quantum/relativistic physics 261
   physics 253
   principle of relativity 95
   relativity 122
   relativity into relativism 153
Einsteinian physics 52, 176
elasticity and improvisation 126–129
emotional
   discharge 9
   experience 4, 9, 11, 21–25, 34, 65–68, 93, 144, 170, 208, 210, 223–224, 234, 240
   situation 11, 21
   tension 11
   theories of thinking 17
   turbulence 243
emotions 40, 55, 68, 80, 89, 91, 104, 189, 199, 203, 208, 234, 239, 244
   in sensitive audience 91
   quasi-conscious manipulations 189
enforcing inclusion 239–240
enlightened-romantic
   achievements 171
   movements 261
entropic homeostasis 189
enzymatic processes 13
epistemology xix, xxii, 5, 10, 86, 91, 114, 135–136, 156, 196
   Bion's 147
   conundrums 197
   definition 137
   Hume's contributions 137
   instrument 203–206
   knowledge 138–141
   posture 138
   practice 136
   psychoanalytic fable xxii, 144–148
   psychoanalytic view 136
epistemophilic instinct 66, 144, 146–147, 156, 218, 236, 238
Escher, M. C. 53, 69
   drawings 70–71
Euclidean
   bi-dimension space system 27
   coordinates 16, 62
   geometry 49, 51, 54
   representational system 73
   space 8, 11, 51, 54, 60, 62
exclusion-in-itself 241
exclusion of material reality 238
exclusion of psychic reality 236–238
exclusion of real self 235–236

failure of dream work 206–210
Fairbairn, W. R. D. 253
   psychoanalytic vertex 168
fanaticism and slavery 104
Fechner's principle of homeostasis 33
femininity 236, 249, 264
Ferenczi, Sándor 113, 117–118, 120–125, 127–128, 138, 253
   bio-analysis and organic mathematics 120
Ferro, Antonino 40, 252
fictional suspense xxi
Foulkes, S. H. 232, 249–250, 256
four-dimension Grid 8, 53, 68
Frankenstein's monster 92
Frankenstein-like life 141
free associations xxi, 4, 9–10, 22, 24, 36–37, 52, 61, 89, 93–95, 99, 100–104, 106–107, 109–114, 124, 143, 148, 151, 203, 221, 223, 237, 239, 258

abhorrence of 109–110
development of 107
fear of 109
fugacious multi-dimensional 109
life and 104–109
patient's 112
scrutiny of 104
free-floating attention xix, xxi, 4, 23, 37–39, 104, 112, 115
freie Einfälle 37, 89, 92, 101–102, 106, 112
nature of latent content 113
French positivism 10
Freud, Sigmund
abilities and gifts 65
achievements 46
analogical model of mind 219
analysis terminable and interminable 4
analytic function 112
aphorisms 177
as transference 241
atomic bomb = aggression 26
bisexuality 153
cause-effect explanatory episteme 146
contingency and necessity 98
discovery of psychoanalysis 67, 86
effigy 142
empirical science 146
empirical-clinical criterion 8
epistemological approach 147
epistemophilic instinct 66, 144, 146
from enlightenment and romantic movement 90
fundamental contributions 137
fundamental method in psychoanalysis 93
fundamental rule 106
hypothesis 111

in case of Schreber 71
in dreams 61
intuition 65
mechanisms of defence 46
mental functioning 11, 105
multifactorial analysis 97
negative therapeutic reaction 241
Nietzsche's *Beyond Good and Evil* 166
nihilism 122
object and instinctual cathexis 55
parlance 85
personal equation 48
personal factor 48
Plato's numinous realm 146
pleasure/displeasure principle 153, 204, 242
pleasure–pain principle 76
post-1920 modifications 242
post-mortem psychoanalysis 97
pre-psychoanalysis 153
pre-psychoanalytic theory of trauma 242
principle of reality 142
probability 99
projective identification 50
psychic determinism 95–96, 99
psychic functions 65
psychic reality 50, 91
psychoanalysis 31
psychoanalytic endeavour 45
psychoanalytic exercise 97
psychoanalytic pattern 46
psychotic mechanism 114
reality 120
structural theory 266
superego 57, 206
talking cure 5, 203
The Interpretations of Dreams 4
theories with positivist religion 108

theorisation about instincts 168
theory of consciousness 135
theory of instincts 46
unconscious phantasies 147
unconscious system 65
verbal formulations 139
Freud-bashing accusations 224
Freudian
categories of grid 13
psychoanalysis 52
Fromm-Reichmann, Frieda 103
frustration 12–13, 79, 82, 103, 105, 143, 151, 176, 188, 215, 236, 256
intolerance 77
functional determinism 52

German idealism 150, 201
German romantic movement 142
Glover, Edward 138
Gödel's theorem 64
Goethe's *Faust* 143
Gould, Laurence 232–233
greed ⇔ envy, autistic cycles 84
Greek painting, tri-dimensional 43
Green, André 109, 114, 126, 131–132, 138, 143, 154, 258, 266
Grid diagram 40
Grotstein, James 138, 143, 146–147, 154, 158

hallucination xx, 23, 25, 33, 37, 49, 51, 77, 92, 103–104, 107, 117, 127, 132, 140–141, 152, 157, 164, 169, 173, 177, 179, 181–183, 187–188, 190, 200–205, 209, 215, 217–221, 224, 230–231, 233–235, 237–240, 243–244, 247–248, 252, 257, 259
absolute truth 182
appertaining 240
common 173
dream work 204
exclusion 240, 262

expansions, after Bion 218–221
formation of 220
inclusion 241
of appertaining 246
of exclusion 246
phantastic state of 239
pleasure-seeking 190
realm of 49
transformations in 233, 248
Hamann, Johann Georg 126–127, 140, 147, 158, 171
Hamilton, William 57, 61–62
hampering facts 172–173
Hegel 145–146, 201, 244
gist experience 147
Winnicott's paradox 119
Heisenberg's principle of uncertainty 122, 153
here and now 28, 31, 59, 61, 71, 74, 81, 111–113, 128, 132, 148, 157, 222–223
free associations 111
instant 59
hermeneutic powers 200
hermeneutics and post-modernism 96
hermeneutics to function 40
hexa-dimension
grid 45
space 62
homeostatic balance 236
homo excludens 238, 265
homo-hallucinosis 182
homosexual phantasies 130, 175, 223, 237
prevalence of 237
human device and mechanism 64
human sensuous apparatus 8, 13, 52, 73, 121, 206
human unconscious phenomena 196
human willingness 76

Huntington, Samuel 114
hyperbole xx, 50, 243

idealism versus realism 136
idiosyncratic transformations 200
idolater-iconoclast reader 97
individualism 131, 200
infantile
    helplessness 259
    omnipotence 122, 125
    sexuality 124, 159, 180
inferiority complex 198
infinite
    categories 63
    dimensional spaces 62–63
    emptiness 62
    existence 62
    space 54
innate narcissism 217
instinct-dependent motivation 192
International Psychoanalytical
    Association 18, 244
intersubjectivism 129
intra-psychic and relational psychic
    reality 38
invariance 62, 110, 172, 195
    and transformations 62, 125–126,
    132

Jacobs, Theodore 131
Jaques, Eliott 138
Jewish-Bolshevik idea 159
Jones, Ernest 138, 165, 247, 253
Jung, Carl 95, 253–254, 258
    associative experiment 103
    Jewish psychoanalysis 263

Kant, Immanuel xxi, 17, 34, 47, 52, 57,
    65, 84, 86, 118, 121, 126, 139–140,
    142, 144–146, 148–150, 152,
    158–159, 162, 167, 170, 172,
    192–193, 196–198, 218, 221, 244

dialectical antinomies 147
ideas 57
naïve realism xxii, 121
parlance 52
political categorical imperative
    206
Kantian
    amendment 15
    categories 63
    sense 202
Kernberg, O. 230, 245
Kershaw, Ian 250
kidnapping 225, 238, 262
Klein, George 138
Klein, Melanie 26, 42, 138, 142, 146,
    193, 242
    aegis of rivalry 50
    Bion's notation 109
    contributions 27
    discovery of projective
        identification 220
    formulations on paranoid-
        schizoid interplay 139
    legacy 254
    mental positions 110
    observations and profiting from
        psychiatry 47
    paranoid-schizoid and depressive
        positions 11
    personal responsibility 103
    positions 221
    positions theory 46
    projective identification 103, 250
    psychic reality 50
    psychoanalytic vertex 168
    self-feeding cycles of envy and
        greed 94
    sense 79
    supreme creative act 101
    theory of positions 177
    unconscious phantasy 103
Krebs cycle 219

INDEX

Kuhn, Thomas 118, 159, 179, 198, 242, 259, 263
   paradigms 144

Laplanche, Jean 126
Lawrence, W. Gordon 232–233
Leibnizian idealism 150
libertarian force 105
lie and truth, psychoanalytic nietzsche's genealogy 182–187
Liouville, Joseph 61–62

Machiavelli, Niccolò 205
Mackay, C. 58
   extraordinary popular delusions 259
Mafia-like allegiance 216
Mafia-minded criminals 213
mafia-type gang inclusion 238
mafia-type knots 248
malignant narcissism 217
mass psychology phenomena 230
materialisms 149
mathematical notation systems 50
mathematical nucleus of mind 55
mathematical-physical analogy 58
mathematisation of psychoanalysis 49
Mawson, Chris 90
Meltzer, Donald 82, 142, 165, 180, 224, 242
Menninger, Karl 138, 253, 258–259
mental functioning 6, 11, 41–42, 45–49, 98, 105–106, 120, 127, 139, 146, 153–154, 202, 208, 221, 236, 256
momentary relationship 69
Money-Kyrle, Roger 5, 138, 252–253, 266
Monod, Jacques 99
morals and ethics 215–217
mother-baby relationships 149, 230

multi-dimension Grid xx, 1, 73, 79, 85, 99

naïve idealism xxii, 121–122, 148–153, 156, 171, 195–201, 257, 259, 263
naïve idealist 121–123, 153, 155, 157, 181, 197–198, 200–201, 206–208, 214–215, 217, 260
naïve realism xxii, 121, 124, 149, 154–156, 171, 195–198, 217
naïve realist 121–123, 154–155, 157, 197, 200, 206, 208–210, 215–217, 260
   classification 206
narcissism 12, 68, 75, 81, 86, 102, 117, 131, 141, 146, 181, 202, 207, 210, 217, 232, 248, 255–256
   versus socialism 207, 210
narcissistic
   and paranoid psychosis 120
   hallucination 127
   imagination 85
   personality 116, 156
   traits 164, 191
Nazism 70, 114, 116, 150, 181, 266
n-dimension
   Grid 73
   negative Grid 84–85
   polyhedron 73
   psychic reality 73
negativation 84
negative Grid 19, 73, 80–85
   n-dimension 85
negative rationality factor 39
negative sense 83
negative therapeutic reaction 241
neologism xx, 71, 91–92, 114, 152
   Bion's 177
neo-Kleinism 243, 254
neo-Nazism 266
neo-positivism 10, 17–18, 147, 198

INDEX

neurological catchment power 64
neuro-mediators 13
neurophysiology appearance 193
neuro-psychoanalysis 5
neurosis and psychosis 256–257
Newton, Isaac 54–55, 145, 155, 253, 259
   progressive discoveries 54
Newtonian physics 49, 57, 176
Nietzsche, F. 67, 75, 105, 135, 161, 165–169, 182–183, 185–189, 193, 201–202, 204, 263
   Beyond Good and Evil 166
   fundamental insight 188
   On Truths and Lies in a Non-Moral Sense 168
   The Antichrist 168
nihilism 122
non-analysability 107
non-Euclidean geometry 51, 69
non-mental functioning 42, 154
non-psychotic personalities 51, 257
numinous-food 220

odious inhumanity 39
Oedipal
   homosexual phantasies 130
   situation 75
Oedipus
   complex 9
   mistake 214
   myth 67
   phantasies 124
ontogenetic/phylogenetic chain 147
oppressive minorities 244

pain ⇔ growth 74–79
paradoxical
   balance 125
   coexistence 48
   epistemological tool 151
paranoid phantasies 129

paranoid-schizoid
   depressive position 11, 79, 106, 176, 202, 236
   interplay 139
paranoid-schizoid position 39, 41, 77, 104, 145, 164, 191, 200, 207, 230
passionate love xxii, 229, 265
pathognomonic feature of thought processes 84
patient's
   aggression 22, 24
   associative reaction 39
   attitude 22, 66
   capacity 9, 21, 76, 78, 223
   collusive reassurance 29
   destructiveness 30
   free association 112
   Grid 29, 34, 39
   invariants 42
   mental processes 203
   models 223
   parlance 66
   patience 190
   personal equations 125
   personality 3, 12
   professional pair 26
   psychic reality 5, 68–69, 151
   reaction 25, 223
   reality 122
   report 39, 223
   sense apparatus 191
   unconscious features 84
Payne, Thomas 150
personal equation xxi, 48, 119, 121, 125–127, 129, 131
   in two movements 129–131
personal factor xix, xxi, 42, 48, 115, 119–121, 123–125, 132, 201
   abolition of 121
   and reality 124–125
   enthroning of 121
   Kantian criticism 121

phantasies of superiority 107, 243, 264
phase space 57–63, 109, 114
philistinism 82
plagiarism 55, 71
Plato's Ideal Forms 67, 114, 138
Platonic forms 90
Platonic realms 170
Platonic-Kantian categories 12
pleasure–pain primacy 85
political capacity 210
Popper, Karl 86, 118, 158–159, 179, 198, 259
Portuguese-Brazilian motto 67
positive rationalism 145
positivism 17, 47, 54, 65, 77, 95, 97, 121, 139, 198, 259
post-Aristotelian metaphysics 136
post-Einsteinian physics 52
post-Freudian psychoanalysis 52
post-modernism 71, 96, 164, 194, 201, 259
  abuses 144
  chaos 96
  relativism 121
post-sensuous
  perception of reality 205
  tendencies 196
post-structuralism 152
pre-dialectical pairs 244
predictive cause-effect relationships 11
probabilistic indeterminism 52
projective identification 27–28, 50, 75, 78, 103, 123, 130, 141, 152, 175, 200, 203, 207, 209, 217, 220, 225, 235–236, 238, 240, 243, 245–246, 248, 250–252, 255–260, 262–263, 265
  massive 238
  of exclusion 240, 248
PS ⇔ D
  interaction 83

movement 58, 193
pseudo-associations 30
pseudo-loving agreement 28
pseudo-masculinity, infantile stereotypes 237
pseudo-reliance on memory 58
pseudo-scientific deductive systems 30
psychiatric
  and sociological vertex of pathology 47
  entity 206
  practice 42, 191
psychiatric and psychoanalytic diagnoses
  three-dimension grid 40–43
psychiatrists and psychoanalysts 246–247
psychic
  activity 82
  and material reality 62
  change 176
  determinants 164
  equivalents 138, 147
  equivalents of instincts 147
  existence 14
  facts 47
  functions 65, 220
  motivations 116
  non-reality 120, 157
  qualities of unconscious 46
  reality ⇔ material reality 71
psychical qualities 141, 196
psychic determinism 106
  creative product of 99
  principle of 93–101
psychic reality 5, 8–9, 27, 33, 38, 45, 50–51, 68–69, 71, 73, 91, 96, 106–107, 113, 118, 120–123, 127, 137, 139, 141, 151, 157–158, 191, 205, 209, 226, 236–238, 257–258
psychoanalysis
  and free associations 93

art-and-science root of 143
contemporaneous with 108
curative factor 175
Derrida's textualism 159
enlightenment and romantic movement 170
epistemological view 136
exclusion of 242
hereditary traits 170
in community systems 189
misunderstanding 49
naïve idealism 199
nonmedical forerunner 136
non-psychoanalytic models 258
psychoanalytic episteme of 153
Ricoeur's textualism 159
scientific research 3
scientific/humanistic approach 259
therapeutic effect 143
to satisfaction of desire 201
umbrella of 49
psychoanalyst initiating 41
psychoanalytic
    apprehension 4
    approach 247
    congress 187
    constructions, clinical validation 8–10
    controversy 81–82
    endeavour 45, 56, 157
    environment 81
    establishment 76, 243, 257, 261
    ethos 155
    field 146, 183
    function 81
    hypotheses 97
    institutions 233
    intuition 11
    Nietzsche's genealogy 182–187
    object xx, 50, 147
    observation of patients 188
    paradoxes 202
    parlance, pseudo-interpretation 26
    patterns 47
    posture xx, 120, 129, 225
    realm 17, 43, 62
    research and movement 244, 259
    societies 243, 247
    tenet 10
    training 129
    verbal formulations 64
    vertex xxii, 57, 105, 132, 148–150, 163, 168, 170, 173, 181, 184, 189, 231, 256
psychoanalytical sense 205
psychoanalytic couple 185
    basic group 234–241
psychoanalytic movement xx, 5, 31, 47–49, 53, 70, 72, 115, 117, 120, 122, 124, 129, 132, 141–142, 154, 157, 190, 199, 203, 206, 224, 226, 242–243, 245, 252, 257
    into principle of ignorance 122
    naïve realism 154
psychoanalytic theories 75
    evolution of 112
    rational learning 155
psychodynamic diagnosis 41
psychogenesis of thinking processes 13
psychological
    and philosophical schools 180
    oughtism 189
psychologising philosophy 137
psychopathic
    and delinquent personalities 84
    behaviour 12
    criminality 238
    naïve idealist 207–208, 210, 214, 217
    personalities 206–207, 238
    tendencies 206
psychosis 53, 83–84, 120, 150, 198, 206, 216–217, 256–257
    and psychopathy 206–210

psychotic
   breakdown 9, 21, 78
   creation of pseudo-pain 78
   mechanism 114, 183, 231
   moment 41
   naïve idealist 208, 215–217
   personalities 51, 181, 219

quantum mechanics 53, 71
quantum theory and relativity 165
quasi-analytic pair 33
quasi-mathematical
   notation 15, 33–34, 231
   symbols 50

Rank, Otto 165–166
rationalism 142, 145, 150, 154, 159, 170, 249
real psychoanalysis xxii, 9–10, 253
reality ⇔ hallucination 164
Reik, Theodor 138, 253
relational psychic reality 38
relativism 18, 121–122, 138, 153, 165, 170, 196, 207, 244, 249, 259, 263
repression theory 165
Ricoeur, P., textualism 159
Riklin, Franz 95
Riviere, Joan 94, 101
romantic achievements 142

Sandler, P. C. xx–xxii
   Determinism of Causes 99
   Determinism of Functions 99
   International Journal of Psycho-Analysis xxi
   transdisciplinary relationships xxii
Sapienza, Antonio xix, xxii
Schlick, Moritz 5, 10
   neo-positivism 198
Schoenberg, Arnold 116
Schreber, Judge 71, 114, 154
   diary 219

scientific deductive systems 43
scientific-poetic function of mind 93
Searles, Harold 138
   facilitating environment 108
self-feeding autistic cycles of greed ⇔ envy 84
self-importance, phantasies of 84
self-pleasure and desire 69
sense of truth 101, 126, 156–157, 202, 204, 222, 250–251
sense-based realism 149
sensuous impressions 14, 66
sensuous-concretifying 196
sexual activity 68
sexual curiosity 126
six-dimension Grid xx, 8, 53, 61, 63–69, 73
   verbal formulation of 67
sixth basic assumption xix, xxii, 229–230, 232, 240–241, 247–258, 263
   hallucinosis of exclusion/appertaining 230–232
   in larger groups 241–246
social and psychiatric entity 206
social-ism 75, 181, 207, 210, 255–256
socialist ideologies 207
sociological ideas and scientific hypotheses 232–234
splitting 256–260
   factualisation 256
split narcissism 102
splitting and dissidences 243
Stalinism 116, 150, 181
Strachey, Alix 94, 101, 103, 266
Sullivan, Harry Stack 103
superego 57, 206, 215–217
superiority 107, 113, 124, 131, 165, 173, 177, 180, 191, 207, 230, 237, 243, 249–250, 254, 256, 264
   paranoid ideas 256
   phantasies 243

tandem movement PS ⇔ D 109
tandem transience 202
thinking processes xx, 11–13, 15, 28, 51, 54, 80, 91, 102, 140, 237
three-dimension Grid 8, 19–20, 25, 27, 29, 33, 38, 40–41, 43, 66, 68
time-machine 58
tolerance of paradoxes 79–80, 157, 167
transcendent permanence 90
transference neurosis 241
transference phantasies 130, 241
transient glimpse of reality 46
tri-dimension Grid xx, 20, 32, 43, 51, 63, 252
truth and community networks 179–182
truth and mental health 188–190
truth-and-paradox-abhorring expressions 148
truthfulness in untruthful environments 210–215
truth ⇔ lie 164
Turquet, Pierre 232
two-dimension Grid xx, 7, 19–20, 27, 29, 63–64, 79–80

ultra-idealistic solipsism 122
unauthorised incursions in German language 110–111

unconscious
    awareness 236
    goals and pursue 95
    mind xxii, 138–141
    memory 37
    mental processes 46
    phantasies 12, 46, 106, 124, 138, 147
    principle and functioning 111
    processes 95, 128
    thoughts 38, 176
Ur-pre-psychoanalysis 155

Venn diagram 47
verbal formulations 5, 25, 53, 64, 90, 113, 139, 164, 202

Wallerstein, R. S. 230, 245,
wars among psychoanalysts 241–246
wars of psychoanalysis 241
Weber, Max 232
Wilde, Oscar 235, 249, 251
Winnicott, Donald 4, 16, 33, 46, 50, 52, 103, 124, 138, 141, 147–148, 156, 158, 234, 241–243, 248, 254, 263
    good enough mothering 108
    sense 27
Winnicottians 103
Wisdom, John 138

For Product Safety Concerns and Information please contact our EU
representative GPSR@taylorandfrancis.com
Taylor & Francis Verlag GmbH, Kaufingerstraße 24, 80331 München, Germany

www.ingramcontent.com/pod-product-compliance
Lightning Source LLC
Chambersburg PA
CBHW070301010526
44108CB00039B/1442